THEOLOGY FOR

The Everlasting Song

PEW AND PULPIT

THEOLOGY FOR

The Everlasting Song

PEW AND PULPIT

BY JOSEPH A. BASSETT

Ragged Edge Press

This Ragged Edge Press publication was printed by
Beidel Printing House, Inc.
63 West Burd Street
Shippensburg, PA 17257

In respect for the scholarship contained herein, the acid-free paper used in this book meets the guidelines for permanence and durability of the Committee on Production Guidelines for Book Longevity of
the Council on Library Resources.

For a complete list of available publications please write:
Ragged Edge Press
Division of White Mane Publishing Company, Inc.
P.O. Box 152
Shippensburg, PA 17257

Library of Congress Cataloging-in-Publication Data

Bassett, Joseph A., 1940-
        Theology for pew and pulpit : the everlasting song / by Joseph A.
Bassett.
            p.   cm.
        Includes bibliographical references and index.
        ISBN 0-942597-90-7 (alk. paper)
        1. Public worship--Reformed Church.   2. Reformed Church--Liturgy.
3. Reformed Church--Doctrines. 4. Pastoral theology--Reformed
Church. 5. Calvin, Jean, 1509–1564. 6. Taylor, Edward, 1642–1729.
7. First Church (Chestnut Hill, Mass.) 8. Chestnut Hill (Mass.)--
Church history--20th century.   I. Title.
BX9427.B38   1996
264´.05--dc20
                                                        95-46836
                                                             CIP

PRINTED IN THE UNITED STATES OF AMERICA

To The First Church in Chestnut Hill
Who took up the melody and sang the Song

Table of Contents

Preface

In the winter of 1987 I enjoyed a three-month sabbatical at the Presbyterian College in Montreal. The task at hand was defined by a sentence in the book review section of The Eden Seminary Newsletter.

> One looks in vain for a practical
> theology of the congregation, that is
> critical reflection on the local church
> that brings its activities into dialogue
> with biblical and historical theology.[1]

This book addresses that void by commenting upon selected liturgical texts in the context of the liturgical year and a congregation's worship.

This is a practical theology in that it is based upon liturgical prayers that are heard in a church on Sunday morning as well as prayers that the people of God may say in the course of a week. The texts of these prayers are taken primarily from the *United Church of Christ's Book of Worship,* published in 1986; the Presbyterian Church (U.S.A.) and the Cumberland Presbyterian Church's *Supplemental Liturgical Resources Series,* published from 1984 to 1992; and their *Book of Common Worship,* published in 1993.

This is by no means a comprehensive commentary on the liturgical rites that the worship books of the United Church of Christ, the Presbyterian Church (U.S.A.) and the Cumberland Presbyterian Church advocates. Instead this book takes up some of the essential prayers and actions that members of a worshipping Christian congregation encounter on Sunday morning, during Christmas and Easter seasons, or in a hospital room. It pays particular attention to prayers of confession, a prayer over the water at baptism, the communion prayer, collects and pastoral prayers.

In addition to these liturgical texts, various ecumenical dialogues contribute to the local congregation's theological understanding. This book draws upon the conversations of the World Alliance of Reformed Churches with the Orthodox Churches, the World Alliance of Reformed Churches and the Secretariat for Promoting Christian Unity in Rome, the Anglican and Reformed Churches in Great Britain, the Roman Catholic/Presbyterian-Reformed Consultation, the International Reformed/Methodist Consultation, the work on *Baptism, Eucharist and Ministry* by the Commission of Faith and Order of the World Council of Churches, and the Consultation on Common Texts's *Revised Common Lectionary,* published in 1992.

This is "a theology of the congregation" in that it centers on the nucleus of a Christian church, namely, the presence of Word and Sacrament in the course of the year. It is a theology written in the Reformed corner of the vineyard as the Presbyterian and United Church of Christ liturgies attest. The particular congregation from which this book springs is the First Church in Chestnut Hill where I have been minister for twenty-five years.

Located near the Brookline and Newton town line, the First Church is a small stone structure with twenty-seven pews and an adjacent parish hall. As you enter the church there is a balcony overhead with a newly built and installed pipe organ. The windows used to be clear until various parishioners dedicated stained glass to the memory of their family members. In the vestibule the original smoky clear glass can still be seen. One or two of the real old-timers make sure newcomers see the original glass. The baptismal font is in the front of the sanctuary. There is a split chancel with a communion table between pulpit and lectern.

Being in a metropolitan area, the First Church draws from the neighboring communities and beyond. Some come because they are looking for a small church. Others are parents who have recognized that the church is where their children can hear biblical stories and celebrate Christian holidays. They may have found the church in the yellow pages, or come across it while out running. They may have heard about it from a newsletter, or attended a wedding or funeral in the sanctuary. The result is a wide variety of interests, opinions and backgrounds in the congregation. While stereotypes abound based on the way it used to be "when Hector was a pup," anyone involved in the First Church can easily separate past recollections from the unfolding present.

The First Church manifests the dynamics of a small church. Worship on Sunday morning is the congregation's primary activity. On any Lord's Day, members of the congregation can tell you who was in church, where they sat and who the new people were. When one young man called to make an appointment to talk about getting married, he said that he and his fiancée had been attending church for the last few weeks. I replied:

"Oh, you're the guy with the beard."

"Yeah, I'm the guy with the beard."

After being married in the church, one of their children was baptized alongside the grandchild of a family that had been in the congregation for generations.

An Old Testament professor asked, "Is there room for Amos in Chestnut Hill?" The answer is "Yes," provided it is the Word of Amos and not the gospel of *The New York Times* or the *Wall Street Journal* pasted over some handy text. People who attend the First Church on Sunday are well aware of the ways of the world. When I preached my candidating sermon, I made a reference to some hearings in Washington. I noticed that one of the parishioners snickered. When I asked who she was and heard the answer, I realized that she was much closer to the capital than I would ever be. She didn't come to church to hear what she already knew better than I. She came to church to hear the Word of Scripture and Tradition and how that might bear upon what she knew.

In the pews beside the *Pilgrim Hymnal* there is a small prayer book. These slender black volumes contain an order for morning prayer and a psalter, both substantially revised from the Book of Common Prayer. On Communion Sundays, the liturgy follows the shape found in the United Church of Christ's *Book of Worship* and the Presbyterians' *Book of Common Worship*. In a word, the congregation worships with a set liturgy.

The service begins with a sung doxology following the prelude. Then the congregation says a prayer of confession and the Lord's Prayer. The Psalms are read responsively, followed by an anthem. After two Scripture lessons a series of prayers are said. Some of the prayers are collects and thanksgivings from the *Book of Common Prayer*. To these, several other prayers and a weekly pastoral prayer are added. After the prayers the morning offering is taken and the offertory anthem sung. The sermon is given between two hymns. The service concludes with a benediction and postlude.

This form of worship might initially appear to be confining. Although the prayer book provides the basic shape of the Sunday service, within that shape there are a number of variables. The psalms, the Scriptures, the hymns and anthems, collects and pastoral prayers vary each Sunday. The prayer book's structure provides in John Williamson Nevin's words "a real emancipation into the liberty of the children of God."[2]

A wise seminary student decided to spend three weeks with the congregation in the pews before leading worship. He came back astonished at that man one third of the way down on the right. Exclaimed the student, "He doesn't need the book!" He surely did not. This was a person who, knowing and trusting the rhythm of the service, was free to feel the tug of the Word. For him Sunday was not always comforting. He once told the minister, "I don't like being compared to a sheep!"

As a "practical theology of the congregation" this book is written to point out the glory and wisdom of Christian worship among the sons and daughters of John Calvin. It is my hope that people who read this book will come away with a renewed sense of what takes place in church on Sunday. Those who are called to lead worship will hopefully learn what they can expect in a congregation. Those who attend church regularly will gain renewed insight into familiar actions and words. Those preparing for marriage or a stay in the hospital may become aware of the resources that a worshipping congregation provides. Finally, I hope that readers of the book, whatever their situation, will gain an increased appreciation of recently published liturgical texts.

I have been in dialogue with historical theology throughout this book, primarily with John Calvin, Edward Taylor and Samuel Sewall. These three figures have left us different writings about the faith. I have taken up Calvin's *Institutes of the Christian Religion* and some of his commentaries for their succinct insights. I have pondered and pressed Edward Taylor's poetry for its profound appreciation of parish life. In order to gain an historic sense of the faithful's daily life, I have consulted Samuel Sewall's diary. All three of these people articulate a sense of the tradition in which the First Church lives.

At the very beginning of my ministry during a summer program in New Hampshire, I dramatically encountered Calvin. As divinity students, we were to work with a minister for the first six weeks of the summer and then remain when the minister went on vacation in August. One week in July the minister called me in and said that he had just received a call that a fifteen-year-old boy had died. He went on to say, "I'll do the service. But suppose I couldn't, what would you do?" He then left me to spend the rest of the afternoon finding an answer to that question. I read everything I could find in the pamphlets and books in the church library that I thought might be helpful. It was all terribly soft and vacuous. Finally, at the very end of the day I decided to look in the text we had read in introductory theology—Calvin's *Institutes of the Christian Religion*. I looked up "death" in the index and was directed to a passage entitled, "Meditation upon the future life." Having exhausted all other avenues, I dutifully read it. I was quite surprised at what I found. Calvin knew what it was to live in a world where fifteen-year-olds die. He also spoke of something called "the power of the resurrection." That was a phrase I found worthy of study.

When I returned to Divinity School in the fall, I made my way to the theology professor's office and blurted out my story. To which he replied, "Well, Mr. Bassett, I'm glad that you discovered that Calvin is a pastor. For that's what he is in a very real sense." Therefore, I have cited Calvin at critical points because of his insights into the life of the faithful rather than as the founder of a school of theology. Although he certainly is a beautiful theologian, Calvin is first and foremost a pastor.

Recognizing that there were subsequently many kinds of "Calvinists," I have chosen to listen to Edward Taylor, the minister of Westfield, Massachusetts 1671–1725. Taylor is recognized as an early American poet. But indispensable to his poetry was Edward Taylor's ministry. His poetry sprang from a lively sense of Word and Sacrament and delineated the beauty at the heart of a Congregational Church.

I have sometimes juxtaposed the diary of Taylor's college roommate and lifelong friend, Samuel Sewall 1652–1717 with the poetry of the Westfield pastor and poet. His diary notes provide insight into significant events like eclipses and the questions of young children. Too often the homely texture of early New England church life is lost under phrases like "The early Puritans" and "Congregational Polity." Taylor and Sewall correct that bias by giving us a sense of Word and Sacrament, encountering Congregationalists where they lived.

To read Taylor's poetry and Sewall's diary is to realize that our faith is not unique. They remind us that we are not called to invent the church for the twentieth or even the twenty-first centuries. Rather we would do well to learn from the faithful of the seventeenth and other centuries, joining them at pulpit and table so that we might be more faithful in our own time. When a facile colleague opined that, "Of course, all theology has to be rethought," someone quite rightly replied, "No, I don't think we have to reinvent the hypostatic union." While it is certainly the obligation of each generation in the church to appropriate the faith of the historic church, we need, first of all, to know what that faith is. Here John Calvin, Edward Taylor and Samuel Sewall are instructive.

Each chapter has a five-fold structure. First, there is a pastoral situation that most church-goers will recognize, for example, the Christmas pageant. Second, a liturgical text is introduced, an opening doxology or a communion prayer. Third, commentary upon the text follows. In some chapters this section may be too detailed for some as, for example, the discussion of the lectionary texts in the second chapter. If that turns out to be so, members of a congregation might enjoy discussing these details with their minister. She might be able, for example, to mention the way she chooses Scriptures to accompany the Gospel reading. Fourth, particular attention is paid to the dynamics of the Holy Spirit in the liturgy. While recognizing that the Three Persons of the Trinity cannot be separated one from another, the accent in this book falls upon the Third Person as in the prayer before baptism or the prompting to worship. The reason for singling out the Holy Spirit is that the attention given to the first Two Persons of the Trinity has more often than not all but suppressed the Third Person. Finally, throughout the book there is a running conversation with Edward Taylor. This is a way of gaining a perspective on contemporary Sunday mornings. Listening to Taylor's meditations, we hear the voice of another generation and time encountering the Word. The first chapter is primarily given over to Taylor because in subsequent chapters his poetry will be quoted and commented upon with a minimum of biographical context.

The list of those to whom I am indebted is long. I am especially grateful

to the First Church Standing Committees who granted my sabbaticals;

to the Presbyterian College in Montreal for their hospitality;

to Jerry who said on the lawn with a gleam in his eye that it could be done electronically;

to Sandy who paid for the upgrades on his computer that Jerry said would do the trick and also offered timely advice;

to Ginny and Howard who knew when to push the print button;

to Marion, Lelly, Joan, Horace, Helen, Mary, Gabe, Uncle Bill, Esther, Art, Fred, Scott, Harold, Lisa, and Alan who read the manuscript and made suggestions;

to Martin Gordon who edited the manuscript;

to the Wednesday congregations of Word and Sacrament at the Wellesley Hills Church, presided over by Craig Adams who realizes the presence involved;

to Llewellyn Smith, Jim Chase, Scott Axford, Herb Davis and Ken Clarke and Martha Stone who week after week open up texts in ministry;

to Molly who did the illustrations, and without whom this book simply would not have been possible;

to Nancy who quietly stated the fact of the matter, and supplied the commas.

Brookline, Massachusetts
Lent A.D. 1994

CHAPTER 1

The Signs in God's Acre

$\mathfrak{C}$alvin was right. Whenever we pass an ancient burial ground we are impressed with the transience of human life. We may either wax philosophic ourselves or chuckle as we read the inscription of a man who was:

> Well, sick, dead
> in one hour's space
> in the fifty-fourth year of his life.

But Calvin knew whatever thoughts that come to mind concerning the vanity of life are fleeting at best. Once we return to the world and its busy streets, he noted any philosophy that we may have exercised in God's Acre evaporates "like applause in the theater for some pleasing spectacle."[1]

Communities maintain these sacred spaces by lining the grave stones up in neat rows and enclosing them with a fence. A plaque placed outside by local historians may identify the old burying ground and name a few famous people therein. The stone carvers' names may also be noted on the fence for those interested in colonial folk art. In addition, a sign may state that a meetinghouse once stood nearby and has since moved to another location. Beaten paths lead to the resting place of those whom the world deems worthy of note. At Memorial Day, patriotic groups will decorate the graves of those who fought in the American Revolution and other wars with a flag.

These stones in a burying ground are signs very much like the stones Joshua arranged at Gilgal. Gilgal was the designated meeting place for the tribes of Israel in the period of the Israelite Settlement. That site was located in a corner of the Jordan River valley near where they crossed the Jordan River and entered the land. It was a regular meeting place for the tribes of Israel from the latter half of the thirteenth century on.

Joshua had commanded that twelve stones taken from the river bed by representatives of each of the twelve tribes be put in a circle. Since the root of the word Gilgal means to roll, some said that the name Gilgal came from the circle of twelve stones. In the Book of Judges 3:19 there is a reference to "the sculptured stones near Gilgal." These may be the circle of stones that Joshua had commanded to be put in place when the tribes passed through the Jordan.

Joshua said that the stones there were "a sign" and "a memorial." [Joshua 4:6] A sign is that which brings something other than itself to mind. In the words of Augustine:

> ...a sign is a thing which, over and above
> the impression it makes on the senses, causes
> something else to come into the mind
> as a consequence of itself. [2]

The stones were put in a circle at Gilgal to bring something else to mind—the crossing of the Jordan. Joshua declared the stones would prompt the children who came with their families to Gilgal for the festivals to ask the question, "What do these stones mean to you?" Then their parents would tell them the story of Israel's crossing of the Jordan. In that way the stones served as a sign.

3

The stones at Gilgal were also called a memorial because they called to mind ritual actions. These ritual actions delineate particular events and commandments that define the religious community. There were two such rituals at Gilgal, an initiation rite, and Israel's first Passover in the promised land. These were not routine services, but took place in "faithful response to the claims of covenant."[3] Seeing the circle of stones at Gilgal, later generations would remember the initiation rites and the celebration of Passover as well as crossing the Jordan.

And yet, even though Israel gathered there for generations and there were signs and memorials at Gilgal, no Temple was ever built in that place. The old campground was superseded by David's Jerusalem where Solomon built the Temple in the middle of the tenth century. But the memory of Gilgal as a meeting place for the people of God lingered on after the destruction of the Temple in Jerusalem. At least until the days of the prophets Amos and Hosea in the eighth century Gilgal was known as a significant meeting place for the people of God.

The gravestones of an old burying ground are signs as were the stones at Gilgal. Grave stones bring to mind congregations of people who knew and enjoyed God. They recall the names of the people of God who lived in the community years or even centuries before. People like Mrs. Hannah Gibbs who died in 1783 at the age of 84 and whose slate stone in Newton announces:

Rich in faith and good works
and fully ripe for Heaven.
She quits her earthly Tabernacle
to dwell with God.

In addition to bringing to mind the names of God's people, some of the stones recall the rituals that members of the congregations carried out. In Northborough the stone of Paul Newton reports that he faithfully served the Church of Christ in that town as a deacon for more than 30 years. As deacon in addition to being responsible for the bread, wine and vessels of holy communion, Mister Newton was also responsible for the minister's salary and the welfare of the poor. In the words of the Cambridge Platform of 1648, deacons served "the *Tables* which the church is to provide for: as the *Lord's Table*, the table of the *ministers*, & of such as are in *necessitie*."[4]

The tombstone of the first minister in a neighboring congregation brings to mind more pontifical memorials. The inscription on the tombstone of Ebenezer Parkman announces he was "The First Bishop of the Church in Westborough." Was this by virtue of close New Testament exegesis or did this pastor anoint the children he baptized?

The original meetinghouses of these congregations have long since disappeared. Some congregations have settled in other parts of town. Others have replaced the meetinghouse two or three times. Just as no Temple was established at Gilgal so no comparable structures have been erected by the graveyards. A sign may state that the church's original meetinghouse used to be here. If the church is nearby, somewhere it is noted that this is the third building.

Further west, in the Connecticut River Valley in the old burying ground of Westfield, a modest stone marking the grave of their first minister, brings to mind The Reverend Mister Edward Taylor. Edward Taylor reached New England in 1668, thirty-five years after John Cotton, and thirty-eight years after John Winthrop. He was a Reformed Pastor serving a congregational church in western Massachusetts, an area known for its piety and strong ministers.

In 1937 Taylor was recognized to have been a poet as well as a pastor. Thomas H. Johnson pursued a passing reference to poetry in a biographical sketch of Taylor and uncovered a manuscript of Taylor's poems in the Yale University Library. Johnson published several selections in *The New England Quarterly*. Subsequently, he published a collection of Taylor's poems in 1939. Later in 1960 Donald Stanford edited *The Poems of Edward Taylor*. This collection of the Westfield minister's poetry can be found on many a library shelf. In response, four years later on Memorial Day 1964, the Western Hampden Historical Society posted a plaque by the gate of The Old Burying Ground pronouncing Edward Taylor to be "the greatest poet of colonial America."

Calling Edward Taylor "the greatest poet of colonial America," ignores the fact that his poetry sprang from his life as a pastor who preached the Word and celebrated the sacraments in Westfield. Taylor faithfully lived his life in that particular town, in that specific religious community. Rooted in the life of Westfield, Taylor's poetry sang of God's glory realized there. As minister of the Church of Christ in Westfield for fifty-eight years, Taylor enjoyed an extraordinary sense of Word and Sacrament. To read his poems is to understand the way he, as Westfield's first pastor, and the town's first settlers approached the Lord's Table. His writings attest to the Word and Sacrament that dwelt among those seventeenth-century saints and shaped their days.

Edward Taylor's poems provide insight and instruction for the people of God who go to church today. His poems are a witness to the presence that continues to dwell with Christians on Sunday mornings. Reading his poems, contemporary Christians become aware of certain liturgical dynamics and theological distinctions that constitute Reformed tradition. Therefore, it is not enough to laud him as a colonial poet. It is necessary to hear Edward Taylor's piety as well.

Since Taylor's poems are not abstract treatises, but spring from the life of his congregation, it is helpful to know something of how he came to be minister in Westfield, what his life was like in the community as well as who the people were with whom he gathered in the meetinghouse each Lord's Day. Moreover it is instructive to note some of the chords in his poetry. These can still be heard in the worship of Reformed churches.

The Pastorate of Edward Taylor

Aged

His gravestone tells us that Taylor was "aged" in 1729. He was eighty-seven years old when he died. Born in a Midland village north of Coventry, Taylor decided to migrate to New England, for some unknown reason. He embarked late one Sunday night, April 26, 1668, when he and a gentlewoman took a boat from London's Execution Dock at Wapping and boarded a ship for New England.[5] It was almost three weeks later on Thursday, May 21 when the ship cleared Land's End for the open sea.[6] Then six weeks later on the first of July Taylor noticed New England rockweed in the water. On the third of July, those on board ship caught more mackerel than they could eat in one day. On the fourth of July, Taylor noted in his diary that he could see "Land on both hands, Plymouth on the Left and Salem on the Right..."[7]

The name Salem was a variation on the Hebrew word "Shalom." It attested to one of the most striking characteristics of New England piety, namely, the way those Calvinists associated themselves with the biblical people of Israel. The same could be said of Plymouth. In his history *Of Plymouth Plantation* William Bradford compared his community on their arrival with the Israelites reaching the promised land. Bradford praised the loving kindness of God by adapting the opening verses of Psalm 107 to the situation of his community in Plymouth. Wandering in the wilderness and finding no city in which to dwell; being hungry and thirsty; their spirits being overwhelmed within them, were all descriptions of Israel in Psalm 107 that Bradford found to fit the experience of the Pilgrims just as well. As God had manifest a divine loving kindness to the people of Israel, so God manifest loving kindness to the early New England settlers. Thus, the Pilgrim congregation in Plymouth took up the refrain of the psalm:

> Let them praise the Lord because he is good:
> and God's mercies endure forever.[8]

To declare that the experiences of God's people in Israel and Plymouth are similar is to think in terms of analogies. Analogies fall in two basic catagories: analogies of proportion and analogies of attribution. In an analogy of proportion the juxtaposed figures share a similar action or form. In an analogy of attribution the two figures share an attribute. The Pilgrims' experience is analogous to that of the biblical Israelites in terms of both forms of analogy. First, there is an analogy of proportion in that both communities of faithful people were journeying to a new land. When Bradford read of Israel's wandering in the wilderness, he recognized the experience of his band anchored off Plymouth. That would be an analogy of proportion. But there is an analogy of attribution involved as well. The Pilgrims and the Israelites shared a common attribute. Both communities waited upon God and praised God for the mercies they enjoyed. That is not an attribute the Israelites shared with Canaanites nor the Pilgrims with the crew of the Mayflower. In the end when the Israelites and the Pilgrims were peacefully and safely settled, they both praised God in terms of a psalm.

At five o'clock on the fourth of July in 1668, Taylor and his companions sighted the islands in Boston harbor.[9] Some of them stayed up all night so as to go ashore as soon as possible. Taylor elected to try and sleep in his cabin before he disembarked. He had brought several letters with him to Boston which, the morning he landed, he set about delivering. The first was to the Reverend John Mayo of the Second Church in Boston. After dining with this minister, it was arrranged that Taylor would lodge at the home of the other minister of Boston's Second Church, Increase Mather. Taylor remained until July 7 and then delivered two letters to Mr. John Hull from his relatives. Hull was a goldsmith who sixteen years earlier had been appointed mintmaster of the colony. He produced willow tree, oak tree and pine tree shillings for the colony, keeping every twentieth coin for himself.[10] Hull urged Taylor to stay at his home and to store his chest in his warehouse until Taylor could settle in at the college. Hull was so insistent that Taylor remained at his home a little over two weeks until he was admitted to Harvard on July 23.[11]

Taylor attended Harvard for three and a quarter years. For the duration of that time he was the college "Buttler" which meant he was in charge of the public rooms, managed the buttery and kept accounts of the college's vessels and utensils. Taylor's roommate, i.e. "chamber fellow," was Samuel Sewall. The friendship between Taylor and Sewall lasted all their lives. In 1675–76 Sewall married John Hull's only daughter, Hannah. Sewall kept a diary in which glimpses of Edward Taylor are recorded every now and then. Both graduated in the class of 1671, Mr. Taylor having been given advanced standing. After graduation he was persuaded to remain in residence at Cambridge as "scholar of the house."

Venerable

To the people of Westfield, Taylor was "Venerable," that is to say, he was worthy of respect. Their respect was in part due to the fact that he was their first minister and that his call was more arduous than that of most ministers. On November 16, 1671, Thomas Dewey arrived in Boston in Massachusetts Bay from Westfield on the Connecticut River. He was seeking a minister for Westfield. Dewey attended the Boston Lecture delivered on Thursdays by one of the local ministers, where he met with "eight or nine Elders." When he asked them to recommend a candidate, the elders recommended Edward Taylor. So the next day Mr. Dewey went to Cambridge and pressed his case upon the recent graduate. Taylor was hesitant. He asked for five days to consult others to be able to give his decision on the next Tuesday.

The advice of his friends and members of the faculty was initially mixed. But on Saturday, two of the ranking ministers in Massachusetts Bay encouraged Taylor to accept the Westfield invitation. Dewey took heart on Monday that, although Taylor would not leave that week as he had hoped, nevertheless, the candidate's preparations appeared "to be sufficient to raise his expectations."[12] On Thursday a snowstorm arrived and continued through the weekend. Nevertheless, Taylor did set out for Westfield with Dewey on Monday, the twenty-seventh:

> ... not without much apprehension of a
> tedious and hazardous journey, the

snow being about Mid-leg deepe,
the way unbeaten, or the track filled up againe,
and over rocks and mountains, and the journey being
about on 100 miles;[13]

The trip was as arduous as Taylor had anticipated. They went from Cambridge to Marlborough. They left Marlborough at a half an hour before sunrise and by ten o'clock they were lost for about three or four miles. They finally got back on the trail, spotting the marked trees, but feared they would not be able to reach Quabog in the Nipmuk country. However, by eight that night they were safely at Quabog.

From there they set out for Springfield and arrived without incident. The next leg took them over the Connecticut River. This involved crossing the river on the ice with their horses. Taylor did not like this idea one bit. When the ice, which he estimated had been frozen for two days, cracked with every step, he confided to his diary that he liked the idea even less. However, the party did make it over "to the wonder almost of all that knew it."[14]

Arriving in Westfield on December second, the travellers and especially Taylor were cordially welcomed. He notes that he had never known such gusts of wind as those that rattled the house of Captain Cook.[15] Taylor preached his first sermon in Westfield on December 3, 1671. His text was Matthew 3:2: "'Repent ye; for the kingdom of heaven is at hand.'"

Taylor continued to preach in Westfield for fifty-five years. He came to know the people of the parish for better and for worse. They came to know him in the same way. In the course of his pastorate, Edward Taylor was married twice. Of the eight children the first Mrs. Taylor bore, five died as infants.[16] The six children by his second wife all survived to adulthood.[17]

Not until 1722 did the congregation consider a colleague for him. Nemiah Bull was ordained in Westfeld, having acted as school master and the pastor's assistant before being ordained on October 26, 1726. Taylor lived for another three years. In December 1728 the town voted 10 pounds for his daughter Hitable Taylor "to inable her to provide help to tend Mr. Taylor." [18] He died on June 24, 1729 "after he had served God & and his generation faithfully for many years."[19] The stone placed on his grave declared him to be:

The Aged, Venerable, Learned and Pious
Pastor of the Church of Christ in this town.

As their "venerable" pastor, Taylor was intimately bound up with the people of Westfield. The church records indicate that there were times when Taylor was embroiled in conflicts over disciplinary matters which involved egos besides his own. All of which attests that he knew his flock and they their pastor. However, that did not mean that they always agreed.

Taylor noted in the church records that the summer he had hoped would open the door to a church being gathered, opened instead onto King Philip's War. He was very much present during the raids that took place in the Connecticut River Valley in the course of that war. When in April 1676 the suggestion was made that the inhabitants of Westfield move to Springfield, Taylor was among those who protested against the move. When the war was over, the Westfield Church was gathered on August 27, 1679. This was the occasion when members of a congregation affirmed the covenant that made them a church and they were recognized to be a church by other congregations.

Taylor's work as a pastor included cases of church discipline. For example, twelve years after he had come to fetch Taylor from Cambridge, Dewey went out one morning and cut down a dam up river from his own and hid the competing miller's tools.[20] But after hearing a sermon on Romans 12:19, Dewey was convinced of the error of his ways and confessed his fault to the church. His confession was accepted.

In 1697 one Abigail Bush, the youngest of eight children, was charged for saying of her father before he was to remarry that "he married not for Love. And that he was as hot as a Skunk, & the woman as hot as a Bitch."[21] The church accepted her confession as well. Fifteen years later she was again accused of upbraiding her father, who judging by the records was not an unblemished character.[22] This time Abigail denied the charge. When people from the church came and asked to speak with her, Abigail went "about her business" in the garden and refused to talk about the charge. As a result the church placed her on a time of trial for two months. In that time "no thing appearing of unworthy carriage", she was absolved of the charges.[23] Taylor's testimony in a court case regarding the support of Abigail's father, offers a description of what life was like in those days. Taylor said of Walter Lee:

> For tho' the man is not able to mannage
> strong worke as Plowing, Carting etc.,
> yet when his land is plow'd he plants, Woods,
> hill, & gathers his Corn: Reaps his Winter grain,
> pulls his Flax, makes his hay,
> buys what he needs, of Merchants, Shoemakers,
> Taylors, & payes them, is rated in the town, & payes
> his dues.[24]

In the course of his ministry a pastor could offend people as Taylor offended Benjamin Smith. Recording the proceedings of a disciplinary case in the summer of 1713, Taylor notes:

> Benjamin Smith being of a fever sent for me & I was at
> his house I saw his fever so high I thoug[ht] him in danger
> of Dea[th] and so advised . . . myself to advise him to
> looke into his life, & soul & se what was amiss therein; &
> renew his repentence before God & so apply himselfe to
> Christ by faith. I saw his Spirit rise hereat & he asked me
> whether I had anything against him. I told him, that I
> doubted not but if he searched into his life he would find
> that his life had not been so Even but that he might finde
> matter of repentance, etc.[25]

Taylor, the minister physician, later had reason to believe that this exhortation so offended Smith that he bore a grudge against him. When Smith claimed that Taylor had defamed him, Taylor suspended the celebration of Holy Communion in the Westfield Church until the issue was resolved to his satisfaction. This raised a hue and cry in the parish.

Smith ended up taking his case to the neighboring ministers and magistrates. The Magistrate Col. Samuel Partridge wrote to Taylor and advised him to settle with Smith, telling Taylor somewhat indelicately that such action "may much disturb yourselfe in your old age."[26] The issue was finally resolved when, meeting at a neighboring minister's home, Smith read a confession of his maligning Taylor. Although he did not consider Smith's confession adequate, it was put before the church and they accepted it. Taylor then appointed a Lord's Supper Day which the church duly celebrated.

Westfield endured the traditional New England dispute about where to build the second meetinghouse. The community's first meetinghouse had been built in 1673. When the time came to rebuild it, there were competing proposals as to where it should be located. The town voted to establish a committee which would select a suitable site in January of 1716. However, after three years of trying to decide where it should be located and getting nowhere, the town's people asked Partridge to arbitrate the dispute and the town to be bound to accept his judgement. The colonel made his determination on December 21, 1719.[27] The decision was to build a new meetinghouse less than a mile up the road from the river toward the burying ground. Although Taylor was invited to be present and invoke the Deity at the first raising in June of 1720, he still remained partial to the original site. So persistent was Taylor's resistance to the new meetinghouse that his college friend Sewall noted in his letter book:

> He had an aversion to it, because it was not built just in
> the same spot the former sorry house was. The new one is
> built upon a little knowl, that it might be out of the way of
> the Overflowing of the River. I writ Mr. Taylor to incline
> him to remove to his New House.[28]

This may have been a sign that Taylor was slipping. The following year, 1722, a committee of two deacons and a captain of the militia had gone to see whether Taylor was willing "to lay down preaching."[29] Negotiations were begun with Issac Stiles in New Haven to see if he would become Mr. Taylor's colleague. Stiles had married Taylor's daughter Keziah. But the couple decided to remain in Connecticut.[30] It wasn't until four years later that the Reverend Bull was ordained Mr. Taylor's successor.

Learned

The grave stone called Taylor "learned." On the frontier, he was accustomed to copy texts and bind them into books, creating a remarkable library. Thus, for example, he transcribed a work of Origen, second-century theologian from Alexandria. References to Justin Martyr and Cyprian in some of his sermons indicate that Taylor had access to other volumes of the Church Fathers.[31] His library also contained descriptions of China by Jesuit missionaries, a dispensatory with four hundred plus pages on the healing qualities of herbs and a history of metals.[32]

Like many ministers after him, the first minister of Westfield participated in the regional controversies concerning what was required for church
membership. Solomon Stoddard, the Minister of Northhampton, was the dominant churchman in the Connecticut Valley. To some in the Connecticut Valley
he was known as Pope Stoddard. He had been the college librarian while Taylor was the buttler at Harvard. From the very beginning of Taylor's Westfield
ministry, Stoddard had been ready to advise his neighbor's parishioners on
various and sundry matters.

When at the end of August 1679 the Westfield Church was gathered,
Solomon Stoddard, the Minister from Northhampton, participated in the rite
by giving Taylor the Right Hand of Fellowship. This was a sign of ecclesial
recognition taken from Galatians 2:9. On that day, however, Edward Taylor,
without mentioning Stoddard's name, preached a sermon that criticized
Stoddard's understanding of the Lord's Supper. Taylor also noted that at the
gathering of the Westfield Church they would have spent more time on the
founder's personal relations of faith had not Stoddard and his colleague from
Hadley "drove on to the Contrary."[33] The elders and messengers from neighboring churches, who constituted the church council that presided at the gathering of the Westfield Church, did not consider profession of the doctrine in the
Westminster Catechism an adequate profession. They required even Taylor to
make a personal profession of faith.

Soon after the Westfield Church was gathered, Stoddard proposed a significant alteration in the approach to Holy Communion at the Synod of 1679.[34]
Subsequent discussions and correspondence with Stoddard prompted Taylor in
1693 to preach a series of eight sermons in which Taylor set forth his disagree-
ment with Stoddard. Westfield's first minister and Pope Stoddard were rarely, if
ever, in perfect agreement. Stoddard was less insistent upon an experience of
grace being a requirement for participation in communion than was Taylor.[35]

The Piety of Edward Taylor

In addition to being aged, venerable and learned, his gravestone in the old
burying ground declares that Edward Taylor was "pious." In modern parlance
this word has the connotation of affectation or excessive religiosity. But, in the
strict sense of the word, it means faithfully carrying out religious duties, or, in
the words of Samuel Johnson, being "careful of the duties owed by created beings to God."[36] Like many ministers, Taylor found a way to nurture his own
religious life that was unknown to many of his parishioners. He wrote poetry.

Eucharistic

The pastor of Westfield was particularly pious when it came to celebrating
the Lord's Supper. He had prepared himself to carry out that art of his ministry by
writing metaphysical poems. He entitled them:

Preparatory Meditations
before my Approach to the Lords Supper.
Chiefly upon the Doctrin [sic]
preached upon the Day of administration.

There are two series of Preparatory Meditations. The first begins on July 23, 1682 and continues until February 26, 1692. The second series begins in 1693. Taylor's last dated meditation is in October 1725. It appears that later that year or maybe in 1726 the Westfield pastor gathered up his poems and bound them.[37] The poems were passed through the generations of his descendants until they came to rest in the Yale University Library.

In the Preparatory Meditations from 1693 to 1699, Edward Taylor pondered the many similarities he discovered between the Old Testament figures and the worship of his Westfield congregation. His juxtaposing of those figures in Scripture with the Person of Christ in preparation for celebrating the Lord's Supper was, technically speaking, an exercise in typology in which the figures of the Old Testament were the "type," and the figure of Christ or the New Testament was the "antitype." Taken together they constituted a meaning that was significant for Taylor celebrating the sacrament.

In his meditations, Edward Taylor would more often than not juxtapose the person of Christ with a person or event from the Old Testament, e.g. Jesus and Joshua. In a meditation he wrote in February of 1694, Taylor pressed the similarities between Joshua, the type, leading Israel to cross the Jordan, and the leadership of Jesus, the antitype, in the New Testament Church. Taylor made several fruitful discoveries; the first being that the names of Jesus and Joshua are both rooted in the Hebrew word "to save." Second, he discussed the number twelve; twelve men raised twelve stones as a sign and a memorial at Gilgal. Taylor believed that corresponded to the twelve apostles of Jesus who he believed wrote the twelve articles in the Apostles' Creed. Third, there was the river Jordan itself. The Israelites crossed the river in which Jesus was baptized. Fourth, the worship of God affected the life of the people of the Exodus as the worship of God shaped the life of Christian congregations. Taylor expressed that fact in two succinct lines.

As Joshua fixt Gods Worship, and envest
Them with the Promise. Christ thus his hath blest.[38]

One of the significant marks of Taylor's piety was his love of music. The poet pastor repeatedly concluded his meditations with a musical figure. For example, in the closing stanzas of an undated poem, "The Return," Taylor articulated the decisive dynamic of saving grace in musical terms.

Be thou, Musician, Lord, Let me be made
    The well tun'de Instrument thou dost assume.
And let thy Glory be my Musick plaide.
    Then let thy Spirit keepe my Strings in tune,
    Whilst thou art here on Earth below with mee
    Till I sing Praise in Heaven above with thee.[39]

Taylor cast the relationship between divinity and humanity in terms of God as musician, that is to say, in terms of play. Divinity is cordially involved with humanity as God plays men and women. God is neither a distant cause nor a relentless bookkeeper but musician. In this aesthetic metaphor of music God still dominates but in a mode other than oppressive politics.

> ...Lord, Let me be made
> The well tun'de Instrument thou dost assume.
> And let thy Glory be my Musick plaide.
> Then let thy Spirit keepe my Strings in tune,...

TRINITARIAN

Who is this "Lord"? At first glance, it would seem to be Christ, since the Second Person of the Trinity is the one who "assumed" humanity. If Christ is this "Lord," the glory of Taylor's poetry would be in the praise of Christ. "Thy Spirit" would be the Spirit of Christ, sometimes known as the Holy Spirit, who follows and completes what Christ does.

But "The Lord" of Taylor's poetry may not be that simple. "The Lord" of Taylor's meditation is the Triune God. "The Lord" is neither One Person nor a simple abstract divine essence. Rather "The Lord" of Edward Taylor is a God whose dynamics involve all Three Persons of the Trinity. Given that the doctrine of the Trinity maintains that Three Persons constitute One God, there is a telling choice as to where the accent in the praise of this Lord rests. Which will be accentuated—the One Essence of God or the Three Persons of God? Western Christians prefer to start with the One Essence of God. Eastern Christians often begin with the mission of the Three Persons. It has been observed that these two accents are radically different.

> These two views begin from different
> starting points: the Eastern version with the
> distinction of persons; the Western version with
> the unity of the divine essence. They cannot be
> made to coincide.[40]

Reformed theology has allowed the distinct dynamics of the Three Persons in the One God to fade. The 1984 Anglican Reformed Dialogue, "God's Reign and Our Unity," acknowledged that the distinct dynamics of the Three Persons had been too long ignored. Conversations with Orthodox Christians prompted the candid statement:

> Though this doctrine of the Trinity, fundamental to our
> faith, has never been denied in either the Anglican or the
> Reformed tradition, yet we confess that it has not
> occupied the central place which belongs to it and which
> it has held among the Orthodox. The image of God in the
> minds of many people in our churches is a unitary one—
> the solitary creator, the prime mover of the philosophers
> consequently the doctrine of the Trinity has been
> regarded as an incomprehensible mystification of
> something simple.[41]

Taylor's "Lord" can be understood in terms of the personal missions of the Triune God. The personal mission of all three is set forth in these verses.

Be thou, Musician, Lord, Let me be made
The well tun'de Instrument thou dost assume.

The mission of the Second Person is the assumption of human nature. Here Taylor describes this assumption of humanity in musical terms. The humanity Christ assumed is described as being "The well tun'de Instrument." This figure goes back to Patristic tradition. Clement of Alexandria, at the end of the second century, delivered an "Exhortation to the Greeks" in which he described the humanity which Christ assumed in the Incarnation as a multi-toned instrument.

And He who is of David, and yet before him,
the Word of God,... makes melody to God on this
instrument of many tones...."

Clement then explicitly says that he means by this "instrument" humanity:

A beautiful breathing instrument of Music the
Lord made man, after his image.[42]

The metaphor of people being "a beautiful breathing instrument" is anything but a static understanding of human nature. This musical metaphor enables Christians to think of their life in terms of notes and chords, all of which are taken up by the Second Person of the Trinity and played by Christ in the Incarnation.

Taylor prays that the Lord will let thy glory be the poet's "Musick plaide."

"And let thy Glory be my Musick plaide."

The Lord's Glory being set forth in this line is not simply the praise of God the Creator. It is the holy beauty known in the dynamic relationship between the Second and Third Persons of the Trinity with the First Person. The glory of the Lord being "plaide" is not a celebration of the ground human beings walk upon nor the air they breathe. The melody of Taylor's piety involves the praise of God who is known in the Person of Christ and the Holy Spirit. The glory being played has to do with the myriad surprising and delightful ways that God meets and reaches people in the world. Taylor's piety delights in the music of God's presence being played by the Persons of the Trinity among God's people in the world. In short, the glory that resounds in Taylor's poetry is closer to "Love Divine All Love Excelling" and "The Spacious Firmament on High."

Epicletic* [43]

A repeated mark of Taylor's piety is his invocation of the Holy Spirit. Hence, the line in "The Return": "Then let thy Spirit keepe my Strings in tune." The tuning of humanity to God's glory is one of the missions of the Third Person of the Trinity. It is the Holy Spirit that pitches Christian life to the glory of God. If the mission of the Second Person of the Trinity is to assume human nature, then the mission of the Third Person of the Trinity is to keep Christian life tuned to God. Therefore, at critical points in their worship the sons and daughters of Calvin invoke the Holy Spirit.

Thomas F. Torrance has noted "the epicletic dimension" of the life and worship of Reformed congregations.[44] He was referring to the "epiclesis," that is, the prayer to the Holy Spirit in the communion prayer. But those prayers to the Holy Spirit are not restricted to the communion service. At other decisive points in the worship of Reformed Churches, for example before baptism, there are prayers requesting that the Third Person of the Trinity enable a congregation's rites to glorify God rather than themselves or the world they have made. This feature of their worship stems from the fact that Reformed congregations never forget that God comes from Heaven above rather than from Earth below. It is from a realm of being beyond their own, i.e., from Heaven above, that God impinges upon those who on Earth do dwell.

This refrain of Reformed piety can be heard in the concluding couplet of the first seven stanzas of "The Return":

Oh! that thou wast on Earth below with mee!

Or That I was in Heaven above with thee.[45]

God in Heaven above is not confined to, nor defined by, nor confused with "Earth below." This vehemently maintained distinction accounts for the austerity of Calvinist worship as well as this tradition's truculent "no" to human enthusiasms. The sons and daughters of Calvin are ever wary of identifying God too closely with earthly materials, customs, or practices. For Reformed Christians "The Lord" is sovereign of creation, not part of it.

And yet, in the next to the last stanza, Taylor says of his Lord, "That thou hast been on Earth below with mee." In that stanza the poet and pastor specifies where and how God's presence has dwelt with him.

But I've thy Pleasant Pleasant Presence had

In Word, Pray're, Ordinances and Duties; . . .[46]

In other words, he encountered God in the Word preached, the prayer offered, the ordinances celebrated in their meetinghouse, as well as in his duties done in the midst of Westfield. The rituals of Taylor's congregation in Westfield realized the promised presence of God in their midst as did the memorials of Israel at Gilgal. In their worship God was known, enjoyed and glorified.

The congregation's worship has continued for over three centuries. Having moved pew, pulpit, font and table in that time, the congregation of Old First finds themselves situated in what Calvin called the "orchestra of the world." In his commentary on Psalm 135 Calvin maintained:

All the world is a theater for the display

of the divine goodness, wisdom, justice and

power, but the church is the orchestra as it

were...[47]

The Genevan preacher and teacher had in mind a Greek amphitheater where the chorus occupies the orchestra in the very front part of the theater. In the course of the drama the chorus would comment upon the action. Calvin's figure suggests that the church is that place in the world where the people of God play the chorus and comment on the display of God's goodness, wisdom, justice and power in the world.

Indeed churches usually are situated so that the realms and forms of the world in which God plays pass before them. The second building of the First Church in Chestnut Hill was built near the junction of Hammond Street and the commuter train station. Many dramas are played out in that one site. The maples are bright in the fall. In the winter they can be identified by their shape against the sky. In the spring the Garden Club's flowers and shrubs bloom. In the summer the day lilies flourish along the stone wall. All sorts and conditions of human beings have left their mark on the area. Arrowheads recall peoples who lived in the region from the tenth to the thirteenth century. Hammond Street is named for a family that arrived four centuries later. The bend in the road is associated with George Washington, and the train station with Lincoln's assassination.

Now while the trains come and go more or less on schedule, the cars thump over the bridge, and the post office trucks back up to their platform. At any point in the day, people are running or walking down to the train or returning from the train. Some are children coming out to school talking of math and Spanish tests. Some are headed into town to work. Others come out to work; the man who rides his old bicycle to the fish market, the women who come to clean houses, and the people who build foundations or paint houses. Others come to play, hang out, carouse, shout, smash and pound. The church is in the orchestra of this theater, holding up and commenting upon God's goodness, wisdom, justice and power being displayed.

On the first day of the week when the church's bell rings out over the neighborhood, various folk respond. In Taylor's Westfield people walked or rode to church. But today some come to church in Chestnut Hill by getting off the train and walking up the parking lot of the train station; others drive down Hammond Street from Route Nine, some walk up Suffolk or Middlesex Road. They all enter the sanctuary while the prelude is being played, slip into a pew and take their place in the chorus of God's people.

Chapter 2

The Word in the Meetinghouse

$\mathcal{A}$t the front of the sanctuary is a font, a table, a lectern and a pulpit. The lectern and pulpit declare these are a people of the book. Anyone with curiosity can go up behind either and find there assorted slips of paper, old orders of service, glasses partially filled with water, and taped-down prayers. A large Bible lies above everything else. The first page or cover is usually inscribed with the name of the person in whose memory that particular volume was given to the congregation as well as the date of the gift.

If it is a large Bible, more often than not, it will be the Authorized Version or as it is popularly known, "The King James." However, that translation may well have been replaced by one more recent. The old Bible is then carefully put on a shelf with others like the American Standard Version of 1901. But sometimes the old Bible isn't replaced. The old translation remains open on the pulpit and the reader sets the new translation on top of it.

In the pews there is another book—the hymnal. That contains the hymns which John Williamson Nevin, Mercersburg theologian, called:

> ...perpetual sermons. Texts of Scripture stuck in mind like
> proverbs, enforce their own lessons when all commentar-
> ies are dumb or forgotten.[1]

The hymnal might be a relatively recent hymnal like *Rejoice in the Lord*, or an old standard such as *The Pilgrim Hymnal*. *Rejoice in the Lord* bears the subtitle, "A Hymn Companion to the Scriptures," which means it is a commentary upon the biblical narrative. In the preface the hymnbook committee declared:

> The plan of this book is very simple:
> the canonical order of the Bible has provided the outline
> for the selection and arrangement of hymns.[2]

To underline this scheme, *Rejoice in the Lord* cited a passage of Scripture at the bottom of each hymn page. The hymnal divided the biblical narrative into four parts:

Part I: The God of Abraham Praise
Part II: Behold the Lamb of God
Part III: Spirit of Truth, Spirit of Power
Part IV: The Hope of Glory

The 1958 *Pilgrim Hymnal* arranged its hymns under much broader headings:

Worship
God The Father
Our Lord Jesus Christ
The Holy Spirit
The Trinity
The Bible
The Church of Christ
The Christian Life
The Kingdom of God on Earth

Seasons
Special Services and Occasions
Children
Youth
The National Anthem
Service Music.

During the organ prelude those sitting in the pew may check the hymns up on the board to see what they will be singing and perhaps the psalm for the day. Members of a congregation are not indifferent to the chosen hymns. Comments like, "What wonderful hymns this morning! They were familiar, ["O Master let me walk with Thee"] and not that dirge we sang last Sunday ["Lord, Thou Hast Searched Me"]," can be heard at the end of church.

After the organist concludes his prelude, he glances up to be sure the minister has entered by the side door and taken his seat. Then the organist modulates to the doxology. With the notes of that venerable tune everyone stands to sing. The worship of God has begun.

There is a note to the suggested order of service in the back of *The Pilgrim Hymnal* which reads: "The doxology may be sung in place of the Call to Worship or at the offering."[3] The First Church exercises the first option and begins with the doxology. After singing the Doxology, the congregation and minister say a prayer of confession together. Those two notes of doxology and confession constitute the opening moves of the People of God when they gather in church on the Lord's Day.

THE DOXOLOGY

The Doxology in *The Pilgrim Hymnal* consists of words sung to the tune of "Old Hundredth." It is called "Old Hundredth" because it is the tune to which Thomas Sternhold and John Hopkins set Psalm 100 in their 1562 edition of metrical Psalms. When their edition became known as the "Old Version," the tune linked with Psalm 100 became "Old Hundredth."

"Old Hundredth" originated in Geneva. It is thought to be the creation of Louis Bourgeois, the man who wrote tunes the Calvinists sang in that city. Since then the sturdy old melody has been set to other words, including Ralph Waldo Emerson's Concord hymn about rude bridges and shots fired around the world.

When sung as an offertory, the doxology ("Old Hundredth") is joined to the words written by Thomas Ken in 1695:

Praise God from whom all blessings flow;
Praise him all creatures here below;
Praise him above, ye heavenly hosts:
Praise Father, Son, and Holy Ghost.

A doxology may refer to the words of praise sung at the end of psalm or anthem. "The Doxology" was originally written as the conclusion of three hymns that

Ken wrote. It is the last verse of Ken's hymns "All Praise to thee, my God this night" and "Awake, my soul, and with the sun." "The Doxology" as found in *Rejoice in the Lord* and *The Pilgrim Hymnal* [4] consists of Ken's words and Bourgeois' tune. It is associated with bringing forward the morning offering. Visitors in a congregation hearing the familiar melody will listen for the words, "Praise God from whom all blessings flow," before heartily joining in the singing.

At the beginning of the morning service at the First Church the tune is "Old Hundredth" from the Old Version but the text is taken from Tate and Brady's "New Version" of 1669 which is a refrain from Psalm 57:5.

> Be thou, O God, exalted high,
> And, as thy glory fills the sky,
> So let it be on earth displayed,
> Till thou art here, as there, obeyed.

In this doxology the congregation's words cordially acknowledge God amid realms and forms of being that the people of God encounter in their world and worship.

Edward Taylor understood a doxological opening of Sunday worship. In the fall of 1696 Taylor wrote a preparatory meditation based on words from the last chapter of the Epistle to the Hebrews, "We have an altar." [The Epistle to the Hebrews 13:19] In the second stanza Taylor offered a playful statement of being distracted from the worship of God.

> Mine Heart's a Park or Chase of sins: Mine Head
>   'S a Bowling Alley. Sins play Ninehole there.
> Phansy's a Green: sin Barly breaks in't led.
> Judgement's a pingle.
> Blindman's Buff's plaid there. [5]

By the time he concluded the meditation, Taylor returned to the melody from Tate and Brady's doxology.

> ...do make my tunes as fume,
>   From off this Altar rise to thee Most High
> And all their steams stufft with thy Altars blooms,
>   My Sacrifice of Praise in Melody. [6]

In other words, a sung praise of God emerged from the secular recreations of Taylor's heart.

A sung doxological opening of worship stands in marked contrast to opening greetings like "Good Morning." Such opening words embody the temptation to begin worship in terms of human being rather than God's being. These beginnings may be didactically orthodox. For example,

> Why are we here?
> We have responded to the gospel of God's love for us in
> Jesus Christ. [7]

Nevertheless, the accent remains on the congregation rather than God. A doxology or doxological hymn at the beginning of worship strikes a very different chord.

"BE THOU O GOD EXALTED HIGH"

The doxological figure of God being "exalted high" is well-known. It can be heard in a favorite opening hymn of praise such as "O Worship the King," the second hymn in *Rejoice in the Lord*. This eighteenth-century paraphrase of Psalm 104 by Sir Robert Grant carries a congregation's praise out and up to God with its opening line, "O worship the King, all glorious above." Grant entered the British Parliament in 1818. One year after writing this hymn he was knighted and appointed governor of Bombay.

Both that hymn and the Tate and Brady paraphrase may be criticized for these exalted figures of speech. More than one modern soul, when thinking of heaven, has imagined a five star hotel. The opening line of "O Worship the King, All Glorious Above" doesn't describe any such place. Nor does the line "Be Thou O God exalted High" speak of such a locale. Both the lines ardently praise the Divine Lord who is out in the world and then some, well beyond humanity's grasp.

Nevertheless, objections have been raised against the figure of God as "King." With increased awareness of the gender issues, that line of a traditional hymn may become the target of sharp criticism and informed suppression. A congregation may feel compelled to change the opening words of Grant's hymn "O worship the King, all glorious above," to "We worship Thee, God, all glorious above," and substitute that text in the order of service. Many orders of service are supplied with current revisions of traditional hymns. Having learned from the objections and sung revisions that have been offered, the church needs to evaluate both the criticisms and the alternatives. This means considering the way words work in lines of hymns where God is praised as a "King," in terms of translation and analogy.

The question of translation is primary. "King" is the way Grant chose to translate the four letters that in Hebrew signify God. The single word "King" is an eighteenth-century man's rendition of what the 1640 Bay Psalm Book translated "exceedingly great art thou" and the 1985 Jerusalem Bible chose to translate "how great you are"! Since the word "king" is not found in the opening Hebrew line of Psalm 104, the suppression of the word "king" could be pressed simply on the grounds of translation alone.

But subtler objections can be raised in terms of religious language, specifically in terms of analogy. Analogies between human communities are one thing, as for example, comparing the pilgrims of Plymouth to the people of Israel.[8] Analogies between human experience and God are quite another matter. In such analogies "a verbal expression is put for something that by definition transcends verbal expression."[9] When God is one element of an analogy, then certain distinctions are traditionally made. Not all analogies are the same.

First of all, there are analogies of proportion and analogies of attribution. In analogies of proportion the analogy turns on an action or form. In analogies of attribution the analogy turns on an attribute. Therefore, in any analogy the initial question is whether it is an analogy of proportion or attribution.

However, analogies of proportion and analogies of attribution each hold two forms within them. Within analogies of proportion there are analogies of proper and improper proportion. Analogies of proper proportion juxtapose two entities that are proportionately alike. An example of an analogy of proper proportion would be to say that someone's love for their cousin is analogous to their love for their brother. The action of the analogy is love. Cousins and brothers are both human. Therefore, the analogy is one of proper proportion.

Analogies of improper proportion juxtapose two entities that are decidedly not alike. An example of an analogy of improper proportion would be to say that someone's love of her boat is analogous to her love of family. Again, in this analogy the action is love. But since a boat is not human and families are, the analogy is one of improper proportion.

Analogies of attribution can be separated into analogies of intrinsic attribution and analogies of extrinsic attribution.[10] In analogies of intrinsic attribution the attribute of the analogy is intrinsic to both elements of the analogy. Even though it may be more marked in one element of the analogy than the other, still the attribute is intrinsic to both. An example of an analogy of intrinsic attribution would be to say that the houses in New Amsterdam were analagous to those in the Netherlands. That is to say the colonial structures shared the attributes intrinsic to Dutch architecture. Thus, the analogy is one of intrinsic attribution.

In analogies of extrinsic attribution, while certainly shared, the common attribute is decidedly extrinsic to one. The attribute in the second is dependent upon the first. An example of an analogy of extrinsic attribution would be to say that the government of New Amsterdam is analogous to that of the Netherlands. The attributes of government in New Amsterdam were certainly Dutch, but they were primarily known in Holland. Thus, the analogy is one of extrinsic attribution.

The analogies of proportion and attribution are found in the church's language for God. Discussion of figures for God like "King" in hymns, such as "O Worship the King," are knowingly or unknowingly based upon analogies of proper and improper proportion or analogies of intrinsic and extrinsic attribution. The discussion is usually initiated by calling the word "King" in the first line of Robert Grant's hymn, "O Worship the King, All Glorious Above," a metaphor for God. But metaphor works on an analogy of improper proportion. Thus, those who object to "O Worship the King" as a metaphor are objecting to the figure of God as "King" as an analogy of improper proportion. That is to say, in a metaphor two radically different entities are juxtaposed. The entities are usually so different that, when taken together, an imaginative new meaning results. To call the figure of God as "King" a metaphor is to speak in terms of an analogy of improper proportion and maintain that "God" and "King," properly speaking, have nothing in common. But when the two are juxtaposed, a meaning does emerge. If Grant's "King" in the opening line of the hymn is based upon an analogy of improper proportion, then God is most definitely not a king. Being a metaphor, "King" is decidedly different from God.

However, the more likely objection to the figure of God as "King" does not have to do with "King " being a metaphor based upon an analogy of improper proportion. Rather the protest may very well be against the figure of God as "King" as an analogy of proper proportion. In that case, Grant is claiming that there is a similarity between the actions of God and the actions of a king. While "King" and God are not simply identical, nevertheless an analogy of proper proportion maintains that a similarity does exist in terms of the relationships both God and "King" elicit. Grant may indeed have felt he should act in church as he acted in court. If the word "King" in his hymn is based on an analogy of proper proportion, then one should praise God the way one praises the King of England.

However, suppose the figure "King" in Grant's hymn is based on an analogy of attribution either intrinsic or extrinsic. If the juxtaposing of the God and "King" is based on an analogy of intrinsic attribution, the claim would be that even though God and "King" are decidedly different, nevertheless there is an attribute, for example power, intrinsic to both divinity and monarchy. Did Grant, living in 1833, believe that God and monarchs exercised a similar kind of power? He might claim that the power in question resides first and foremost in God, and only dependently in kings and queens in any real way. That would declare the hymn's juxtaposition of God and "King" to be an analogy of intrinsic attribution.

If, on the other hand, the figure of God as "King" rests on an analogy of extrinsic attribution then the attribute, power for example, resides primarily in God and any sharing of that attribute with human kings or queens would have to have been authoritatively articulated by God. The attribute in question, for example power, is in no way intrinsic to human being. It is utterly extrinsic to human being and can only be attributed to human being from God. If Grant translated the name of God as "King" with an analogy of extrinsic attribution, he could only have done so having learned from an authoritative source that God was a king. Presumably he did so on the basis of psalms and other canonical scriptures. That would be an analogy of extrinsic attribution.

Given these four kinds of analogy: an analogy of improper proportion, an analogy of proper proportion, an analogy of intrinsic attribution, or an analogy of extrinsic attribution, the word "King" as a figure for God could be eliminated on the basis of any one of these four analogies. More than one congregation has tried to revise hymns in a way that will remove offending metaphors. Different forms of revision have been carried out. It is not unusual for a Sunday congregation to find a revised text of a hymn in their order of service. In that way the line of Grant's hymn "O worship the King, all glorious above" might appear as to "We worship Thee, God, all glorious above." Why would a worship leader make that change?

They might eliminate the figure of God as "King" on the grounds that it is an impoverished metaphor. In twentieth-century hymnals the royal metaphor for God has become a cliché. Modern folk hear about kings in church. So much so that the metaphor has lost its impact. Since it is preferable for Christians in any era to

> **Analogy of Improper Proportion God as King:** meaning that God really isn't at all like a king, but juxtaposing God with "king" creates a metaphor that produces a meaning.

use living metaphors for God rather than clichés, Grant's hymn needs to be revised. This is to speak in terms of the analogy of improper proportionality.

A second argument could be made on the basis of an analogy of proper proportion. In point of fact, members of a contemporary congregation no longer recognize what relations to a monarch involve because they are seldom, if ever, in the presence of a king or queen. They derive no meaning in regard to God from royal analogies. Since the figure of "King" is not one that is any longer understood, it is not a good figure to articulate a person's relation to God. That is to say, Grant's "King" based on the analogy of proper proportionality is to be rejected.

> **Analogy of**
> **Proper Proportion**
> **God as King:**
> meaning that God acts the way
> King George III did.

The third argument could be made that modern Christians no longer believe that monarchs inherently share attributes of God, such as power. Therefore, they reject Grant's paraphrase of the psalm. The rejection of any analogy of intrinsic attribution might well be deemed necessary in order to maintain the distinction between divinity and humanity. The sons and daughters of Calvin are reluctant to identify any human quality with divinity. This would be to confuse the sense of God in Heaven above with rulers on earth below. In that case the figure of God as "King" would be rejected in terms of rejecting any analogy of intrinsic attribution between divinity and humanity.

> **Analogy of**
> **Intrinsic Attribution**
> **God as King:**
> meaning that God and kings share
> an attribute intrinsic to their being,
> for example, power.

A fourth choice remains. If the figure of God as "King" is based on an analogy of extrinsic attribution, then the figure can be rejected by rejecting the authority that articulates that particular analogy. To call God "King" is a biblical figure. However, on the basis of religious experience the biblical figure of God as "King" might be overthrown and therefore rejected. Some critics would argue that figures like "King" from the Scripture and tradition are too rooted in another era and another culture to have meaning for Christians today. On the basis of contemporary experience such figures are to be replaced. Thus, "King" becomes "Thee."

Those congregations centered in religious experience will revise hymns in order to fit their experience of God. Thus,

> **Analogy of**
> **Extrinsic Attribution**
> **God as King:**
> meaning a canonical figure describing
> the dynamics of divinity.
> Any such dynamics are found
> primarily in God and only
> secondarily in human monarchs.

the revision "We worship Thee, God, All glorious above" says much more than that these people do not understand God to be like a king. The first word "We" affirms the congregation's experience. The hymn's opening line is no longer an invitation to worship God. It is a description of what is being done. Moreover, God is now much more personable, more approachable as a "Thee" rather than a "King." In other words, the distance between divinity and humanity is closed in this revision. Presumably the singers' experience of God finds God much closer to them than a monarch would be. At this point the critical question arises, does a church only praise God in terms of names that only fit that generation's experience or current ideology?

To reject Grant's word "King" in terms of an analogy of extrinsic attribution has serious implications for Reformed theology because much of Reformed worship is informed by biblical figures of speech. If those biblical figures are overthrown and revised in terms of a congregation's experience, that means that our understanding of religious language is informed not by Scripture but by current experience and culture. In other words, the Word addressing a congregation in Scripture is no longer primary. Marjorie Procter-Smith has clearly stated this position.

> An alternative understanding of the Bible locates authority
> not on the Bible as a book, or even in selected texts in the
> Bible, but in the suffering, struggle, and survival of
> women and men who are oppressed.[11]

Which is to say that the attributes of God are not primarily known in terms of the Word in Scripture. For this reason, Karl Barth maintained the only appropriate analogy for religious language is for it to be the analogy of extrinsic attribution. Barth rejects the other analogies because they in one way or another limit the dynamics of God. Moreover, he notes how easily divine attributes are domesticated by humanity in the analogies of intrinsic attribution as well as by analogies of proportion, both proper and improper.[12]

In a congregation where the knowledge of God is informed by the canonical Scriptures, biblical metaphors, names and analogies of God are not suppressed. For these congregations the opening line of Grant's hymn "O worship the King all glorious above" rests on a biblical analogy of extrinsic attribution. That is to say, the word "King" in that hymn refers first and foremost to God's relationship to humanity. Biblical metaphors for God are not convenient labels that various people have chosen to express their experience of divinity. The figure of God as "King," coming from the Scriptures, articulates the dependence of humanity upon God, before it says anything about human government or community. Any such references are decidedly secondary and derivative. Therefore, Grant's word "King" is not to be rejected as an analogy of extrinsic attribution. On that ground it is a perfectly appropriate analogy. To reject the word "King" on the basis of the other three kinds of analogy is to overthrow the role of Scriptural language in the knowledge of God.

"ANd As THy qloRy fills THE sky"

The Doxology's second line introduces the figures of space and light. The reference to God's glory filling the sky speaks to the magnitude of God's glory. The magnitude of God's glory is to be understood not in terms of mechanical power but of space and light. This paraphrase is a reflection of Psalm 57.

The second verse of "O Worship the King," paraphrasing Psalm 104, has a contemporary ring when it refers to God's canopy as "space." God's being encompasses the space that humanity has so recently begun to explore. Both references to sky and space keep the accent out there with God rather than on the angle of human perception.

Both the second line of the doxology, "as thy glory fills the sky," and the second verse of Grant's hymn, "whose robe is the light," introduce a key analogy in the biblical descriptions of God's glorious being. God's glory is likened to light. For example, in Psalm forty-three, verse three, it is written:

Oh send out your light and your truth;
let them lead me,
let them bring me to your holy hill
and to your dwelling!

Also Jesus' transfiguration presents one of the most dramatic examples:

And he was transfigured before them,
and his face shone like the sun,
and his garments became white as light.
[Matthew 17:2]

In the doxology from Tate and Brady's New Version the reference to light is indirect "as thy glory fills the sky." In the second verse of "O Worship the King" God's splendor is directly described in terms of light, "Whose robe is the light...". When light is juxtaposed to the glory of God, which of the four kinds of analogy is involved?

It is not an analogy of improper proportion. Light is not another metaphor for God. The light humanity experiences in the world is not taken from the world and projected upon God. Nor is the light of God's glory an analogy of intrinsic attribution. There is no innate quality of light that is shared with divinity. There is nothing intrinsic to the light that plays in the sky that is identical with the glory of God. That would be to identify God with the first product of creation.

However, the action of light is sufficiently similar to the dynamics of God's glory to appear as an analogy of proper proportion. Light can be a figure for the dynamics of divinity. Instead of being a massive pile, a huge lump or a first cause, divinity is a moving presence. God moves and plays among the realms and forms of being that constitute reality. Since the speed of light in point of fact measures the time and space in which humanity dwells, the speed of light may serve as a figure for the magnitude of God's glory.

Taylor certainly thought so. He repeatedly cited light in terms of the analogy of proper proportion. In December of 1694, one of his meditations indicated that the minister had been playing with a mirror outdoors. Perhaps he had tried to observe a noted solar eclipse in June with a mirror and "button moulds of clay" over his eyes. Turning the mirror Taylor caught the sunlight and it so dazzled his eyes as to make them water.

He connected that experience with the dynamics of God. The flashes of light bespeak the dynamics of divinity.

> Good God! what grace is this takes place in thee?
> How dost thou make thy Son to shine, and prize
> His glory thus? Thy Looking-glass give mee.
> And let thy Spirit wipe my Watry eyes.
> That I may see his flashing glory darte
> Like Lightening quick till it
> infire my heart.[13]

In other words, Taylor associated the blinding flashes of the sun's reflection in the hand-held mirror with the reflections of glory between the persons of the Trinity. The glory within God is such that it enables the First Person to manifest the Second Person. "How dost thou make thy Son to shine...."? The Third Person's mission is to enable the poet pastor to catch a glimpse of God's lightning-quick glory in the world. "And let thy Spirit wipe my Watry eyes." Having overcome that obstruction, divine glory will infire his heart, that is give him the note that will set him singing in the world.

However attractive the analogy of proper proportion linking the glory of God to light in the Scriptures may be, that still is not the primary analogy upon which this figure works. The primary analogy is that of extrinsic attribution. Taylor recognized this fact when he wrote his initial preparatory meditations in the second series. In the course of that meditation, Taylor acknowledged the glories of the world. He recognized the beauty and power of what can befall human beings. But he concluded that:

> The glory of the world slickt up in types
> In all Choise things chosen to typify,
> His glory upon whom the work doth light,
> To thine's a Shaddow, or a Butterfly.

In other words, whatever may be said about the glory of God in terms of the world and the lights therein, whatever can be said about the good experiences of creation known to humanity, Christ's

> ... glory doth their glory quite excell:
> More than the Sun excells in its bright glee
> A nat, an Earewig, Weevill, Snaile, or Shell.[14]

For Taylor the glory of God impinging upon humanity in the event and dynamics of Christian redemption is far superior to anything the world might display or that the world might offer. The light of God's glory is properly the glory of the Trinity, not whatever light there might be in the world. This would mean that light as a figure for God's glory is ultimately an analogy of extrinsic attribution.

"So let it be on earth displayed"

The third line of the doxology states that the people of God expect to enjoy a measure of God's glory in this world. If the glory of God is brighter than that of the creation's sun, then how can the glory of God be seen when it is displayed on earth? The answer is found in one of Calvin's best figures:

> The splendor of the divine countenance, which even the apostle calls "inapproachable" [I Timothy 6:16], is for us an inexplicable labyrinth unless we are conducted into it by the thread of the Word.[15]

THE GLORY OF THE WORD

Those who come to church on Sunday expect to hear two or three readings from Scripture; one from the Old Testament, one from the Epistles and one from a Gospel. When the preacher does not personally select the Scripture readings, they are taken from what is called a lectionary. One of the most far-reaching actions of the Second Vatican Council was the publication in 1969 of a lectionary for the Sunday Scriptures in which one Gospel is primarily read in the course of a church year. In one year (A) it is Matthew, and another year (B) it is Mark with some help from John, and yet another year (C) Luke. Thus, in Year A, B or C certain Scriptures are read on the particular Sunday of the church year, for example, on the first Sunday after Pentecost, known as Trinity Sunday. In Year A the Gospel reading in most congregations would be the Great Commission in Matthew 28 where the Trinity is explicitly mentioned. On the same Sunday in Year B the congregation would hear the story of Jesus' encounter with Nicodemus in John 3. In Year C the Gospel would be from the Fourth Gospel chapter 16, verses 12–15 speaking of the Spirit of Truth.

This arrangement of reading the Gospels for Sunday was adopted in one form or another by other churches in North America, beginning with the Presbyterians who included a version of this arrangement of Scripture for Sunday in *The Worshipbook 1970*. Other liturgical books followed. The Roman lectionary was evident in the Lutherans' 1978 *Book of Worship* and the Episcopalians' 1979 *Book of Common Prayer*. In other churches the readings from the lectionary were printed on bulletin covers as well as in planning calendars.

This shared lectionary touches families in surprising ways. A visiting grandmother and grandfather may attend Mass on Saturday evening only to hear the same Gospel being read when they attend the church of their child's spouse on Sunday morning. The differences in church lections are more likely to be heard in the Old Testament lessons. The differences could be easily identified in a publication like the *Proclamation Series A*. This 1975 series of studies on the lectionary texts for the church year presented at the top of each page the readings for the particular Christian communities. The same format continues in the 1988 *Proclamation*.

Although the Gospel reading "calls the tune," other notes are definitely heard in a Sunday's readings. With every Gospel lesson there is a reading from the Old Testament as well. These passages articulate the dynamics of God. For example, on Trinity Sunday in Year A the creation story from the first chapter of Genesis 1:1-2:4a accompanies the Great Commission from Matthew. In Year B it is Isaiah's vision of the seraphs calling out, "Holy, holy, holy is the Lord of hosts; the whole earth is full of his glory," that accompanies the story of Nicodemus. In Year C the personification of wisdom present at the creation is the reading juxtaposed to the promise of the Spirit of Truth. These texts being heard on the same Sunday of Year A, B or C proclaim that God's people live out of a complex and sometimes baffling sense of divinity.

The exchange between Jesus and Nicodemus dramatizes the fact that a Christian's knowledge of God involves more than the teachings and signs of Jesus' ministry. Like Joseph of Arimethea, Nicodemus was a pious Jew who had marked well Jesus' signs and teachings. For some reason he met Jesus at night. In the course of their conversation the words that stand out are found in the Authorized Version's phrase "born again." "Except a man be born again, he cannot see the kingdom of God [3:3]." The New Revised Standard Version translates that same line, "No one can see the Kingdom of God without being born from above/ or born anew." That figure speaks to the radical reordering that being an adult Christian convert means.

Nicodemus is not the only person to be puzzled by what a particular element in the story said about God and humanity. Listening to the biblical lections in a season of Sundays, people in church begin to realize that their ideas of God do not match God's ways. After hearing the stories for three or more years, those in the pew and pulpit find that there is more in the biblical narratives than their favorite ideas about divinity.

The people of God enjoy a keen insight into the nature of reality. In large part this comes from their hearing the biblical narratives Sunday after Sunday in the course of at least three years including their holidays. These Scriptures of the church year can be heard as the descriptions of events in which God is intimately involved. The biblical texts also hand over venerable ideas about God that have been passed on from generation to generation. Part of a congregation's listening is to grasp the form of the biblical story. Instead of coming away with only a vague sense of the story, those with ears to hear recognize the limits of detail. They discover that the narratives of Jesus' baptism differ in terms of where he was when the voice from heaven was heard or that in Luke he says more in the Nazareth synagogue than he does in Matthew or Mark. These details hold meanings that resonate on other Sundays in the same year.

The biblical narratives can also be heard in terms of recurrent human situations. There are all sorts of basic figures of human experience, emotions and sage wisdom that some preachers are most adept at emphasizing. Members of their congregations come away on Sunday with a sense that there have been times when they too have walked in the night, having been impressed by what someone has said or done and wanting to know more. The experience of birth or new beginnings would be another sense of the Scripture that resonates with a parishioner. Juxtaposing contemporary experience with biblical narratives tells people that they are far from being alone. The biblical stories can also declare the intentions and power of God.

With a touch of the Holy Spirit these folk begin to understand, like people who hear a joke and understand it without someone having to explain the joke to them. Their understanding becomes manifest in a wider embrace of the realms and forms of being in the world than they were capable of before. They have also been led by the thread of Scripture to a decided sense of God's complex being. They are open to the dynamic presence of God in the world.

Many are either too busy or preoccupied with their own affairs to change their routine and sing praises to God. When the church bell rings on Sunday mornings, many aren't around to hear it or, if they are, they are too busy to put down what they are doing and head for church. Weekends have become a time to relax from the press of the week. They enjoy themselves and take their pleasure.

One church member candidly told his minister, "For you church is first priority, but for everyone else it's second, or third." Passing that remark on to a colleague the response was, "Of course it's second or third. Where else? After family and work." Passing it on to another member of the congregation the response was, "Oh no, it's not second or third, Reverend. It's way down there— sixth, seventh or eighth. Church comes after lots of other things." But not for those people who recognize some measure of God's glory. For them personal programs once pressing and satisfying are set aside or postponed on Sunday. One such person observed, "I used to say I had better things to do on a Sunday morning. Then I discovered that wasn't so." Such awareness is a mark that the Holy Spirit has reached that person and disturbed a routine.

The disturbance reaches into summer Sundays as well. In the Sundays following Pentecost, the differences in the Old Testament readings among congregations are the most pronounced. The Roman Catholic, Episcopal and Lutheran communions choose readings from the Hebrew Scriptures for each Lord's Day that resonate with the Gospel lesson. However, the Common Lectionary of 1983 chose to read significant segments of the biblical narratives in semi-continuous manner. The stories of Abraham and Sarah through the death of Moses are read in Year A. The stories of David are read in Year B. The Elijah-Elisha stories as well as the prophets are read in Year C. With the exception of Noah, Job, and Esther, the figures in these readings are historical people. Even though stories may have gathered about them in which they loom larger than life, still they did live and walk in a particular time and place. In the history of God's people the glory of God is displayed on earth.

These basic sequences are presented in the Revised Common Lectionary of 1992 as well. However, these semi-continuous readings are accompanied by a second set of Old Testament readings drawn from a variety of Scriptures. For example, instead of Abraham's call, Hosea's exhortation to repentance may be read to accompany Matthew's call and Jesus' being criticized by the Pharisees for eating with sinners.[16] On the Sunday between July 14 and July 30 in Year B, Elisha's feeding a crowd accompanies John's account of Jesus' feeding of the five thousand rather than the story of David's murderous adultery with Bathsheba. On the Sunday between July 3 and 9 in Year C, verses from the prophet Isaiah with a figure of feminine comfort accompany Luke's sending out of the seventy. This provides an alternative to the cleansing of Naaman. These alternate readings do not provide a sustained narrative but present figures that resonate with the Gospel. This is a way of accentuating the Gospel as that Sunday's major chord.

When the semi-continuous narratives of Old Testament figures or their alternatives are juxtaposed to the Gospel narrative, other notes are struck. It is virtually impossible to program all of them in advance. Therefore, during the summer Sundays when there is a definite ongoing narrative, any number of connections and insights can occur in the pew. On any particular Sunday morning the thread in the lives of lectionary figures will lead both the preacher and members of her congregation through many different turns. The insights are not always obvious.

The reading and preaching of the Scriptures on the Lord's Day is certainly not the private preserve of the preacher. More important than any sermon title is a listing of the Scripture readings for a particular Sunday. That is why sermon-soaked saints want to see the Sunday lessons printed in the church newsletter. Ushers arriving early have been known to step up to the lectern and check the reading. Those listening carefully will notice which hymns go with the day's Scriptures. As one member of the congregation said to a minister, "If I have a chance to read the lessons before church and I get here early enough to check out the hymns, I think I can figure out what the sermon will be about."

Others will listen carefully to the choir's anthems on Sunday morning. They are commentaries on the Word. The choir director reads the lections before he chooses the Sunday music. Drawing upon the music in the choir's library, he chooses anthems and choral responses that will accentuate portions of that Sunday's Scriptures.

Parishioners often feel free to criticize the minister for switching translations, even when done in the interests of didactic clarity. After all, they only hear it once every three years and it may be a puzzling passage. One woman who came to church every Sunday startled her minister by asking for an explanation of why he had switched a translation. It had to do with the status of Anna, and he had made the move for clarity. King James read, "She was of a great age and had lived with a husband seven years after her virginity." Better, he thought, to read from The New English Bible, "She was a very old woman, who had lived seven years with her husband after she was first married." Not so. The faithful woman informed the minister that she read the Scriptures over every Saturday evening. On Sunday she listened for the Word, having sorted out any textual confusions or difficulties before she came to church. The minister need not take it upon himself to pick and choose translations at the last minute on the assumption that otherwise nobody in the church would understand. Critical comments of that kind declare the Scriptures to be common ground.

Preachers are often surprised to learn how the biblical narrative speaks to a sermon-soaked saint. For example, one parishioner told his minister that he was "sick and tired of the rich being criticized Sunday after Sunday." Watching this faithful member of the church walk to his car, the minister could recall no such references in recent sermons. He hadn't even recently preached on the topic. Then the preacher remembered. This was Year C. That meant the Gospel was Luke. His parishioner, being attentive Sunday after Sunday, had caught the basic tone of Luke's Gospel, which is a decided preference for the poor.

At other times people become caught up in the extended narratives of the summer time. On an August Sunday a visiting preacher changed the Old Testament lesson in the order of service. At coffee hour she was surprised when a member of the congregation noted that she had altered that lection.

"Yes," answered the minister, "I thought it went better with my sermon than the 2 Kings 2. "

"I suppose so," replied the parishioner, "it's just that I was looking forward to hearing how Elijah died."

At that point the visiting preacher realized here was a person who had been following the narrative of Elijah stories for several weeks. The narrative had carried this person along in ways that probably surprised them both. Who would have thought that the change in lessons would be felt as such a decided loss? So dynamic and complex is the process that it is impossible to predict when, where or in what way the Holy Spirit and the Word of Scripture speak to people in a given congregation.

At weddings, people publicly share their sense of the Scripture. Hearing the lessons the bride and groom have chosen for their wedding, the congregation comes to appreciate the insights that have reached the couple. The United Church of Christ's *Book of Worship* and the Presbyterian *Supplemental Liturgical Resource 3 Weddings* both suggest texts other than the evergreen I Corinthians 13.[17] Preparing their wedding, a couple sits down and reads through their lists of suggested readings. This exercise is an important step in placing their relationship in the context of God's people.

Reading various scriptures and choosing one for their wedding, a couple becomes sensitive not only to their present situation, but to their religious background as well. Certain passages may be familiar from weddings they have recently attended. When they recall where a Scripture was read, they become conscious not only of the text, but also of the church in which the wedding was celebrated. In this way the different accents among the people of God begin to emerge.

A couple will often discover parts of the Bible that neither one has known before. More than one couple has asked, "Where is Tobit in this Bible?" This may raise a question about the Bible that one of them received from their church.

They discover that not all Bibles are the same. The various new translations provide alternatives.

When they come back to the minister, the discussion centers on the passages that they have chosen as possibilities for their wedding. The conversation turns on which of the Scriptures provides the best context for the love that this bride and groom are celebrating before God and their guests. The pastor's homily at the wedding is based upon the couple's reasons for choosing a particular text.

In that way their wedding is more than a celebration of their personal relationship. A wedding sets the couple's love in the context of the way others have known and enjoyed God. If the Gospel they have selected is a passage from John 15 that begins, "This is my commandment that you love one another as I have loved you," they are affirming a love that involves sacrifice. When a divorced man and woman choose verses from Jeremiah 18—the allegory of the potter— as a Scripture reading, the sensitive in the congregation realize the hope of this marriage. When a young couple choose verses from the Song of Solomon, "Look, he comes, leaping upon the mountains, bounding over the hills...Arise my love my fair one and come away," or "Love is strong as death, passion as fierce as the grave," then the congregation is reminded of the way in which the people of God enjoy and embrace human sexuality.

Led by the Spirit, a man and woman will share not only their own joy but a measure of the beauty set forth in Scripture as well. When the Scriptures they have chosen and commented upon are read at their wedding, the couple acknowledges a share in the glory of God. When people come up afterwards and say to the minister, "That was a beautiful wedding!" an appropriate response will direct people's attention to the couple's choice of Scripture which sets the tone of the wedding. That thread of the Scripture and the Spirit will lead the couple back to a Sunday congregation after their wedding day.

"Till Thou art Here, as there, obeyed."

The last line of the congregation's opening doxology strikes the note of obedience.

> Be thou, O God, exalted high,
> And, as thy glory fills the sky,
> So let it be on earth displayed,
> Till thou art here, as there, obeyed.

When followed by the words of the prophet Micah, "What doth the Lord require of thee but to do justly, to love mercy and to walk humbly with thy God," the final line's opening word "Till" sounds a note of warning. Members of a congregation are reminded that they do not dwell one with the angels Isaiah glimpsed in the Temple. In the course of the week they are very much bound to earth. Not infrequently they have wandered in ways other than holy. They have pursued goals far short of God's glory. Consequently, a prayer of confession follows the doxology at the beginning of every Sunday worship service.

The Prayer of Confession

Edward Taylor repeatedly began his meditations with a vehement confession of sins. As a poet he did so in striking terms. In the opening of his October 1696 meditation Taylor described and acknowledged the wandering ways of his life in terms of seventeenth-century games that people played for recreation. He placed certain games in parts of his mind. Then he went on in the same meditation to speak of "Blindeman's Buffs" being played with his judgement.[18]

The people in a Sunday congregation rarely acknowledge their sins in such radically poetic terms. Instead they do so by saying a prayer of general confession. This prayer acknowledges that the congregation has failed to live their lives with the measure of God's beauty made known to them in the world and Word.

> Merciful God,
> we confess that we have not loved you with our whole heart.
> We have failed to be an obedient church.
> We have not done your will,
> we have broken your law,
> we have rebelled against your love.
> We have not loved our neighbors,
> and we have refused to hear the cry of the needy.
> Forgive us, we pray,
> and free us for joyful obedience;
> through Jesus Christ our Lord.[19]

After the prayer of confession has been said, where is the forgiveness mentioned at the conclusion of this prayer realized? At times a biblical sentence from the epistles is spoken by the minister to remind the congregation of God's forgiveness. For example:

> Hear the good news!
> If we have died with Christ,
> we believe that we shall also live with him.
> So you are to consider yourselves dead to sin
> and alive to God in Christ Jesus.
> Friends,
> believe the good news.
> In Jesus Christ, we are forgiven.[20]

In this dialogue, an interpretation of the atonement from Paul's Letter to the Romans is set forth and the congregation exhorted to believe it as good news. Their concluding response would indicate that they have accepted it as such.

Sometimes a psalm will be read to declare the forgiveness of God. For example, in the United Church of Christ's *Book of Worship* there is an assurance of pardon taken from Psalm 32.

> I acknowledged my sin to you
> and I did not hide my iniquity:

I said, "I will confess my transgressions to God"
then you forgave the guilt of my sin.[21]

This is a description of the act of confessing one's sins followed by a statement of God's forgiveness. Psalm 103 can likewise be invoked after a prayer of confession as a poetic statement of God's forgiveness:

The Lord is merciful and gracious,
slow to anger and abounding in steadfast love.
He does not deal with us according to our sins
nor requite us according to our iniquities.
For as the heavens are high above the earth,
so great is his steadfast love toward
those who fear him;
as far as the east is from the west,
so far does he remove
our transgressions from us.[22]

One way to realize the forgiveness of God is to hear it described in biblical language.

Another way is to appropriate the Word. In one of their services, the United Church of Christ's *Book of Worship* calls for a dramatic presentation of God's forgiveness. The story of the woman taken in adultery from the Gospel of John is paraphrased so that what happened to her by analogy happens to the congregation. No one in a congregation is sufficiently without sin to cast the first stone at someone else in the pew whose sins they may or may not know. In this rite, after a prayer of confession, the minister says:

Jesus looked up and said to a sinner:
where are your accusers?
Has no one condemned you?
Neither do I condemn you;
go, and do not sin again.

The congregation responds:

Thanks be to God.[23]

This narration of Scripture serves as an assurance of pardon by drawing on an analogy between the congregation and the woman taken in adultery. The analogy may either be one of proportion or attribution. Those saying a prayer of confession may have committed sins like the woman or they may have recognized within themselves the attributes that lead to sin. The dialogue brings the congregation like the sinner in the Gospel of John before the person of Christ.

The forgiveness is realized in terms of an analogy of extrinsic attribution. Both the woman and the congregation receive the forgiveness of their sins from Christ. The woman from her encounter with the person of Jesus. The congregation from their encounter with Christ not in the person of Jesus from Nazareth, but in terms of Christ's presence with them. This assurance of pardon is based upon Christ Jesus' promise that where two or three are gathered in his name, he will be in the midst of them. Thus, the members realize forgiveness in terms of

their encounter with Christ who is among those who gather in his name on the
Lord's Day. They enjoy faith as Calvin defined it, namely:

> a firm and certain knowledge of God's benevolence
> toward us, founded upon the truth of the freely given
> promise in Christ, both revealed to our minds and sealed
> upon our hearts through the Holy Spirit.[24]

"The benevolence of God toward us" is communicated in the words of Jesus,
"Neither do I condemn you; go, and do not sin again."

But it is not enough to hear the words spoken and think about them. A
measure of persuasion is involved. That is the meaning of the promises being
sealed upon our hearts by the Holy Spirit. The recipient has to be able to hear the
word of forgiveness in the promises of God. Many times the promises fall on
deaf ears. Sometimes they are waved away as so much talk. The personal mission
of the Holy Spirit enables the promises of God's benevolence to be heard. Few
can peg down just when that measure of persuasion occurred. Rather those in a
Sunday congregation are people like Rahab, the stranger who became part of the
people of God.

Even though she was a stranger to the people of Israel, Rahab hid their
two spies on the roof and sent the Jericho authorities away with a classic "they
went that-a-way" story. Rahab had heard that God had enabled Israel to escape
through the waters of the Red Sea. Although others had heard the story too,
Rahab took it to heart. She decided to cast her lot with the Israelites. Rahab
was persuaded that the God of Israel was the source of salvation not only for
them but for herself and her family as well. In short, Rahab recognized the way
in which the divine goodness, wisdom, justice and power were about to act in
her city and behaved accordingly.

Before she let the two spies down the wall, Rahab made them promise that
they would spare herself and her family when they took Jericho. They agreed
upon a sign. She would tie a red thread to the window of her rooms in the city
wall. [Joshua 2:18] When Joshua and Israel conquered that city they would see
that thread and it would bring to mind Rahab's kindness and trustworthiness.
Then the Israelites in turn would deal kindly with her and her family. According
to the Book of Joshua that is what happened. [Joshua 6:22–25]

Rahab was not forgotten by the tradition. Taylor described Rahab's incorporation into the people of God writing in his February 1694 Meditation that she
was implanted into God's "Golden Stock."[25] In the Gospel of Matthew, she is one
of the women mentioned in Jesus' family tree. The Letter to the Hebrews [11:31]
listed her act as an act of faith. Her act of faith involved the personal mission of
the Holy Spirit, which Calvin called, "the inner teacher by whose effort the promise
of salvation penetrates into our minds,..."[26] The mission of the Holy Spirit involves the exertion of divine energy that reaches a person where they live, turning them to hear the promise within the divine power, goodness, beauty and
justice being played out in the world. The Holy Spirit enabled Rahab to hear a

promise in words where her neighbors heard only a threat. She took up the melody and became part of the chorus. Of the others it could be said, "We played the flute for you and you did not dance." [Matthew 11:17]

Many of the people in the congregation of the First Church weren't born in that particular congregation. Once strangers, now they are members. Somewhere in their sojourn, they heard stories about the ways of God. The Holy Spirit persuaded them that the promises of God in those stories were in fact trustworthy. At some point they became part of the chorus that is the church.

A faithful member of the congregation, sitting in church during the prelude, notices someone who is there for the occasion. Being in church most Sundays, and not seeing this stranger, she assumes that he is generally somewhere else on the first day of the week. Maybe he went to another church and has dropped in for some reason or other. She will try to say a welcoming word before leaving.

The stranger's presence prompts her to consider how meaningful the service has become over the years. But just how had Sunday worship in this church come to mean so much to her? There certainly were no blinding flashes along the way, no dramatic reversals or seizures of conviction. She knew she had not been "born again" in the evangelical sense of that phrase. Instead she was struck by how gently the persuasion of the Word's meaning had come over her. Hearing the familiar notes of "Old Hundredth," she stands just a few seconds before the visitor to sing the doxology.

Chapter 3

The Blessing of Baptism

One of the events which a congregation of God's people most enjoys is a child's baptism. Baptisms are celebrated on the festival days of particular seasons, for example, the Sundays after January 6 or the Sundays of Easter, most especially Pentecost. But, more often than not, the dynamics of family schedules and visits set the date; the Sunday nearest the day when who will be visiting whom, or a day with special meaning for the clan.

When the members of the regular congregation arrive, they notice that the front pews are strangely filled. They expect someone is being baptized. While the hymn is being sung, parents come to the front of the church and draw near the font with their child. The couple and members of the Sunday congregation await the Holy Spirit's bringing home the Word so they can once again realize the vitality and bond of being the people of God.

The minister has the distinct advantage of being able to see the congregation beaming and craning their necks.

"What a cute baby..."

"So that's who that couple is..."

If a cry is heard, the parents look at one another and carry on an intense non-verbal exchange.

"Do something."

"Maybe you should hold him?"

All in all, it is a most cordial occasion.

There will be people in the pews like Samuel Sewall who on the first Sunday of February in 1704 made his way to the Brattle Square Church instead of the Old South Meetinghouse. He noted in his diary, he went that he "might see my little Grand-daughter baptized."[1] Sewall heard the 15th and 16th Psalms as well as the last chapter of I Peter. The sermon text was Matthew 26:38, "And then saith he unto them, My soul is exceeding sorrowful, even unto death: tarry ye here, and watch with me." Apparently, the minister, The Reverend Mr. Benjamin Colman, was continuing a sermon series. But Judge Sewall noted with some satisfaction that the minister "pray'd excellently at Baptisme for the Child, Mother and all." His daughter Elizabeth was confined at home in the care of a nurse and reckoned herself very ill. "Betty" was twenty-three when her first child was born. Sam had spent the day before fasting and praying for her health and that of the child whom they named Mary after the father's mother and Betty's younger sister. The mother-in-law was present at the baptism in Brattle Square. The nurse had brought the child over to the church and the father, Mr. Grove Hirst, held her up. Grandfather Sewall noted that "Though the Child cried before, did not cry at Mr. Colman's pouring on the Water."Nineteen years later,[2] Judge Sewall would officiate at this granddaughter's wedding. At this point all he could know was that Mary had been baptized.

Children are brought to be baptized in a particular church for any number of reasons. Sometimes the parents have a family connection with the congregation.

41

Sometimes the parents seek out the minister who married them. At other times, it is because this is where they go to church. When a couple stand before a congregation to participate in the baptism of their child, the assumption is that they have heard the stories of the Old and New Testaments and in these have gained some sense of God's goodwill toward them. In the conversations with the minister in preparation for their child's baptism the parents will describe what some of those events might have been. They may have been touched by the Word of those promises when they were growing up in this congregation. They may have cordially consented to the promise somewhere along the way and been drawn back to church, perhaps in the ministry of a congregation far from home. Or perhaps they heard the Word when they were enthusiastically planning their wedding. It is difficult to know just when or where they consented to be counted among God's people.

Two or three meetings with the pastor are required to prepare for the baptism of their child. Since Christian baptism incorporates a child into the Christian Church, at the initial meeting with the parents a minister tries to determine from what corner of the vineyard they are coming. An article by Daniel Stevick describing different types of baptismal piety is very helpful. Reading that short essay parents can usually spot one or two of Stevick's descriptions of the sacrament as being close to where they are.[3] Parents not only recognize where they are in the church but they also learn that their particular understanding of baptism has a history. More often than not people's church backgrounds influence their choice.

Stevick's essay not only presents different accents of baptism but cites Scriptures that set forth those diverse understandings. There is a wider selection of baptismal texts than many might suppose. If the baptism is on the Sunday after Epiphany or Pentecost, the Scriptures on those Sundays address baptism in a very straightforward way. The Sunday following Epiphany the Gospel describes Jesus' baptism by John. The last Sunday of Easter, Pentecost, narrates the pouring out of the Holy Spirit upon the first Christians. But the readings suggested for Consultation On Church Union's 1973, *An Order for the Celebration of HOLY BAPTISM with Commentary,* suggests the call of Abraham, the *Shema,* as well as Jesus' commissioning of the disciples as Scriptures that touch upon different elements of baptism. The sermon for the day will take up the Word in the Scriptures for that particular day and season as it bears upon the life and future of a child in that community. This is an opportunity for the minister to articulate the understanding of baptism that emerged from his discussions with the parents. Many in the congregation are surprised at how much can be said about baptism from Scriptures other than Jesus taking children in his arms and blessing them.

The minister discusses the family's personal understanding of baptism in the context of the ecumenical understanding of this sacrament. This conversation presents liturgical alternatives that shape the baptismal service. The World Council of Churches in Faith and Order's Paper No. 111 "Baptism, Eucharist and Ministry" stated five meanings of baptism: participation in Christ's Death and Resurrection; Conversion, Pardoning and Cleansing; The Gift of the Spirit;

Incorporation into the Body of Christ and The Sign of the Kingdom. Of those five meanings two stand out in a congregational church, "Incorporation into the Body of Christ" and the "Gift of the Spirit."[4] The members of a congregation witnessing the baptism of a child become aware of: the covenant of baptism that includes this child, the prayer over the water which articulates the blessing of the event, the dynamics of baptism understood in terms of the renewed image of God and subsequent life in the congregation.

INCORPORATION INTO THE BODY OF CHRIST

When it came to discussing who were the subjects of baptism in 1662, the Massachusetts Congregationalists found passages in the Old Testament where children were included in the covenant and drew analogies to the church. This tradition of covenant theology understood Christian congregations to be analogous to the covenanted communities of Israel. Covenant constitutes the Christian Church as well as the People of Israel. New England Congregationalists cited the covenants of Abraham and Sarah, the covenants that fired the reform of Josiah or the revolt of Jehoida as well as Nehemiah and Ezra's covenant upon returning from exile, to describe the nature of a Christian congregation.

A key citation was the covenant renewal at Moab. It is written in Deuteronomy:

> You stand this day all of you before
> the Lord your God; the heads of your tribes
> your elders, and your officers, all the men of
> Israel, your little ones, your wives, and the
> sojourner who is in your camp, both he who
> hews your wood and he who draws your water,
> that you may enter into the sworn
> covenant of the Lord your God, which the Lord
> your God makes with you this day;
>   [Deuteronomy 29:10–12]

Since children, "little ones," were included in that covenant of Israel, so children were included in the covenant that constituted a Congregational Church. As a result, they were to be baptized.

Calvin noted that engrafting into the covenant was the primary efficacy of a baptismal service. "Nothing more," he said:

> of present effectiveness must be required
> than to confirm and ratify the covenant made with
> them by the Lord. The remaining significance of this
> sacrament will afterward follow at such time as
> God himself foresees.[5]

In other words, it is all but impossible to tell when and in what way the divine promises in Christ will intrinsically take hold of the child being baptized. The congregation only knows that the one being baptized has become part of the covenanted community by virtue of the promise of God that is extrinsic to them.

Covenant theology is another example of the way the actions of the people of God in the Old Testament informed the life of a people of God in the New Testament. This juxtaposition is based upon an analogy. At first glance, this would seem to be an analogy of proper proportion. Just as the people of God gathered on the Plains of Moab and made a covenant before they entered the promised land, so too the New Englanders understood themselves to be a covenanted community entering a new land. The covenants of early New England congregations enjoyed the same ring of place about them. For example, the First Church in Boston began its covenant by declaring they had "been brought together into this part of America, in the Bay of Massachusetts."[6] Their covenant acknowledged their arrival in a new land.

> Wee whose names are hereunder written, being by His
> most wise, & good Providence brought together into
> this part of America in the Bay of Massachusetts,[7]

But more is involved than an analogy of proper proportion. The Boston Puritans and the people of Israel shared an attribute—namely—the promise to Abraham. The Massachusetts congregations understood the covenant made at Moab to be a renewal of the covenant with Abraham. The root of that covenant was God's promise to Abraham:

> I will establish my covenant between me
> and you, and your offspring after you throughout
> their generations, for an everlasting covenant, to
> be God to you and to your offspring after you.
> [Genesis 17:7]

This meant that the covenant of a local Congregational Church went back to the covenant on the plains of Moab and back still further to the covenant of Abraham. The element in Abraham's covenant which the New Englanders repeatedly accentuated was the divine promise "to be God to you." Thus, whatever covenants were being discussed in Scripture the promise of God to be the God of these people constituted the essential element. When the 1662 Synod declared:

> The covenant of Abraham as to the substance
> thereof, viz. that whereby God declares himself to
> be the God of the faithful & their seed, Gen:17.7.
> continues under the Gospel...[8]

this moved the connection between the congregation and those gathered at Moab beyond an analogy of proper proportion to one of attribution, the attribution being the substance of Abraham's covenant.

The story of Abraham emphasizes that the promise of this covenant was decidedly extrinsic to Abraham and Sarah's nature. Therefore, the analogy the people of God share with Abraham and Sarah is an analogy of extrinsic attribution in that in both cases the divine covenant comes from outside their being.

In the covenants of Congregational Churches the initiative of God is accentuated. God has promised to be that congregation's God. The promise has not only been heard but in some measure realized, when God's benevolence is addressed to children on the basis of their being part of the covenanted community. Being unable to ask a child questions of belief, the questions are directed to the parents. These questions may be cast in the terms of the congregation's covenant. After professing their faith in terms of a traditional creed or other affirmation, parents might also be asked to promise that they will bring the child up within the community as defined by its covenant. In this way, the covenant is heard in the baptismal service as part of the questions put to the parents. For example:

> Do you desire to participate in the communion of
> this congregation under the Lord Jesus Christ?
> Do you promise to live your lives as peacemakers
> and thus to be known as the children of God?
> Will you do so in mutual love and respect so near
> as God shall give you grace?

It is important that the declaration of the parents' intentions not dominate the baptism. If the accent falls too heavily upon what the parents promise to do, then the initiative of God in the covenant is suppressed and a service of baptism takes on the air of a dedication service in which parents celebrate and express their intentions toward the child.

Therefore, the questions directed at the congregation are significant. The members of that particular congregation are asked if they will instruct, support and nurture the child that is being brought into their midst. When children are being incorporated into the church as the Body of Christ, the congregation is asked in the service:

> Do you, who witness and celebrate this sacrament,
> promise your love, support, and care
> to the one about to be baptized,
> as she lives and grows in Christ?[9]

At that point, members of the congregation promise to provide appropriate Christian education and nurture for the little one being baptized. This attests that this event involves more than a family gathering. However, it is the prayer before the baptism articulating God's initiative in terms of the gift of the Holy Spirit that checks that particular temptation to leave it all up to the parents.

The Gift of the Holy Spirit

Although most Christian communions affirm that baptism signifies the receiving of the Holy Spirit, *Baptism, Eucharist and Ministry* notes that they "differ in their understanding as to where the sign of the gift of the Spirit is to be found."[10] In the United Church of Christ's *Book of Worship* the gift of the Spirit is invoked most decidedly in the Prayer of Baptism before the act of baptism. This prayer has two distinct parts: the first thanks God for various events in the history and the second part invokes the Holy Spirit. By giving the pastor the option to say just the first part of the prayer or the two parts together, the United Church of Christ's liturgy distinguishes between these two segments of the prayer. Both parts are telling. What historical events are thankfully recalled? What is the verb that invokes the Holy Spirit? Different communions give significantly different answers to both questions.

The United Church of Christ's baptismal service begins with the congregation and minister reading responsively an account of Jesus' anointing by the Holy Spirit at his baptism.[11] This establishes the context for baptism in terms of Jesus' own baptism. After the hesitation of John the Baptist to baptize Jesus is narrated, the minister says:

> As soon as Jesus was baptized, he
> came up out of the water. Then heaven
> was opened to him, and he saw the Spirit
> of God coming down like a dove and lighting
> upon him.

At which point the people respond:

> Then a voice said from heaven, "This is
> my own dear Son, with whom I am well pleased."[12]

Placing this narrative at the beginning of the baptismal service affirms the personal mission of the Holy Spirit in terms of action upon a human being.

The Holy Spirit descending upon Jesus in the Jordan is noteworthy, not only because it affirms the Personal mission of the Holy Spirit in the world, but because it specifically does so in terms of action upon a human being. The Holy Spirit descending upon Jesus in the Jordan represents the Third Person of the Trinity anointing Christ's human person. Edward Kilmartin has noted the ramifications of that action:

> The way is opened to understanding the Holy Spirit
> as the one who sanctifies the humanity of Jesus,
> created by the Godhead as such, elevating that
> humanity to union with the Word who assumes
> it.[13]

Narrating Jesus' anointing by the Holy Spirit at the beginning of the baptismal rite, recalls the point of contact between humanity and the Holy Spirit at baptism. In the United Church of Christ's *Book of Worship*, it is the Prayer of Baptism that invokes the gift of the Holy Spirit.

THE PRAYER OF BAPTISM

Beginning with the creation and the flood, the first part of this prayer recalls specific biblical events associated with water. The prayer continues by remembering the Exodus and Jesus' baptism in the Jordan. The prayer specifically describes crossing the Jordan River and entering the land as well as the Exodus from Egypt.

> In the time of Moses, your people Israel
> passed through the Red Sea waters from
> slavery to freedom and crossed the flowing
> Jordan to enter the promised land.[14]

This accentuates not only liberation from oppression but entering the promised land to enjoy a new way of life. The reference to the Jordan brings to mind Israel's meetings at Gilgal.

When it comes to Jesus, the prayer sets forth a particularly refreshing cluster of recollections. It touches upon his person, in the fullness of time he was sent and "nurtured in the water of Mary's womb"; his works, he "became living water to a woman at the Samaritan well and washed the feet of his disciples"; and, his teaching, he sent the disciples forth to "Baptize all the nations by water and the Holy Spirit." Since water is the common element, in this part of the prayer, the rubric states that, at this point, the water may be clearly poured into the font. The water in the font provides an occasion in which the congregation recognizes and praises God for the glorious, faithful and personal union of divinity and humanity. The pouring of the water concludes the first part of the United Church of Christ's Prayer of Baptism.

The second part of the Prayer of Baptism articulates the invocation of the Holy Spirit. Here the particular verb is very telling. Theological traditions differ. In the Presbyterian *Book of Common Worship* the word is "send." "Send your Spirit to move over this water that it may be...."[15] In the *Book of Common Prayer* the verb is "sanctify." "Now sanctify this water, we pray you, by the power of your Holy Spirit."[16] But in the United Church of Christ's *Book of Worship*, the word is "bless." "Bless by your Holy Spirit, gracious God, this water."[17] "Bless" is an old English word whose etymology goes back to marking with blood, i.e., to consecrate. However, in the translation of the Christian Scriptures the English word, "bless," came to stand for the Latin *benedicere* which was the Latin word that translated the Greek word *eulogein*. Both of those words on occasion translated the Hebrew word *berak*. Therefore, "bless" carries strong connotations from the three languages of Christian tradition.

There are at least four distinct actions described by the word "bless." One meaning is to praise God. A second sense of "bless" is to authoritatively state divine benevolence. A third sense of "bless" is to invoke divine favor. And yet a fourth meaning is to impart divine favor.

In biblical translation "bless" does not always depict the same action. For example, it is written in Matthew 26:26, "While they were eating, Jesus took a loaf of bread, and after blessing it he broke it...." It is written in Mark 10:16, "And he took them up in his arms, laid his hands on them, and blessed them." These two blessings do not delineate the same action. The first text from Matthew describes blessing as the praise of God while the second text from Mark describes blessing as the impartation of divine favor.

When it is said that Jesus "blessed" the bread, it means that he said a prayer, a grace, a blessing. Professor Thomas Talley of General Theological Seminary sought to grasp the meaning of the word in terms of subsequent Christian liturgical practice. According to Talley, at this point Jesus said a *"motsey,"* i.e., the traditional Jewish table blessing over the bread.[18] As a Jew, Jesus would have said a blessing the thrust of which was to praise God directly for the production of bread. The saying of a blessing over the bread is to praise God directly. This sense of blessing resonates with the *Book of Common Prayer's* opening of Psalm 103 where the Hebrew word *berak* is translated "praise," i.e., "Praise the lord, O my soul...."

However, when Mark narrates that Jesus took children in his arms "and blessed them" [Mark 10:16] the word "bless" is understood in terms other than praise. Mark is describing blessing as the impartation of divine favor. Mark gives the impression that by his very touch Jesus bestowed divine favor. This is a familiar theme in Mark's Gospel. Jairus asked Jesus to lay his hands upon his ill daughter "so that she may be well and live." [Mark 5:23] Mark tells us that Jesus cured a blind man in part by laying his hands upon his eyes [Mark 8:25] and in Nazareth the surprised neighbors reportedly commented not only upon Jesus' wisdom but "the mighty works wrought by his hands."[Mark 6:2] In that context, to say that Jesus blessed children by laying his hands upon them, gives the impression that his very touch is a divine source of well being.

That impression certainly became part of popular piety. On his way to restore Jairus' daughter, Jesus is intercepted by the hemorrhaging woman who says, "If I touch his garment I shall be made well." [Mark 5:28] This line has passed over into hymnody with the line in John Greenleaf Whittier's hymn, "Immortal Love, Forever Full" declaring:

We touch him in life's throng and press;
And we are whole again.[19]

Did Jesus blessing the children brought to him mean actually imparting God's benevolence at the touch of his hand? The Gospel of Mark certainly gives that impression. That fits the definition of "bless" as the impartation of divine favor.

However, in parallel passages Matthew tones down Mark's blessing by touch. Consider Matthew and Mark's account of Jesus' visit to his hometown. Matthew does not say that Jesus laid his hands upon a few people in Nazareth and healed them. Mark does. [Mark 6:5] According to Matthew, the people of Nazareth do not speak of the mighty works wrought by Jesus' hands as they do in Mark. In the First Gospel, the people of Nazareth marvel, "Where did this man get this wisdom and these mighty works?" [Matthew 13:54] not, "What mighty works are wrought by his hands!" as in Mark. [Mark 6:2]

In Matthew the children are blessed by Jesus in terms of declaration and invocation of God's favor. In the First Gospel it is written that people brought them to Jesus, "that he might lay his hands on them and pray." [Matthew 19:13] Was this a blessing in the sense of authoritatively declaring God's benevolence or blessing in the sense of invoking divine favor? The gesture of Jesus' hands with the words of his prayer could have constituted a blessing as either a declaration, or an invocation of divine favor. The sort of blessing Jesus bestowed when he took children in his arms and laid his hands upon them has implications for the Baptismal Prayer.

The Holy Spirit blesses the water of baptism first, by prompting an act of praise by the congregation. The words of the prayer praise God in terms of saving events in the history that are associated with water. Thus, the water is blessed in the context of the congregation's praise of God. The water itself is not praised for simply being water. Rather the water brings to mind the events of Creation, the Flood, the Exodus, and the Incarnation in which God has acted. This water signifies the way God's benevolence is made known. By participating in the praise that these saving events elicit, the water is blessed.

The water in the font is also blessed in that it becomes the occasion for an authoritative declaration of God's benevolence toward the people of God. The sequence of events in the Prayer of Baptism is vitally important. The events of Creation, Flood, Exodus and Incarnation constitute a decidedly Christian narrative. These are not random events having to do with water. The way these events inform and resonate with each other can be heard throughout the year in the congregation's worship.

Moreover, the Prayer of Baptism places these events within the context of time.

Before the world had shape and form....

In the time of Noah...

In the time of Moses...

In the fullness of time....

Those introductory phrases not only declare a sense of history, they place the biblical events in a particular order not unlike the stories told at Gilgal. That particular historical order constitutes the blessing in the sense of being an authoritative declaration of God's favor.

Baptism does not occur in a "magic moment." If the prayer is altered so that the Creation is somehow assumed, the Flood ignored, and instead of the Exodus and the Incarnation being narrated, several contemporary poems on the beauty and meaning of water are read, then the prayer would cease to be a blessing in the second sense of the word. Without the structure of biblical history, such a statement of divine benevolence would lose its authority for Christians. For Reformed Christians, to be authoritative, a declaration of God's favor must be tied to a biblical sense of history. The congregation will teach and pass along the history of these events to the child being incorporated into the church.

However, the third and fourth meaning of the word "bless" can be heard in the second part of the Baptismal Prayer as well, namely, to invoke and impart God's well-being. Care must be taken that blessing, in the sense of the impartation of divine favor, is not identified with the touch of the ordained hand or even the baptismal water. If Mark's pericope about Jesus taking the children into his arms and touching them is read at a baptism, and then the minister takes a child in his arms and touches the child, an analogy of proper proportion is dramatically suggested. Does this action not suggest that, just as Jesus' touch imparted divine favor to the children, so likewise does the touch of the one acting in Jesus' name?

That is for most congregations much too direct an analogy. The actions of the minister and Jesus are not at all comparable, even if the act of blessing is the imparting of divine favor.

If there are homiletic explanations or poetic impressions about the meaning and significance of water, a congregation may be led to assume that the water somehow imparts divine favor. This involves either an analogy of improper proportion, whereby the water serves as a metaphor for the divine blessing, or by means of an analogy of intrinsic attribution whereby the water is said to share some intricate power with divinity. The Prayer of Baptism checks both of these analogies.

When the Holy Spirit is invoked in the United Church of Christ's liturgy, the water of baptism is blessed. The minister prays that God will be present in the ritual action of baptizing the child. The Holy Spirit does not bless the water in the sense that it changes or impacts the water. In other words, the invocation of the Holy Spirit does not direct or summon the divine to alter the water at hand. Rather the Holy Spirit is invoked that those gathered at the font realize the glorious dynamics of God in their life together.

Blessing in the sense of the impartation of divine favor occurs when the child is baptized with water in the name of the Father, Son and the Holy Spirit and she becomes part of a community of God's people who affirm the benevolence of God in terms of the promises of Christ made known to the mind and sealed upon the heart by the Holy Spirit.[20] Those baptized in the name of the Father, Son and Holy Spirit are incorporated into the dynamics of God known and expressed in the name of the Trinity. While the parents and the congregation are witnesses to the promise of God's benevolence toward that child, and their teaching and nurture will introduce him or her to the person and ministry of Christ, it is the personal mission of the invoked Holy Spirit that will seal the blessing of God's favor upon the child.

Killian McDonnell knew whereof he spoke when he maintained that, for the sons and daughters of Calvin, "Beyond the objectivity of the Spirit in act, there is, in the sacramental economy, no objectivity."[21] In other words, Christian Baptism is a transaction driven by the Holy Spirit. The water and words of the prayer are not sufficient to impart the blessing of God's favor upon the child being baptized. The Third Person of the Trinity connects the waters of a baptism with the waters of the events narrated in the prayer. The Holy Spirit is the extrinsic connection between the events of the prayer and the life of those gathered at the baptism. Ultimately, the blessing of baptism depends upon the gift of the Holy Spirit. The Prayer of Baptism and the act of Baptism in the name of the Father, Son and Holy Spirit provide the context for that gift.

This decidedly extrinsic dynamic in the transaction of baptism is stated in the lines of the Prayer of Baptism:

> By your Holy Spirit
> save those who confess
> the name of Jesus Christ
> that sin may have no power over them.

> Create new life in the one/all
> baptized this day
> that she/he/they may rise in Christ.[22]

The fact that the parents have brought their child before the congregation to be baptized should not be too quickly dismissed, when it comes to *confessing the name of Jesus Christ.*" Given the secular pluralism of modern life, given that religious education is not an accepted part of education, for a couple to stand before a congregation and state their intention to raise their child in a church is a form of confession. It is an indication that the parents feel themselves to be in some sense part of the church community that is not identical with the community at large.

Baptism involves participating in a community in which people on Sunday definitely live and move against the mores of secular culture. Having brought their child to the congregation, the family is asking for help in telling the child the biblical stories and celebrating the Christian holidays. When a congregation voices their assent to assist a family in the Christian education of their child, they too are making a public confession. The congregation is declaring that these children will be told the stories of the Old and New Testaments. They will come to know Christmas and Easter as not just vacation time, but a season for pageants, plays and special services at church. The child's religious education will lead to youth groups and summer camps which provide a definite alternative to popular youth culture and its media. When the baptized person encounters the "mystery of iniquity" working in the world [II Thessalonians 2:7, King James Version], it is the very terms of this faith: the benevolence of God, the person of Jesus Christ and the seal of the Holy Spirit that keep the members of a congregation from falling by the wayside, and gives them roots, not only to withstand the heat of life, but to thrive as a lily amidst the thorns.

The saving action of the Holy Spirit can be described as renewing the image of God within a person. Both John Calvin and John Wesley saw "the restoration or renewal of the image of God in humanity as a major category for describing salvation."[23] Calvin maintained "that the end of regeneration is that Christ should reform us to God's image."[24] When speaking of the image of God, there is a tendency to define the image of God in terms of a specific human faculty. To correct that usage the Reformed commentary on one of the statements in the 1981 Roman Catholic/Presbyterian-Reformed Consultation "Ethics and the Search for Christian Unity" recalls that the basic meaning informing the phrase "image of God" is reflection.

> ...the basic concept of image-bearing is
> reflection, i.e., that to be human is to
> experience dialogue with God.[25]

This is the sense in which Edward Taylor understood the term.

On the very same day that Samuel Sewall attended the Brattle Square Church to witness his granddaughter's baptism Taylor wrote a meditation on the phrase "baptized in the cloud" taken from Paul's First Letter to the Corinthians. The meditation began:

> Wilt thou enoculate within mine Eye
>   Thy Image bright, My Lord, that bright doth shine
> Forth in the Cloudy-Firy Pillar high
>   Thy Tabernacles Looking-Glass Divine?[26]

The Westfield minister recalled the way the cloudy pillar rested on the tabernacle. It is written:

> On the day the tabernacle was set up,
> the cloud covered the tabernacle,
> the tent of the covenant;
>
> [Numbers 9:15]

Pondering the way in which the pillar of cloud would settle on the tent of meeting, led Taylor later in the meditation to a delightfully homely metaphor. He likened the descending cloud to a woman sitting on a stool with full skirts.

Taylor wrote that the brightness of God's image shone out as light from a mirror. Following the Apostle Paul's comments in II Corinthians 3:18, Taylor thought a mirror captured the meaning of God's image. The brightness in the cloudy, fiery pillar came from the tabernacle's "Looking-Glass Divine." Since a mirror is nothing if not reflective, Taylor articulated the basic meaning of the "image" of God. Later on in the meditation this looking glass is said to be "Christ's Looking Glass."

It is that image, reflecting God's glory like a mirror, that Taylor wanted implanted in his eye. Hence the beginning of the meditation:

> Wilt thou enoculate within mine Eye
>   Thy image bright...

In the seventeenth century the term "enoculate," now spelled inoculate, was primarily a horticultural term. It described a graft. Not until the eighteenth century did the word come to be associated with public health and the injections that produce immunity. The buds on a stock were called eyes, a usage that has remained in speaking of "the eyes of a potato." Thus, both the verb "enoculate" and the term "eye" in the opening line of his meditation have basically horticultural connotations.

However, these words also articulated figurative meanings. From its reference to grafts, the word "inoculate" came to mean the insertion of one thing into another, resulting in a vital union. In an earlier meditation, Taylor spoke of Rahab being engrafted into the stock of Israel. This figure informs the meaning of baptism as a person's ingrafting into Christ. Taylor notes that being so inoculated means bearing the image of Christ so that the one baptized reflects the glory of God and is transformed from one degree of glory to another. This is the hope that informs a congregation when anyone is baptized.

The concluding petition of the invocation is that the Holy Spirit "create new life" in the person being baptized that they "may rise in Christ." That transaction takes place in the context of church. The baptized learn what has been handed down as a faithful interpretation. In the words of Basil, the Cappodocian theologian:

... we are bound to be baptized in the terms we have
received and to profess belief in the terms in which
we are baptized.[27]

Contrary to popular opinion, being a child of God is not a natural endow-
ment. In the words of Tertullian, the North African Christians "are made, not
born."[28] Christians participate in the benevolent dynamics of divinity given in
Christ's promise revealed to the mind and sealed upon the heart. The glory of
God that the baptized enjoy is a glory that is realized by participating in the life
of a congregation that gathers on the first day of the week. Being baptized in the
name of the Father, Son and Holy Spirit means being part of a congregation
where the stories told on Sunday as well as the celebrations of the holidays become occasions upon which they will reflect upon the being and persons of God.
In other words, the baptized do not live out of some vague sense of God, a generic spiritual belief. Rather God as Father, Son and Holy Spirit becomes known
to them in the course of their nurture, education and life. They will learn to pray
the words "Our Father." They will come to appreciate the story of Jesus so that
they know not only the teachings of the parables but the person as well; para-
digms wherein suffering is bound up with divine benevolence; not only the story
of Christmas, but the narrative of Easter's fifty days as well. In the course of
hearing prayers and stories as well as singing hymns, some words will stick and
become trustworthy.

Those baptized reflect their faith in the way they respond to other persons.
There is a sense of humanity among them that treats people as more than numbers or animals. These folk place their neighbor in the context of God's intentions for the world. This can lead to protests of the way the world is structured. It
can prompt them to respond to others in ways that the world's calculus fails to
understand. Thus, the people of God live and move as a chorus in the theater of
the world.

The baptized persons' capacity to enjoy and glorify God in the world is
easily lost or forgotten. It can be pushed aside by all kinds of activities on the
weekend that take precedence over church attendance. Education in terms of value
clarification can become a substitute for religious education so there is little time
to teach the more subtle issues of church history and theology. Nevertheless, a
beginning will be made. A child's years in Sunday school do make an impression.
If someone wanders off, by virtue of her baptism she remains part of the people of
God. The day may come when she will return to a congregation.

The doxology which concludes the Prayer of Baptism affirms the glory of
God in terms of time.

Glory to you, eternal God,
the one who was, and is, and shall always be.

Praise is given to God for the fullness of being which encompasses and sustains
human life in its passing day by day. With God at the beginning and at the end of
life as well as being present, those baptized can live out their days in the words of
a contemporary collect:

> Gracious and ever blessed God,
> through whose shaping in our mother's womb we had
> our beginning, that with one purpose
> we may return to thee at the close of our earthly
> day: Grant us resurrection on the day of thy
> choosing, that we may awake in Christ Jesus our
> Lord.[29]

In the meantime, the baptized enjoy a sense of God's glory in the world about them. That means a sense of delight in the way that the Christian faith unfolds among the people of God reaching and touching them in the stories they will hear from the canonical Scriptures, from the narrative that begins at the beginning and continues unto the end of time.

The Act of Baptism

When the minister asks the child's name, her parents respond with the name by which she will be known in the community. Someone in the pew might nod, recognizing that was her grandmother's name. Hoping that she will receive the water's touch as graciously as did Mary Sewall, the child is baptized in the name of the Father, Son and Holy Spirit.

In the Name of the Father, Son and Holy Spirit

Recently there has been criticism of the words "Father, Son and Holy Spirit" and alternatives have been offered. The objection to baptism "In the Name of the Father and of the Son and of the Holy Spirit" is that such language is male and hierarchical. An alternative is found in *An Inclusive Language Lectionary*'s translation of Matthew 28:19 where a radical paraphrase reads:

> Go therefore and make disciples of all
> nations baptizing in the name of [God]
> the Father [and Mother] and of Jesus Christ the
> beloved Child of God and of the Holy Spirit...[30]

Still another alternative is to baptize in the name of God "the Creator, the Redeemer and the Sustainer." These alternatives are designed to overcome the male dominance and hierarchical thinking that is heard in Father, Son and Holy Spirit and at the same time articulate the Christian Triune God.

Critics of the traditional words and the proponents of alternatives assume a very close relationship between the language about God and language about humanity. For these critics the language of the traditional formula is analagous to human experience. What is said about God is in some way related to what is said about humanity. But how are the two ways of speaking related? In other words, what kind of analogy is being assumed?

The critics of the traditional formulation think in terms of the analogy of intrinsic attribution, charging that there is a shared quality of fatherhood and sonship in terms of both divinity and humanity which the words Father and Son articulate. A continuity is said to exist between the words "Father" and "Son" in Matthew and those same words as they are currently used in social and political parlance. In other words, the Father and the Son in the Trinity share intrinsic attributes with fathers and sons in patriarchal culture. As a result, when the word Father or Son is spoken of the First and Second Persons of the Trinity, those words bring to mind a quality of father and son experienced in human terms. Thus, when people hear father and son at a baptism they will immediately think of their male social relationships. The analogy of intrinsic attribution correlates language about God and humanity.

Battista Mondin has noted that one of the characteristics of an analogy of intrinsic attribution is that such analogies articulate a relationship of cause and effect.[31] Consequently, the argument is made that Father, Son and Holy Spirit produce hierarchical and male dominated churches. By the same token, the alternatives "Father and Mother God and Jesus Christ beloved child of God and of the Holy Spirit"; or "Creator, Redeemer and Sustainer" are put forth in order to create more egalitarian and inclusive communities.

However, in analogies of intrinsic attribution the accent can slide from one part of the analogy to the other. Since language about divinity and humanity share intrinsic attributes, there is a very real danger that the accent may shift from the attribute in divinity to the attribute in humanity. Since attributes are intrinsic to both, it is tempting to take one's bearings from the laudable attribute which is near at hand. So, for example, the equality of the Persons of the Trinity is affirmed out of protests against human sexism or participating in a political struggle. Since in the context of that human protest or political struggle words like father and son are believed to be oppressive, then they are to be suppressed in the baptismal rite and alternatives tried. But this raises the question of whether the accent hasn't slipped from the attributes of the Trinity informing humanity to the Trinity being given the attribute of a desired human community.

Analogies of extrinsic attribution block such slides. While acknowledging that there is a close relationship between the way we speak of God and the way we speak of humanity, in these analogies the accent remains ultimately and steadfastly extrinsic to human experience and upon divinity as attested in Scripture. In the case of baptism, "Father" and "Son" are spoken at a baptism because these are the words found in the Great Commission. First and foremost, they attest to the being of God. Being an analogy of extrinsic attribution, when push comes to shove, there can be no free flowing, two way traffic between the words father and son as addressed to divinity and as spoken of humanity. The meaning of the words Father, Son and Holy Spirit in the act of baptism have primarily to do with God, not the people in or before the congregation. If there is a shared attribute between the two, it is because God impresses that attribute upon humanity in the transaction of word and sacrament. It does not go the other way round. In an analogy of extrinsic attribution, any equality of persons is primarily found among the Persons of the Trinity. Only in God would mutuality and coequality be truly and really present. Such mutuality might well be present among the people of God but only from the impression that the glory of God makes upon them.

For all the criticism of the words to baptize "in the name of the Father, and of the Son and of the Holy Spirit," they remain essential to the baptismal rite. The words "Father, Son and Holy Spirit" articulate the dynamics and relations of divinity made known in the events which the Prayer of Baptism recalls. When reflecting upon and considering God's presence in the world in biblical events such as Creation, the Flood, the Exodus, and the Incarnation, Christians think in terms of Father, Son and Holy Spirit. The dynamics involved in these events cannot be reduced to the simple actions of God. The biblical narratives that present these events are not flat formulas. The stories involve references that, when pondered and pressed, lead to a presence of Word and Holy Spirit. This prompted Prof. Thomas F. Torrance, Reformed theologian, to note in a comment on the "Agreed Statement on the Trinity between the Orthodox and Reformed Churches":

> While there is no formally explicit teaching about the
> Holy Trinity in the New Testament, belief in and worship
> of God the Father, the Son and the Holy Spirit clearly
> belong to the essential content of the Gospel which the
> Apostles proclaimed and taught.....a definite doctrine
> of the Trinity was found to arise out of faithful
> interpretation of the New Testament and of the Church.[32]

Consider the baptism of Jesus. The dynamics of that event involve the other two Persons of the Trinity as well as the Son. The voice from heaven signifies the Father, and the dove the Holy Spirit. While it is certainly possible to interpret that event without invoking the Trinity, a Christian seeking to understand the divine dynamics of that event would do so in terms of the Three Persons.

Father, Son and Holy Spirit articulate the relationship one Person has to the other as well as their unity. Suggested alternate wordings have been found inadequate in terms of enunciating the inner dynamics of divinity. This is one of the most commonly noted limitations of baptizing in the name of "God, the Creator, the Redeemer and the Sustainer." Creator, Redeemer and Sustainer speaks in terms of what God does in terms of the world but says nothing about the relationship of the Three Persons. The traditional terms "Father, Son and Holy Spirit" bring to mind not only God's relationship to the world but the dynamic relationship of the Persons of the Trinity among themselves as well as their unity.

The figures stating the Personal dynamics of divinity are crucial. It is not enough to say that the Trinity speaks of the relationship between the Persons. That is obviously true. The key question is, in what terms is this relationship set forth? Clearly, not in terms of a mathematical order nor even a logical order. The traditional answer is that the relationship between the Persons of the Trinity is one of a dynamic origination and reciprocation.[33] This is the meaning of the words in the Nicene Creed which describe the Father, as "the Almighty, maker of heaven and earth, of all that is, seen and unseen," and the Son as "eternally begotten of the Father...begotten not made" and the Holy Spirit as "the Lord and giver of life, who proceeds from the Father."[34] These phrases translate words having to do with origin, generation and procession, words that articulate the inner dynamics of God. To be sure, these terms are not topics of everyday conversation in the church parlor, office or even the Christian Education wing.[35] Nevertheless, they are heard whenever the Nicene Creed happens to be recited in worship. They are implicit whenever the Trinity is affirmed as Father, Son and Holy Spirit. The major task of any alternative statement of the Trinity is to discover how to state the relationship of the Three Persons of the Trinity in terms that articulate the same Trinitarian dynamics as Father, Son and Holy Spirit. A satisfactory alternative has yet to be found.

After the baptism has taken place, the family returns to their pew. The congregation sings a hymn under the shadow of the Holy Spirit. These are the first notes of the melody that a baptized child enjoys as one of the covenanted people of God. In the words of Edward Taylor,

> But as to Cana'n I am journeying
> I shall thy praise under this Shadow sing.[36]

Chapter 4

The Light of Christmas

$\mathfrak{T}$he Christmas Eve Candlelight Service is the most popular service of the year. This is one service that many will attend. Those who attend regularly on Sunday will lose their seats to others, if they do not arrive early. The church is packed. Neighbors, party goers, parishioners, spouses, visitors, and total strangers, all want to know the time of the service. They ask in person or on the telephone. The answer is four-thirty. People begin arriving at four or earlier. Mothers will take their children up to the crèche and point out the figures. Families jovially chatter along entire pews until the organist begins his prelude. At four-thirty the sanctuary lights are dimmed and the Christ candle is carried down the center aisle. When the lights are brought up, the congregation sings "O Little Town of Bethlehem." The service concludes with the light being passed, the worshippers holding their own candles and singing "Silent Night." Some of the congregation will take their candles out of the sanctuary into the night.

Those who come only to the Christmas Eve service are but dimly aware of what has come before or what will follow. However, those who attend the Christmas Eve Vespers by way of Advent and the Christmas pageant, and especially those who will be present at the Christmas Eve Communion Service and the baptism of Jesus after the twelve days of Christmas, realize that there is much more involved. The more begins four weeks before Christmas Eve.

ADVENT

The season begins with an appropriately mixed message. The post office issues two stamps for the holidays. One is secular, Santa Claus or a toy. The other stamp is religious, a depiction of Madonna and child. Christmas time is a season of both church and culture; Vespers and Communion on Christmas Eve, Christmas cards as well as the Sunday School pageant beforehand.

More often than not, the first Sunday of Advent occurs the Sunday after Thanksgiving when most congregations are yet but dimly aware of Christmas. Pageant planning on that day is met with low attendance and half-hearted responses. However, by the second Sunday in Advent the season has blossomed and those in church want to know, "When will we sing the Christmas carols?" Ministers may stalwartly resist singing the carols in Advent. This prompts one member of the congregation to tell an impatient parishioner, "The trouble is that you're on the secular calendar and he's on the church calendar."

Congregations sing hymns according to the Advent season, rather than count the shopping days. While canned versions of "Silent Night," "O Little Town of Bethlehem," "The First Noel," "Jingle Bells" and "I'm Dreaming of a White Christmas" are being piped into malls, congregations are singing: "Watchman Tell Us of the Night," "O Come, O Come, Emmanuel," "Comfort, Comfort Ye My People," "On Jordan's Bank." "O Little Town of Bethlehem" and "Silent Night" aren't sung for another three or four weeks.

61

Congregations sing from the hymnal before they sing from the books of carols. For the people of God Advent hymns constitute an act of praise that affirms certain basic figures, figures that more often than not resonate with the Scriptures for the season. For example, three Advent hymns; "O Come, O Come, Emmanuel," "Watchman, Tell Us of the Night," and "Comfort, Comfort Ye My People" take up figures from the prophet Isaiah. These Advent figures articulate the Christians' sense of history, their hope in the future as well as their understanding of the darkness.

"O Come, O Come, Emmanuel" is the translation of John Mason Neale (1818-66). John Mason Neale was an Anglo-Catholic priest who served twenty years as the warden and chaplain of a home for indigent men. A graduate of Cambridge, he was a recognized classical scholar who translated many hymns from the ancient and medieval church. For example, he translated "All Glory, Laud and Honor" as well as "Good Christian Men Rejoice." Neale wrote the words for "Good King Wenceslas" after having read the legend. "O Come, O Come, Emmanuel" is based upon his translation of that Advent antiphon.

Antiphons are short texts, preferably from Scriptures, set to recognizable melodies written to be sung before or after a psalm or canticle. An intricate system had evolved whereby the psalm, canticle, and antiphon for a particular day were interwoven and published in books known as antiphonals. In the evening service of cathedrals and monasteries, in addition to the psalms, Mary's Magnificat would be sung. In the ninth century for the last week of Advent a series of antiphons for the Magnificat known as the "Great O's" had developed. Those were antiphons made up of the personifications of Christmas hope prefaced by O. The seven great O's were: Emmanuel, Wisdom from on High, Lord of Might, Rod of Jesse's Stem, Key of David, Dayspring from on High, Desire of Nations. One of these designations for Christ prefaced by O would be sung during the last week of Advent at Vespers either before or after the Magnificat. Neale translated a thirteenth-century version of these antiphons as "O Come, O Come, Emmanuel." After its publication in 1851, it was set to music in 1852 and gained wide acceptance.

"O Come, O Come, Emmanuel" turns on the figure of Emmanuel from the book of the prophet Isaiah and the Gospel of Matthew. Emmanuel, in the words of Northorp Frye, is "a figure of speech that moves in time."[1] As such it articulates the people of God's sense of history.

The prophet Isaiah noted, during a war, that a child would be born to a young woman in the royal house of Israel. The prophet declared the birth of this child would be a sign. He said the child would be called Emmanuel, meaning God with us. That is to say, the birth of that child would remind those in Jerusalem of the promise of God being with them.

Commenting on the significance of Jesus' birth, Matthew relates the dream of Joseph regarding the birth of Jesus. Matthew notes, "All this took place to fulfill what had been spoken by the Lord through the prophet." [Matthew 1:22] He then quotes Isaiah's name Emmanuel as a designation of Jesus. Thus, the figure Emmanuel is found at two points in the history of the people of God. What is the relationship between the event in the time of Isaiah and the event in the time of Matthew?

A common understanding is that of fulfillment. What a prophet said in the eighth century B.C. came true in the first. The child Isaiah foretold in 734 B.C. was really Jesus of Nazareth born in Bethlehem of Judaea. This interpretation rests on two assumptions; that the prophets of Israel predicted future events, and that the Christian Gospels complete the predictions of the Hebrew prophets. Thus, the son of Mary is seen as Isaiah's Emmanuel. The translation of the Hebrew word for the woman bearing the child is applied to Mary as part of the same argument, namely, the Gospels report what Isaiah said would happen. This gives the impression that the Advent hymn "O Come, O Come, Emmanuel" sings of Jesus being born in Bethlehem of Judaea in the days of Herod the King.

However, that is not the only interpretation possible. There is no reason to assume that when Isaiah spoke of a child being born and being called Emmanuel, the prophet had Jesus of Nazareth in mind. The prophet might just as well have been referring to the child of a pregnant young woman in his own community. The name Emmanuel for that child served as a sign to bring to mind God's presence with Israel.

There is a similarity between the birth of that child and the birth of Jesus. The similarities touch upon more than the women who bore them. The name Emmanuel served as a reminder to both communities of God's promised benevolence. Both Emmanuels were born in the house of David. Both came into the world when the people of God's political structures were threatened. The name Emmanuel fits both Old and New Covenants. Both hear God's declaration, "I will be your God and you will be my people."

In "O Come, O Come, Emmanuel" as in other Advent hymns, there is a close similarity between the people of Israel and the Christian Church, but not an identity. Advent hymns do not mean that the church is Israel, but that the Church is analogous to Israel. That is to say, the Christian people of God have a hope for the future and share a sense of darkness as did the people of God to whom Isaiah spoke. In the words of The 199th General Assembly (1987) of the Presbyterian Church (U.S.A.):

> ...Jews and Christians are partners in
> waiting....Christians and Jews together await the
> final manifestation of God's promise of the
> peaceable kingdom.[2]

There are also analogies of attribution involved when Jews and Christians are juxtaposed one with another. Both communities are dependent upon the word of God that comes to them from beyond their own immediate environment. The Emmanuel of Isaiah and Matthew are two notes in the melody of God's song. Taken together they strike a chord in the divine melody being played in the world. However, the melody does not conclude with that chord. It is not as though once Jesus was born the song stopped. The holy melody will conclude only with the consummation of God's Kingdom.

Those who sing "O Come, O Come, Emmanuel" in Advent conclude each verse in the future tense: "Rejoice! Rejoice! Emmanuel shall come to thee, O

Israel!" For these folk Christmas is not a nostalgic trip back to the days when a decree went out from Caesar Augustus or when Cyrus the Persian told the people of God they could return to their land. The biblical events are remembered and taken up as part of a melody that continues to be played. This is an important check upon the Christmas card temptation to reduce Christmas to something that happened in the past.

An understanding of history results in a positive accent on the future. This interpretation of the future is heard in John Bowering's taking up one of Isaiah's sayings. Bowering (1792–1872), was a member of Parliament and held posts in the Far East under the British Empire. In addition to poetry and essays, Bowering, a Unitarian, wrote hymns, among them, "In the Cross Of Christ I Glory" as well as "Watchman Tell Us of the Night." His Advent hymn is a paraphrase of Isaiah 21:11 where a question is posed of a sentry, "Watchman, what of the night?" That became the recurring line in Bowering's hymn.

However, in the hymn the watchman's response is not the same as in the prophecy. In Isaiah the figure of night is decidedly ambiguous. One cannot tell from the Hebrew text whether the night is beginning or ending. In Isaiah the sentry might be announcing the coming of morning or the continuation of night. In the hymn no such ambiguity exists. John Bowering introduces the "glorious beaming star" from Matthew's Gospel into his hymn. He then elaborates on the significance of the star for three couplets before returning to Isaiah's text.

> Watchman, does its beauteous ray
> Aught of joy or hope fortell?
> Traveler, yes; it brings the day,
> Promised day of Israel.

> Watchman, tell us of the night,
> Higher yet that star ascends.
> Traveler, blessedness and light,
> Peace and truth its course portends.

This hopeful note strikes a chord with the refrain of "O Come, O Come, Emmanuel" which looks for God in the future.

The same note can be heard in another Advent hymn, "Comfort, Comfort Ye My People," a paraphrase of Isaiah 40. This translation by Catherine Winkworth affirms the glory of the Lord being shed abroad to all flesh. Catherine Winkworth (1827-1878) was an advocate of higher education for women. She helped establish Bristol University College and Clifton High School in England and served as Secretary of the Committee on Higher Education for Women. In 1845 she went to Dresden to visit an aunt. While living there she mastered German and subsequently translated a wealth of German hymns into English. The version of "Now Thank We All Our God" is one of her translations. The Advent hymn, "Comfort, Comfort Ye My People," had been written by a seventeenth-century German court chaplain, Johann Olearius. In *The Pilgrim Hymnal* this text is set to the Genevan tune for Psalm 42.

The third verse of "Comfort Ye, Comfort ye My People" sings of the glory of the Lord which all flesh shall see together. Isaiah's line is paraphrased in Olearius' hymn as:

> For the glory of the Lord
> Now o'er earth is shed abroad;
> And all flesh shall see the token
> That his word is never broken.

Martin Luther King, Jr., paraphrased Isaiah's words in the ringing conclusion of his speech at the March on Washington.

Advent expresses the theme that when the time comes, all flesh shall see the glory of God and the presence of God together. The accent upon the future heard in these hymns underlines the point that during Advent the congregation is not only looking back to a past event. They are a people waiting for the full Kingdom to come.

And yet there is still darkness to be found in Advent hymns. In "O Come, O Come, Emmanuel," "the gloomy shades of night" are part of "death's dark shadows,"

> Disperse the gloomy clouds of night,
> And death's dark shadows put to flight.

These figures take up the darkness and shadows of which Isaiah 9:2 speaks. In "Watchman Tell Us of the Night," darkness is associated with doubt and terror. The final verse sings:

> ...darkness takes its flight,
> Doubt and terror are withdrawn.

In "Comfort, Comfort Ye my People" the darkness covers those sitting under the burden of their sorrows.

> Comfort those who sit in darkness
> Mourning 'neath their sorrow's load.

This is a paraphrase of a line from Isaiah 42:7. The darkness in Advent hymns signifies elements with which Christians must wrestle in this world; doubt and terror, death and sorrow.

The approach of Christmas can stir doubts. Psychologists and counselors warn of the difficulties that the holiday season can bring upon people. Memories of Christmases past may be as painful for some as they were for Ebenezer Scrooge. Dickens realized that the fact of death or the threat of death amid loss often caused holiday traumas.

And yet the darkness is never a realm of being beyond the reach of God. In spite of the threatening images of darkness heard in Advent hymns, God rules over both the darkness as well as the light. Evening prayer in the synagogue praises the power of God over both darkness and light.

> Blessed art thou, Lord our God, King of
> the universe, who at thy word bringest on the
> evenings.... Thou createst day and night; thou
> rollest away light before darkness and darkness
> before light; thou causest the day to pass and the

night to come, and makest the distinction between
day and night...[3]

Each figure of darkness in these three Advent Hymns is rooted in the book
of the Prophet Isaiah, which places the figure of darkness in the context of the
canonical Old Testament. Thus, a pervasive religious symbol, darkness, is in the
church's worship situated in the history of a particular people. There is always a
temptation to take the figures of darkness and light well beyond Scripture. In a
pluralistic world, figures like light and darkness slip out of their particular context in Scripture and are placed in many other contexts. When that happens,
Christmas loses its center. While all around them Christians meet various contexts for the symbol of light, on the four Sundays before Christmas this universal
symbol is pondered in the context of a particular history.

In either the second or third week of Advent that particular history is manifest in the person of John the Baptist. An Advent hymn like "On Jordan's Bank
the Baptist's Cry" describes the Christmas event in terms of the first historical
figure in the Gospels—John the Baptist. This Advent hymn is an English translation of an eighteenth-century French hymn written by the sometime Rector of
the University of Paris, Charles Coffin (1676–1749). John Chandler (1806–1876),
a popular translator of Latin hymns, translated Coffin's hymns into English. Chandler was given to somewhat free translations that sang well.

The second verse of "Comfort, Comfort Ye My People" takes up the
Gospel's identification of John the Baptist with the voice Isaiah [40:3] described
crying in the wilderness.

> Hark, the voice of one that crieth,
> In the desert far and near,...

This is an analogy of proper proportion. The early Christians seeking to understand who John the Baptist was, discovered certain similarities in his situation
and these words of Isaiah. First of all, the Baptist was a prophetic preacher—a
voice crying out. Secondly, he was in the wilderness. In Isaiah the phrase "in the
wilderness " was linked to the road being prepared. Christian commentators shifted
the phrase "in the wilderness" to the location of John's preaching, hence the
voice crying "in the desert near and far."

The Judean wilderness was the traditional haunt of critics of the Jerusalem
establishment. When Luke states that "the word of God came to John the son of
Zachariah—in the wilderness" [Luke 3:2], it is like the word of God that came to
Elijah. The word encountered those men and fired them. This was not a word
that blossomed from within; this word seized them. As in the case of Elijah that
extrinsic word of God prompted John to speak out and bear witness against those
who thought that they were in charge.

A note of the Baptist's truculent preaching can be heard in the vehement
exhortation:

> Bear fruits worthy of repentance....
> Even now the axe is lying at the root of the trees;
> every tree therefore that does not bear good fruit
> is cut down and thrown into the fire. [Luke 3:8–9]

John's axe and fire lend a decided sense of urgency to the act of repentance as well as giving a sense of the Baptist's vehement first-century exhortation.

The repentance of faithful members of a congregation before Christmas is not a matter of responding to seasonal charities and appeals. For those who hear the Baptist's words in church, Christ is more than a prophet or messenger of good will. Jesus has communicated a promise of God's benevolence to them. At the same time, remembering some of his parables, they have reason to be disquieted. Jesus' parable about the barren fig tree reverberates with the Baptist's exhortation. The owner of the vineyard finding a tree barren of fruit says to the vinedresser:

Lo, these three years I have come seeking fruit on this fig

tree, and I find none. Cut it down;...

[Luke 13:7]

This parable speaks to the times in the course of the last year when members of the congregation have let slip the connection between the human and the divine. They may have presumed too quickly that God's glory is circumscribed by the world. The location where divinity and humanity actually meet in the world has become comfortably vague and indefinitely hopeful. The "glory of the only begotten of the Father" has not been understood as necessary. That mistaken assumption is purged when the person in the pew, singing Chandler's translation of Coffin's hymn in Advent, is asked to furnish his/her heart for "so great a guest."

Given the realms and forms of being in the world, even the faithful find it all too easy to regard those they meet in the world as being in a "mere state of nature."[4] God is not so much denied as ignored in the world's humanity. The sense of the human person informed by Christ is lost. In its place people live and work out of the secular self, an empty conception into which various definitions of human being can be poured. The result is that the interests of others are invaded and defeated despite the best of intentions and calculations to the contrary. Some people are marginalized as beyond reach, as not having the requisite qualities that entitle them to love and respect. In that modern wasteland the voice of the Baptist reaches a congregation. In church singing Advent hymns, people are urged to change their ways and prepare for the power of Christmas. Those in the larger community are invited to parties and urged to shop.

THE CHRISTMAS PAGEANT

On the last or next to last Sunday of Advent the Sunday School presents the pageant. Their presentation is filled with feeling. Grandparents, parents and members of the congregation love it. Attendance will rarely be higher or cooperation more cordial as together Sunday School teachers and parents work to make sure that the costumes and scripts are ready. This is the time to count how many attend Sunday School because they will all be there for the pageant.

Pageant scripts come in three basic forms: Bathrobe Drama, Bathrobe Drama Plus, and Creative. Bathrobe Drama is a straightforward walk-through of the Christmas story primarily as it is found in Luke. Older children read the passages of Scripture and the other children dressed in what look like bathrobes stand or simply move to illustrate the point. Bathrobe Drama Plus includes the elaboration of certain details, the effort to find the room in the inn, the shepherds' antics in the fields or the gifts of the Magi. Here minor dramatizations fill in the gaps of the biblical narrative. What was it like to be turned away? What were the shepherds doing that night? How many wisemen were there? What sort of gifts did they bring? Were there gifts from others as well? In a Creative Pageant the familiar narrative is cast in radically contemporary terms: the wisemen stop at a gas station for directions, Herod smokes a big cigar, Spider Man costumes are allowed because there were spiders in the manger.

Usually after the Creative Pageant a return to Bathrobe Drama is all but mandatory for the next year. Among Christian congregations the story told by Luke and Matthew is so significant that they do not like it disturbed. In Bathrobe Drama the basic elements of the narrative are front and center. Joseph and Mary, the infant Jesus, the shepherds, the angels, the magi, the decree from Caesar Augustus are figures not to be trifled with or rearranged every year. The alternatives and the parallel stories, delightful though they may be, do not and cannot displace this story.

The pageant is the occasion when children learn the sequence and persons of the narrative. In the process of participating in the pageant, children come to know the story. After his first pageant one father announced, "This year my son was a shepherd, junior grade. Next year they'll issue him a sheep." In Bathrobe Drama Plus teachers engage the children's interest in the characters and incidents of the story. They probably will voice stubborn opinions as to which parts they will or will not play. The Creative Pageant enables the Sunday School folk to interpret the story in their own terms, provided of course, they don't completely overthrow the figures. Joseph and Mary may appear in contemporary clothes; they cannot be displaced.

Carl Sandburg once asked why the story never wears out.[5] One reason concerns the archetypes in the story as Northrop Frye defined them,

> A symbol, usually an image, which recurs often enough
> in literature to be recognizable as an element of
> one's literary experience as a whole.[6]

The light and darkness, the silence, the mother and the child are just five of the archetypes that adults in a congregation recognize year after year. There are undoubtedly others buried in the Christmas story, for example, tyrants, local characters, angels, the family against a callous world. Coming together in the narrative of a pageant, these archetypes present a powerful and meaningful event.

Adults come to the Christmas pageant from the dark streets of the world seeking that light which the world has neither overcome nor managed to put out. For them the Sunday School pageant is a ritual expression of hope centering in a town in Israel that can still be visited and where the powers of the world still clash. Two years after he had visited David's city in Judea, Phillips Brooks captured the sense in which Christians respond to Bethlehem as a spot where their hopes center. The Episcopalian minister wrote "O Little Town of Bethlehem" for the children of the Trinity Church Sunday School in Philadelphia. In the first verse he declared that "the hopes and fears of all the years" annually meet in that particular little town.

The blessings of God's heaven in the world are not obvious for all to see. Nevertheless, Brooks would have the adults attending the pageant believe that:

...in this world of sin
Where meek souls receive him still,
The dear Christ enters in.

Those watching the pageant appreciate its reminder that if they were less callous and busy, if they could get a break from the holiday press, if they would ponder the Gospel, then they would enjoy some sense of Christ's presence at Christmas.

But in the end the hymn reminds the congregation that more than their hopes are involved. The fourth verse of Brooks' Christmas hymn concludes with a prayer that the Holy Child of Bethlehem would descend upon the congregation casting out their sin, entering in and abiding with the people of God as Emmanuel. Thus, no matter how well the story is presented, or how effective the pageant, something else is required. The initiative rests with God.

Anyone who has witnessed a Sunday School pageant knows that this is not the occasion wherein "How silently, how silently the wondrous gift is given!" That definitely does not describe Pageant Sunday. There are too many slipped haloes, flubbed lines, frisky children, and last minute tasks to convey the atmosphere that Phillips Brooks, the bachelor preacher, had in mind. The gift of Christ must await Christmas Eve.

CHRISTMAS EVE VESPERS

At the Christmas Eve candlelight service the mood of "O Little Town of Bethlehem" intensifies. Church members, neighbors, families and friends all gather to share in the candlelight. Luke's narrative is read. A psalm is sung and prayers are spoken. As "O Little Town of Bethlehem" is sung, on Christmas Eve the line "How silently, how silently the wondrous gift is given" is reaffirmed by singing "Silent Night".

The Vespers' highlight, "Silent Night," was originally written to be accompanied on a guitar because the organ in Oberndorf, Austria was broken on Christmas Eve in 1818. The assistant priest at St. Nicholas Church, Joseph Mohr, wrote the words for "Silent Night." The organist Franz Gruber wrote the melody and played it on his guitar.

The opening verse presents with beautiful simplicity two significant notes of Christmas Eve Vespers—"All is calm and all is bright." The calm and the brightness are immediately associated with the singing of "Silent Night" in candlelight. However, the silence and radiance of Christmas Eve run deep in Christian tradition.

The silence of that silent night when "all is calm" extends back through centuries of Christian tradition to a letter that Ignatius of Antioch wrote to the Ephesians before he was martyred in about 107 A.D. He commented that the birth of Christ was one of the mysteries of God wrought in silence to fool the prince of this world. And indeed the silence of the Vesper Service certainly escapes the notice of those who are caught up in the last minute rush. Those who fail to secure a silent spot on Christmas Eve may very well have missed the holiday.

But the silence of Christmas Eve is in marked contrast to more than the music of malls. T. S. Eliot knew the voice of Christ was silent as well. Quoting a sermon that the Anglican Bishop Lancelot Andrewes had preached at White-hall before the Kings Majestie on Christmas Day 1618, Eliot played with the meaning of the unheard Word in his poem "Ash-Wednesday."[7] Centering on the infant Christ checks any idea that the importance of Jesus Christ rests solely on his teachings, his parables, the great commandment and the like. People who sing "Silent Night" with a candle in hand are asked to go ponder much more than a prophet. They are affirming the being of a person unable to speak.

"Silent Night" reveals another archetype, the figures of mother and child. Part of the power of the Vesper service is the basic figure of mother and child of which the carol sings. This phrase invokes the powerful complex of mother, child and birth imagery. As with any of the other figures of Christmas this one can be transposed to other settings. Some interpretations of Christmas do just that. Mary and Jesus bring to mind every other mother and child. When the figures are so universalized, they run into the sand. But Mohr's words check that tendency by singing not about "Round yon gentle mother and child" but "Round yon virgin mother and child," thus making the point that this is not every mother and child.

In the third verse of "Silent Night" the light of the Christmas carols takes on a very specific location, "Radiant beams from thy holy face." The light is found in the face of the Christ child "with the dawn of redeeming grace." Now, as in the earlier Advent hymns, the night is indeed turning into morning but the source of that light is not the star but the face of the Christ child.

The child is designated in the third verse as "Jesus Lord at thy birth" and "Son of God, love's pure light." These are titles given to this person. They may not be titles that we find congenial or even appropriate. Others may come to mind. However, at this time any designation of Jesus as Lord serves to acknowledge him as the dominant figure of the holiday. The singing of "Silent Night" at a Christmas Eve Vespers cordially makes that point. There are those for whom singing "Silent Night" in the candle light is the epitome of Christmas. The carols, the narrative, the candle light touch upon basic archetypes and profound feelings. Taken all together these are said by some to constitute the significance of Christmas.

But for others that is too diffuse a sense of divinity. Archetypes and feelings fail to articulate the power of Christmas that is extrinsic to humanity. The people of God, acknowledging the root and initiative of Christmas that is outside human being, attend the Christmas Eve Communion Service. To give thanks for the inestimable love that is the source of all the Christmas hymns and carols, a congregation gathers at ten o'clock.

CHRISTMAS EVE COMMUNION

The service begins at ten o'clock with the bringing in of the light from the sanctuary where Vespers were held. The Presbyterian *Supplemental Liturgical Resource 5 Daily Prayer* suggests several ways to mark the entry of the light. The worship leaders will choose one of these rites for the Christmas Eve communion service. For example, the person bringing in the light might sing a tune of "Jesus Christ is the Light of the World." A member of the congregation sings in response "The Light no Darkness can overcome."[8] Then the congregation sings "O Little Town of Bethlehem," the candles are lit and the hall is illumined.

Those who gather at the communion service are fewer than the congregation at Vespers. Therefore, the communion service takes place in an intimate space, in a chapel, or before a hearth in the parish hall. The candelabra illumine the lectern and the table. The people who gather for communion are those for whom God is an uncommon concern. They are acquainted with the rudimentary dynamics of grace and have some sense of God in their lives. But they also have doubts, uncommon doubts. For these folk Christmas involves more than holiday spirit and Christianity is more than service and good works. For them God is not simply the source of all being and the cosmic creator. This congregation is aware that at the heart of this festival there is a decisive play of divinity to which the Scriptures bear witness. Seated about the table they listen for that move.

The Scripture Readings

The Scripture Readings at the communion service are decidedly different from what has been heard on Pageant Sunday and at Candlelight Vespers. There are two or three sets of Scripture for the Christmas Eve communion service. In one set the Gospel is from the prologue of John, and the epistle reading from the Letter to the Hebrews. While the Old Testament reading is from the book of the prophet Isaiah, the tone is decidedly different from the Sundays in Advent. Now instead of telling us of the night, the watchman sings of good news.

Hebrews 1:3
The third verse of the Letter to the Hebrews' first chapter presents a critical figure that touches upon Christ's share in the glory and being of God. This verse can be translated several ways. In this case the authorized translation is the most helpful because it expresses the Christological issue most dramatically. The Son is described as being (a) "the brightness of God's glory and (b) "the express image of God's person." Or in the words of the New English Bible, (a) "the effulgence of God's splendor" and (b) "the stamp of God's very being."

This verse affirms that God's glory involves the relationship between Jesus and One whom he called "Abba." The Letter to the Hebrews casts the closeness of their relationship in terms of light. The Son is declared to be the brightness of the Father's glory. In other words, when the glory of God is described in terms of light, Christ is the brightness of that light.

The writer of the Letter to the Hebrews wished to articulate an intimate and intrinsic bond between the Son and the Father. The writer did so in terms of the figure of light. Only here an analogy of intrinsic attribution rather than proper proportion is involved.[9] Just as brightness or effulgence cannot be separated from light because they share a common being, so the Son of God cannot be separated from God the Father. They share a common being as well. As brightness is to light so Christ is to the divine being of God. Reading this portion of the Letter to the Hebrews at the Christmas Eve communion service proclaims that this holiday involves the very being of divinity.

According to the Letter to the Hebrews, Mary and Joseph's first-born did more than reflect the glory of God. His being was informed by the very being of God. Their son embodied the characteristic dynamics of divinity in his person. He bore "the stamp of God's very being." This seems to be an abstraction. One theologically very astute, perceptive pastor noted that most people consider God to be "the great undifferentiated whoosh."[10] Or in the more measured words:

...if there is a God at all, his
reality is absolutely unique and transcendent
so that there can be nothing to associate
with him.[11]

But the being of God in this verse of the Letter to the Hebrews is not God's ethereally transcendent being. Instead Christ expresses the characteristics of divine being that inform creation. Most people are content to express that characteristic as love. But something more is involved than an observed human affection. "The stamp of God's very being" involves the contours of divinity well beyond an exalted human experience. In order to consider the shape of God's being in those terms it is necessary to take up the unusual language of the Fourth Gospel.

John 1:14

The key of Christmas is set in the fourteenth verse of the first chapter of John's Gospel.

And the Word became flesh,
and lived among us, ...

At issue is the nature of the coming of Christ. This is a dynamic event. It is divinity encountering humanity in a decisive way. The initiative of the Christmas event is decidedly extrinsic to humanity. It is not a question of certain qualities emerging out of the historical situation. The gospel for Christmas Eve announces the way divinity and humanity are joined in this event.

The figure of the Word is significant on several counts. Luke narrates that he was born in Bethlehem because Joseph was "of the house and lineage of David." David was called away from herding sheep in Bethlehem's fields to attend King Saul. One of Saul's courtiers had heard that David knew how to play the lyre. Therefore, Saul sent messengers to Jesse, David's father, to send David to the palace in the city. The son of Jesse played the lyre so well that King Saul asked his father if David might remain there with him, which he did. As a result, it is written:

> Whenever the evil spirit from God came upon Saul,
> David took the lyre and played it with his hand,
> and Saul would be relieved, and feel better,
> and the evil spirit would depart from him.
>   [I Samuel 16:23]

These and other stories of David are in the background of the familiar Christmas narrative. The coming of the magi as well as the shepherds is connected with the figure of David.

However, the Word that became flesh in the Fourth Gospel reaches beyond David. The Word is before David. The Word goes back to the very beginning. In other words, John declares that the being of the Word is present in this event at Bethlehem.

The Word declares that the ultimate power of divinity is neither a mute nor abstract force. To speak of the Word attests there is communication between divinity and humanity. That means, Christians do not live in an indifferent universe, but a universe in which the Word plays.

Whereas David took the lyre and played it, the Word took flesh and played humanity. Clement of Alexandria called humanity "this instrument of many tones."[12] His comment resonates with the Fourth Gospel's word "flesh." The "flesh" is humanity with its many tones; for better and for worse, with its limitations of birth and death, its historical limitations, starts and stops. The Word takes up that humanity. However, the assuming of flesh by the Word is not just an occasional gesture. Jesus is the instrument which the Trinity plays without destroying his humanity.

In one of his meditations written on Christmas Day, Edward Taylor pressed the phrase in the second half of the fourteenth verse translated in the King James Version and Revised Standard Version "dwelt among us" but more accurately "tabernacled amongst us." The expression "tabernacling" in the Fourth Gospel comes from Old Testament piety that affirmed God to be the One who tented or encamped with the people of God. That meant moving with them as well as being with them. For that reason, the translation "dwell" sounds too sedate. It implies that God remains ensconced in a temple rather than moving on with the people in a tent or tabernacle. Consequently, one biblical scholar maintains that the translation "dwell" is radically misleading.[13] Taylor heads his meditation with the Greek phrase from John 1:14 but translates the verb "Tabernacled among us."

Taylor's December 25 sermon was another on types of Christ in the Old Testament. The word "tabernacled" in the Gospel made Christ the antitype of the Jewish Festival of Succoth. For the Puritan poet and pastor the tabernacles that Israel dwelt in during the festival of Succoth were a type of Christ's incarnation. Or, to put it technically, the booths of Succoth were a type and the incarnation of

Christ was the antitype. Hence, the primary figure in the Westfield minister's December 25, 1697 Preparatory Meditation was the festival of Succoth.

Succoth is a one of the three major Jewish Biblical Festivals. It is held in the fall and its celebration involved the people of Israel dwelling in tabernacles or booths, that is, structures with boughs for roof so that they could look out at night and see the stars. In part taking meals in a booth or tabernacle during the holiday served as a reminder to Israel of their wandering with God in the wilderness. Hence, the booths of Succoth reminded Israel of the days when the Lord God tabernacled with them in the desert. Those booths or tabernacles reminded Taylor of the Incarnation.

The primary figure is that of the tabernacle or tent. This figure enables the poet pastor to illustrate the nature of the flesh that the Word assumes. This flesh is most definitely not a grand dwelling designed especially for The Logos. Instead God tabernacles in:

> ... a Myrtle bowre,
> A Palm branch tent, an Olive Tabernacle,
> A Pine bough Booth, An Osier House or tower
> A mortal bitt of Manhood,...[14]

Taylor was aware of the shock that divinity should be confined to humanity. It was comparable to seeing "the burning Sun...Ly buttoned up in a Tobacco Box." But this tabernacling resulted in a union between humanity and divinity which Taylor expressed in terms of house and householder.

> Wonders! my Lord, Thy Nature all With Mine
> Doth by the Feast of Booths Conjoynd appeare
> Together in thy Person all Divine
> Stand House, and House holder.[15]

Taylor articulated the intimate connection and exchange between divinity and humanity at the heart of Christmas with a building figure in one very compact line.

> Thou wilst mee thy, and thee, my tent to bee.[16]

This is the full meaning of the admonition in Coffin's Advent hymn that every Christian breast be furnished "for so great a guest." Men and women are not simply visited by God. Taylor knew that Christmas celebrated the fact that an exchange had taken place between God and humanity. Humanity became God's tent. And God became humanity's tent. That means Christians no longer live in a universe where divinity is ensconced in heaven while humanity writhes on the earth below. Rather men and women are exalted in the exchange whereby God becomes their tent and they become God's tent. That exchange is realized in the word and sacrament of Christmas Eve.

At the end of a short homily upon the Scriptures, the congregation stands and recites their covenant and then sings "O Come, All Ye Faithful." While the congregation remains standing, the minister begins the communion prayer which praises God with an extensive narrative of events.

THE COMMUNiON PRAYER

The communion service in many liberal Protestant congregations used to be dominated by the Words of Institution. Fragments of a communion prayer might have been present in the back of a hymnal. For example, in *The Pilgrim Hymnal*, 1958, the SURSUM CORDA AND SANCTUS were printed with a text followed by the lines "PRAYER OF CONSECRATION OR EUCHARISTIC PRAYER" and "THE WORDS OF INSTITUTION" without a text.[17] However, in the United Church of Christ the full texts of new communion prayers were introduced in *The Lord's Day Service*, 1964, *Services of Word and Sacrament*, 1966, and *Services of the Church*, 1966.

At the same time a much older communion prayer was becoming known at ecumenical services. In 1963 at the 19th Ecumenical Student Conference on Christian World Mission, gathered at Ohio State University in Athens, Ohio, from December 27 until January 2, 1964, The Reverend Dr. H. Boone Porter ordered a Service of Holy Communion "According to the Apostolic Tradition of Hippolytus. (Adapted for modern Usage)"

Hippolytus was a prominent bishop in Rome during the early third century A.D. and a prolific writer. It has been suggested that he was born somewhere in the eastern part of the Empire and made his way to Rome. As a church leader he was not eager to accept back into the church those Christians who cracked under persecution, however repentant they might be. The bishop is said to have died in Sardinia where he had been sentenced to labor in the salt mines. *The Apostolic Tradition* is presumed to be a statement of the rites and theology of Hippolytus' congregation. It is dated to about the year 215. The Communion Prayer in *The Apostolic Tradition* aroused considerable excitement because it provided a prayer text antedating not only the Western church's divisions stemming from events in the sixteenth century, but antedating the eleventh-century division of East and West in the Christian Church as well.

After critical editions of *The Apostolic Tradition* became available,[18] various communions incorporated part or all of Hippolytus' prayer into their new liturgies. Phrases of Hippolytus' prayer can be heard in *The Proposed Book of Common Prayer*'s Eucharistic Prayer II B. In the Roman liturgy a version of Hippolytus appeared as Eucharistic Prayer II. In 1978 a full translation of Hippolytus' communion prayer was published in the Lutheran *Book of Worship* as Eucharistic Prayer IV. It appeared in the Anglican Church of Canada's *Book of Alternative Services* as Prayer II. However, given the tangle of manuscripts and different theological traditions, the various churches translated parts of Hippolytus' prayer in different ways.

The Presbyterians' *Supplemental Liturgical Resource 1 the Service for the Lord's Day* in 1984 presented an initial translation of Hippolytus' communion prayer as "Great Prayer of Thanksgiving D."[19] In the 1993 *Book of Common Worship* it appeared as "Great Thanksgiving G."[20] The first part of the prayer attributed to Hippolytus strikes a chord with the Scripture readings of Christmas Eve, praising God for the Person of Christ and what he has done.

Hippolytus' prayer begins with the verb that informs all communion prayers —to give thanks.

> We give you thanks, O God,
> through your beloved Servant, Jesus Christ,
> whom you sent in these last times
> as savior and redeemer
> and messenger of your will.[21]

Designations of Christ

In this opening line there are four designations which state Christ's activities in the drama of salvation: servant, savior, redeemer, and messenger. The fifth designation states who Christ is as a Person, God's Word. Each has its distinct note. These designations for the Person of Jesus prompt those gathered about the table on Christmas Eve to take up the New Song.

Behind the first designation "servant" is the Latin word for child. But because the word is translated "servant" it gives new meaning to the mother and child of "Silent Night." At the communion service the child of Bethlehem takes on the form of the child as servant.

In Mark it is written that Jesus was "in the house" before he asked his disciples what they were arguing about on the roadway. To settle their argument about who was the greatest in Kingdom of God he said, "Whoever wants to be first must be last of all and servant of all." [Mark 9:35] At that point Jesus took a little child and put it among them..." [Mark 9:36]

What was the child doing there? Was he or she helping serve Jesus and his disciples? Did the child's activity provide the setting for Jesus' saying about being a servant? Jesus' subsequent statement "whoever does not receive the kingdom of God as a little child will never enter it" [Mark 10:15] may have less to do with the innocence of childhood than with being a servant. By translating the Latin word "child" in the text as "servant" in Great Thanksgiving G the opening words of Hippolytus' communion prayer strike a serious note amid the boughs of holly.

The next designation for Jesus is "as savior and redeemer." These designations celebrate the fact that Christ renders people victorious over the darkness and sin in their world. Both figures have roots in biblical Hebrew. At the base of the word savior is a Hebrew root meaning "to save." This Hebrew word is found in the names of Isaiah and Joshua as well as Jesus. All three names are different inflections of the root word, meaning "to save." The root meaning upon which this word works is one of health and healing. A savior brings health and healing to the sick and injured. Those sitting around the table singing the second verse of "Silent Night," "Christ, the Savior is born," are more often than not people who recognize a need for healing given the brokenness of modern life. They rejoice that they can turn to the Body of Christ for comfort and healing.

The designation "redeemer" is also rooted in the Hebrew Scriptures. During Advent members of the congregation will probably have heard Handel's *Messiah* at least once with its aria, "I know that my Redeemer liveth," taken from Job 19:25. Redeemer is a political figure and speaks to the dynamic of salvation that repudiates whatever confines and belittles the people of God here and now. Christ as redeemer defies the Herods of this world, be they large or small. Those sitting at the Lord's Table are there in part because in that place they have found a presence in which they have enjoyed a measure of authentic freedom.

The redeemer not only rejects that which separates and grinds down the people of God. The redeemer is also the one who gathers them together from the four winds of the world into the community of the church. Those who come to the Christmas Eve communion table come from all over the metropolitan area. They are grateful not only for their well-being, but for their being there on that night in that place with the others about them. This is a people, in the words of the psalmist, whose lines have fallen in pleasant places.

God is thanked for sending Jesus Christ to humanity "in these last times," a phrase that the author of the prayer may have taken from the opening lines of the Letter to the Hebrews. That reference places Jesus' birth in the context of history and strikes a chord with Luke's historic markers: "When a decree went out from Caesar Augustus that all the world should be taxed...while Quirinius was governor of Syria" [Luke 2:1–2] and the fifteenth year of the reign of Emperor Tiberius when Pontius Pilate was governor of Judea...." [Luke 3:1] In short, there is a definite sense of time informing Christmas. It is not a "once upon a time" event. Rather it is the event by which those in the church measure the years. As they stand and hear the prayer, these folk are locating themselves in time. They are grateful for the measure of time that they have been given and that they have been able to share with their neighbors.

The next designation for Jesus in the communion prayer is "messenger" of God's will. Again the Latin word behind that translation is noteworthy. It is "Angelum," from which comes the English word "angel." There are angels throughout the Christmas story. Angels are among the more popular figures for Christmas cards and stamps. The littlest members of the Sunday School play the part of angels in the pageant. In all of this tradition the basic biblical sense of the word "angel" meaning "messenger" evaporates. Thus once again Hippolytus' communion prayer checks popular holiday clichés and articulates the biblical understanding of angels being messengers of God.

Not that Jesus is an angel. The reading from the opening chapter of the Letter to the Hebrews maintains repeatedly that Jesus is no angel in the sense of being other than human. For those who gather at the Christmas Eve service, whatever is said about the Person of Christ can neither overthrow nor obscure the form of his human being. Being of the flesh and in this world, Jesus' parables and teachings meet people at the beginning of their week and take up their sense of the world. Christ is with the people of God in the world. He doesn't hover over the earth. He walks its length and breadth. Designating the child Jesus as servant, savior, redeemer, messenger, in the first paragraph of the communion prayer sets before the congregation the many ways they have met this person and known his ministry in the course of their own days.

Taking up the designation of Christ from the prologue of the fourth gospel, the child of Christmas is twice said to be God's Word. This is the same Word through whom God made the world and in whom God took delight. Those lines in the prayer hold up the designation of Christ as God's Wisdom. This presents Christ in terms of creation and the beginning of all being. Here the congregation meets the God who not only "beholds all dwellers on the earth" but delights in them. This is the Word at the center of homes and all creation. This "everlasting light" is thankfully acknowledged by those who gather for Christmas Eve Communion.

The prayer describes the Word as "inseparable from" God. This is a figure that resonates with the opening of the Letter to the Hebrews. However, the figure does not spring from the candles at hand but from the Scripture read. To call Christ the Word inseparable from God is an analogy of extrinsic attribution.[22] That is to say, the divine nature is being described in terms taken from the Fourth Gospel and the Letter to the Hebrews. The designation of Christ in the communion prayer as the Word resonates with the prologue to the Gospel of John. To say that this Word is "inseparable from God" is to take up the third verse of the Letter to the Hebrews which speaks of the Son as "the brightness of God's glory" or "the effulgence of God's splendor." This is an especially apt figure for the Christmas Eve communion service which is illumined by candles in four candelabra at the corners of the table. However, the figure in Hippolytus' prayer springs from the Scriptures being read, not from the candles at hand.

Hearing the Word mentioned in the prayer moves those in the congregation to traditional distinctions rarely heard in Christmas carols. Hippolytus' prayer declares that the Word can no more be separated from God's being than the brightness of light coming from candles on a candelabra can be divided into separate portions. Gregory the Theologian, a Cappadocian Father who died in 389, noted he could not "divide or measure out the Undivided Light."[23] The being of the Word is likewise inseparable from God. However, the inseparable Word does not reduce God to a general glow. The very designation "Word" is designed to check any idea of God as a nebulous and homogeneous being.

The Virginal Conception

The Word articulates God's definite dynamic and form. This dynamic and form is narrated in the prayer's subsequent phrases:

> He is your Word,
> sent from heaven into the Virgin's womb,
> where he was conceived,..

This is a virginal conception, not a virginal birth, a topic best left for Communion prayers on Christmas Eve rather than the pageant, being difficult to explain to children or adolescents before or after the pageant. For the pageant, it is prudent to simply mention the passages in Isaiah, Luke and Matthew having to do with the Virgin Mary when the script calls for those passages in Bathrobe Drama and Bathrobe Drama Plus years. Mary's virginity is not a topic for interpretation in the Creative Pageant years. In an era of earnest sex education the Virgin Mary cannot be explained to young people in terms that they understand. The categories of enlightened social science will not do.

The story of Mary in the Gospels is not told in terms of the twentieth-century understanding of human sexuality but rather in terms taken from Scripture and tradition. While the language of the communion prayer is not language which Christians of the twentieth century would use to describe the Incarnation, still, it is notably arrogant for them to assume that earlier Christians were unaware of basic biology. Knowing the facts of human reproduction, they offered this description of the Virgin Birth as a sign to bring something other than gynecology to mind.

On the one hand, the basis of this line in Hippolytus' communion prayer stems from the Gospel of Matthew and the debated translation of the term "virgin" taken from the prophet Isaiah. On the other hand, the communion prayer is speaking in terms other than those of Isaiah. It was in Mary's womb that the Word "took on our nature and our lot."[24] Therefore, it is instructive to recall the teachings from Reformed Catechisms which maintain Mary was not a glass vessel. Instead the catechisms use several verbs to describe this event. Calvin's Genevan Catechism speaks of "assuming our flesh."[25] The Heidelberg Catechism in question 35 says the eternal Son of God "took upon himself our true manhood from the flesh and blood of the Virgin Mary."[26] The Shorter Westminster Catechism speaks of Christ "Taking to himself a true body and a reasonable soul... in the womb of the Virgin Mary."[27] Edward Taylor spoke of humanity being the well tun'de Instrument that the Lord did assume.[28] In other words, the person of Christ took all the attributes of humanity in the womb of Mary. However, those human attributes alone do not constitute "the Word made flesh." Rather those attributes rest on the substance of the Word. Hence, in Hippolytus' prayer the Word "took flesh."

One benefit of mentioning the Virgin Mary in the communion prayer is to make the point that human nature is not solely responsible for the baby Jesus. As the Word of God, the Person of Christ is not even the product of human and divine cooperation. The Word being sent into the Virgin's womb serves as a reminder that the initiative of Christmas is extrinsic to humanity. The holy initiative stays with God.

Liberal religious interpretations of Christmas domesticate the event by accentuating the human elements of the Christmas story and suggesting that the birth of the Christ child is analogous to the birth of all children. The Word of the Fourth Gospel is lost in the glow of a holiday humanity. The Christ child becomes an empty symbol to be filled with the very best of contemporary hopes. But Christmas is centered in the presence of the Word which defines the event.

Hippolytus' prayer declares this child was "revealed to be God's Son." In other words, humanity is not to be confused with divinity. Even on Christmas Eve, Reformed Christians keep the initiative with God and maintain the extrinsic nature of the Word undergirding the whole event.

Christmas involves God dwelling with humanity in a way that brings humanity into touch with God so that they can enjoy God and love their neighbors as themselves. Those at the service become aware that they share a presence with friends and neighbors celebrating Christmas Communion in other sanctuaries that night. This presence will accompany them all out into the world.

The divine initiative of Christmas is underscored by the last phrase in the final line of Hippolytus' prayer narrating the Incarnation. Hippolytus' prayer proclaims the Word "was born of the Virgin by the power of the Holy Spirit." To speak of God's Word being "born of the Virgin by the power of the Holy Spirit" serves as a reminder that this was an event that came from outside the human gene pool. In Matthew and Luke, both Joseph and Mary are told that it is by the Holy Spirit that the power of God dominates this event. The Presbyterian translation of Hippolytus, "born of the Virgin by the power of the Holy Spirit," is a free translation drawing upon verse thirty-five in the first chapter of Luke. This is a reference to the Virgin Birth. But the point of this line is to emphasize that in the life of Christ, the Holy Spirit is involved from the very beginning. This decidedly checks any temptation to equate Jesus' birth with God's Spirit being on others such as Deborah or Sampson. Constituted by the holy being of God the Holy Spirit is present at the incarnation of God's Word as well as at the beginning. In this way the character of Christmas is articulated more radically at the Communion Service than at either the Sunday School Pageant or Candlelight Vespers.

As the bread and the cup are passed among the people in the congregation, they may notice the difference in the congregation from previous years. People who were once present are now absent. Some have died, others have moved away. Noticing these changes around them may prompt people to realize that they too have moved along since last Christmas. For a high school senior this may be the last year living at home. For young parents this may be the year in which a child was adopted. For others it may be the year before retirement. Others may have returned home for Christmas and are coming to church where they were married. Some members of the congregation are people who regularly attend church and who think about what happens there. The presence of God is in the midst of all these folk. When the bread and wine come to them, each person thankfully reaches out to share the signs of communion.

As David touched the strings of the lyre, God touches those gathered about the communion table. Edward Taylor said in his meditation:

> For thou wilt Tabernacles change with mee.
> Not onely Nature, but my person tuch.[29]

Taylor spared no music in the conclusion of his Christmas Day Preparatory Meditation of 1697. In the final stanza of his meditation he invoked Hosannah Songs being raised. Hosannah is another Hebrew word having the same root as the name Joshua, Isaiah and Jesus. With this cordial word, Taylor welcomes Christ at Christmas.

Like the Westfield minister, those seated about the communion table on the night of December 24 do not spare the music. On Christmas Eve they will conclude the service by singing "Joy to the World," Isaac Watts' free translation of the last five verses of Psalm 98. The joy to the world is that "the Lord is come." Where the psalm speaks "Sing unto the lord with the harp," Watts paraphrases, "Let men their songs employ."

The opening stanza takes up an Advent refrain, that every heart should prepare God room. Those who take time out to go to the communion service on Christmas Eve have in part done just that. However, their response is not the whole story. While humanity has prepared room for God, God has made room for humanity in the fullness of God's own being. Calvin noted that the benefits which God bestowed in the Word made flesh, were not for Christ's "own private use but that he might enrich poor and needy" humanity.[30] People at this service are liberated from the demands of those who push them to the side, or simply don't care to understand. Likewise, they shed the status "of those whom the world calls prosperous."[31] Those who come to this service are not defined in terms of zip codes.

The members of this congregation anticipate more in their life than the entitlements of the world. They are enriched from being caught up in the excellence of God. Theirs is an enrichment characterized by an increasing complex and dynamic participation in the realms and forms of being, leading to the fullness of God's being. This congregation, by virtue of being at the table on Christmas Eve, is linked to other Christian congregations on this one night and Christmases down through the centuries. Blessing the bread and wine in the words of a communion prayer that has been handed on from the earliest days of the church means that this congregation is in touch with Christians they have never met. The prayer itself leads to the Word which the Fourth Gospel declares goes back to the beginning and brings into play nuances of the Christian knowledge of God. No one present at the service comprehends the whole text or even large parts of it. But in some measure they do share in these various forms and realms of being of which the communion prayer speaks.

The Christmas Eve congregation shares the signs of communion passed to them in a simple ritual action. As for the parts they don't grasp or that truly puzzle them, they will have time to ponder these. For this congregation the Christmas melody has many notes, striking multiple chords. They hear the new song, when the world has retired.

At some point in the service, those who gather at the table are touched by the Spirit of God. That touch informs the measure of their participation. Those gathered about the table realize a measure of what is being communicated. That is known by their consent, their consent to be there, their consent to listen, their consent to sing and their consent to share in the bread and wine. This liturgy comes together with a dramatic beauty. The people, the prayers, the historical events, the Scriptures, the complex sense of God, all participate in the fullness of God's being playing in the theater of the world from beginning to end. As the chorus in that theater, the congregation reflects the glory of God.

While the people of God do not turn their back on the world, but rather definitely live in the world, they know that there is always more to life than what the world can give. These people at the table have a sense of being sustained and being filled by the presence of God as a dynamic reality that others prefer to ignore. They draw insights and wisdom from people who have been here and are gone. They rejoice at the signs of the coming Kingdom of God. Instead of living by the calculations of either shoppers or social scientists, the people of God live with a measure of hope in the world that materialists neither see nor grasp. In other words, for them Christmas is much more than the presents under the tree and the swing of holiday moods.

Those gathered around the table trust the promises of Christ. When Jesus described those who would be "blessed" in the world, the word behind blessed had a very definite element of happiness. Those who trust the truth of his promises and parables lack the terrible earnestness of those who believe that it is all up to them. They are folk who are called to a life wherein they will understand their neighbors, themselves, as well as the communities where they live and work in terms of Christ's parables of the Kingdom. They are able to enjoy God in the world and make their way through the world responsibly with a measure of graceful abandon. Some have called them playful. They leave the church on Christmas Eve, their hearts having been lifted up.

However, the heart of Christmas is not a secret to stay hidden in a Christmas Eve service that some attend. Isaac Watts juxtaposed the truth and grace of John's prologue with the judgment of God in Psalm 98 to bring out the glories of God's righteousness in the world. Christmas Eve reminds the faithful that God's righteousness is not necessarily what the world calls justice. It is what some in the world call justice with an extra concern for those whom the Caesars and innkeepers of the world ignore.

The last stanza of "Joy to the World" sounds a note of warning to the world. The glories of God's righteousness and wonders of God's love manifest divine justice and power in ways that are beyond the grasp of the world's leaders for whom "God" is a word at the end of a speech. In the United States that seems to be especially true of presidential addresses. Consider, for example, the way John Kennedy concluded his Inaugural Address on January 21, 1961. He asked God's blessing and help, "knowing that here on earth God's work must surely be our own."[32]

"Joy to the World" checks such rhetoric. God's work on earth is God's work. God does God's work on earth despite actions to the contrary undertaken by humanity. God

> ...rules the world with truth and grace,
> And makes the nations prove
> The glories of his righteousness.

But truth to tell, not everyone finds Christmas to be an occasion displaying God's righteousness. Certainly in 1697, Samuel Sewall did not. The new King's Chapel in Boston was celebrating Christmas, much to his disgust. Sewall noted in his diary, that at least, the shops remained open, "Carts and sleds come to Town with Wood and Fagots as formerly." At his morning family prayers, he read Psalms 14, 15 and 16. From the fourth verse of Psalm 16, that would be:

> They who give gifts to a strange God,
>   their sorrowes multiplye:
> their drink oblations of blood
>   offer up will not I.
> Neither will I into my lips
>   the names of them take up.[33]

Samuel Sewall reports that he took the occasion to "dehort mine from Christmas keeping and charged them to forbear."[34] Unlike Edward Taylor, who meditated upon the meaning of Christmas in his own terms, Samuel Sewall would have none of it. The judge may have feared that the extended frivolities of an English Christmas would corrupt his home. Perhaps Sewall was anticipating a riot of leaping lords, french hens and golden rings. He need not have worried.

The Twelve Days of Christmas

Although some people may try to remember what comes after the partridge in the pear tree, most everyone else put the Christmas story away almost immediately. After the first day of Christmas, cultural Christians have renewed their acquaintance with the story in broad enough outline to be quite satisfied. As a result, attendance on the Sundays following Christmas drops off. For those who come to church during the Twelve Days, this is a time to sing the less familiar carols, do services of special music, and recall traditions from forgotten communities like the Shakers. These are the Sundays to hear the lesser known stories of Christmas: Herod's Massacre of the Innocents, Simeon's song at Jesus' Presentation in the Temple. It is time for the youth group to present their version of the mummer's play "St. George and the Dragon" to their younger brothers and sisters. At some later point, they may be surprised to encounter the figure of St. George in a sculpture at the United Nations Gardens. Instead of destroying a comical dragon, he is lancing a dragon with a body of Soviet SS-20 and Pershing II missiles. The old stories have a way of living on.

When they hear the story of Jesus' baptism at the hand of John, members of a congregation know that the Twelve Days of Christmas are over. That is the Gospel lesson for the Sunday following the twelfth day of Christmas, Epiphany. The Baptist has lost none of his roughness. He emerges from the Gospels in January baptizing Jesus from Galilee in the Jordan. The Gospel writers tell us that the Holy Spirit was manifest on that occasion, indicating that this is not simply the action of two earnest and zealous reformers. The presence of the Holy Spirit states that God is intimately involved with this person. In other words, Jesus is not just another prophet. This is a human being upon whom the Spirit of God rests and in whom that Spirit dwells.

In the Jordan, the Holy Spirit anoints Jesus' humanity. Matthew, Mark, Luke and John articulate the intimate and intrinsic bond between Christ and humanity in terms of the story of Jesus being baptized at the hands of John. Jesus' baptism in the Jordan was like the baptism of the others, in that all those John baptized shared the attributes intrinsic to humanity. As John baptized others, so he baptized Jesus. Everyone at the Jordan shared a common humanity. In other words, the humanity of those baptized by John in the Jordan, is the humanity that the Word assumed in the incarnation. That Gospel after January 6 announces the implications of Christmas: in Jesus of Nazareth humanity and divinity are bound one to another. This event manifests the sense of human nature in which Christians rejoice.

When the Sundays that follow Epiphany take up the story of Jesus' ministry, they narrate Christ's "active obedience unto the whole Law."[35] Jesus' teachings, signs and healings in Galilee personify the coming of the Kingdom. The notes of this obedience strike a chord in the people of God that lingers to inform and judge whatever they may do for the rest of the week. When they become involved in the world, they are not marching to a political agenda. They are dancing to the words and tune of "Love Divine, All Loves Excelling." Wherever they go, members of the congregation bring a sense of renewed humanity as well as the way God intends the world to be.

Chapter 5

The Turn of Lent

𝕮hristmas and Easter are the two major holidays of the Christian year. The first always falls on December 25. The second has no fixed date. The Council of Nicaea in 325 A.D. established the rule that Easter is to be celebrated on the first Sunday after the full moon following the Spring Equinox.[1] Therefore, Easter is celebrated on dates that can come "early" or "late" in the spring. Either way, preparation for Easter begins with Ash Wednesday.

In 1696 Easter fell on April 4. In the complete edition of Taylor's poems Meditation 22 is undated. But given that its text from I Corinthians 5:7 is "Christ our Passover is sacrificed for us," this poem may well have served as the Westfield pastor's Easter meditation for that year. Meditation 20 in the Second Series bears the date "7.12m 1696."[2] In the early New England almanacs February marked the end of the year. Thus, when Taylor dated his twentieth meditation "7.12m" that meant February 7. In 1696 that was the first week in Lent. Strange as it may seem, this would suggest that the Westfield poet and pastor kept a holy Lent.

Whenever Ash Wednesday arrives, it serves notice to a congregation that the season of preparation for Easter is upon them. That preparation is reflected in the Christian education curricula. At the First Church in Chestnut Hill fifth graders will prepare an Easter marionette play for the Easter Morning Breakfast. One or two persons will spend Lent preparing to be baptized on Easter Eve. With adolescents, preparation for baptism begins with their Sunday School curricula. An adult's preparation for baptism during Lent involves picking up a thread of Scripture and considering the witness of earlier congregations they have known. Church activities in Lent are designed to meet people where they are on the journey and invite them to deeper participation in that holy communion where sin is defeated and life is victorious.

INSTRUCTION

Members of the fifth grade are old enough to know the story. They will spend Lent preparing a marionette play for the Family Easter Morning Breakfast to pass along their understanding of the Easter narratives to the younger children. The very word "marionette," meaning "Little Mary," suggests that they are not the first people in church to have done so. As early as is possible in the season, given the school vacation schedules, the fifth graders bring the Bibles they received two years earlier and meet with the minister. Squeezing those two or three meetings into the children's busy spring schedules, with the pressures of Little League, swimming, ballet, tennis and vacations, can be a very daunting pastoral task.

After hearing the ways of the four Gospels, the fifth graders decide which one of the Gospel stories of Easter will be the basis of their play. A chronology of the events constituting Easter is put up on the blackboard. This involves a discussion of the difference between the Sabbath and Sunday and when each day begins. A sun is made to rise and set, signifying the days beginning and ending. The fifth graders read through the Passion and Easter narratives thinking out loud in terms of how many marionettes can be made to do what. How to make the tomb big enough to get Jesus in without catching the strings? In this process the particular accent and figures of a particular Gospel are heard. If Mark is the basic text, then the women buy the ointment before going to the tomb. Matthew's angel descending to the tomb offers truly dramatic possibilities. Plastic flowers, wrapped around darts, dropped into a styrofoam block before Jesus produces the Garden of Gethsemane. If it's Year C, Luke's year, the story of Emmaus may balance the Last Supper. If it's Mark in year B, the play comes to a very abrupt ending. Working over the script for their play, the fifth graders learn the events of Easter. "What will you be doing this year?" asked one father. "Everything but the dinner," his fifth grade son confidently replied.

The actual construction of the marionettes takes no more than parts of two meetings. Attention remains on the narrative and who does what when, rather than the actual mechanics of the marionettes themselves. Their heads are made from strips from brown paper bags with simple cloth bodies and two simple strings on one rod. Two or three sessions are spent telling the story with the marionettes coming on and off the stage. When there is a question as to what should be done, the Gospel text is checked. The directions are surprisingly explicit. For example, "The soldiers came and took him away." Soldiers enter left, Judas enters right and approaches Jesus. The marionette heads bob toward each other. Jesus exits, swept before a cluster of soldiers whose faces are made from the bottom of an egg carton.

The minister promises to stand in front, narrating the marionettes' actions, thus relieving any stage fright. As the rehearsals progress, the fifth graders themselves may volunteer to take a line here and there. "Is it I?...Is it I?...Is it I?" On Easter morning the narrator may say "Jesus said" only to be followed by silence as marionettes are being lifted back and forth backstage. So the narrator is forced to repeat, "And Jesus said...," waiting and hoping for a voice to be heard. Belabored expositions of the Sabbath are not uncommon as the sun seems to have been misplaced after the Good Friday scene. Given the simplicity of the marionettes, strings can be untangled and the show go on without a total break in the narrative.

The fifth graders, putting on the play for the younger children, understand the chronology of the events. After rehearsals and the production, they have the story of the less well known holiday in mind. This is a narrative that they will not study in school. Taken together, the Christmas pageant and the Easter marionette play provide children with the basic Christian story.

At the beginning of Lent an announcement in the church bulletin reminds people that this is the season when Christians have traditionally prepared for baptism and invites any who might like to do so to meet with the minister. Responding to that invitation, one or two people may come forward. In small congregations this preparation is done individually rather than in large groups.

PERSONAL CATALOG REQUEST and RELEASE INFORMATION

White Mane Publishing Company, Inc. would be happy to add you to our growing list of readers. For your personal copy of our book release information please return this card with your complete mailing address information.

FROM: _____

_____

_____

I purchased this book through:
A. Direct Mail
B. Bookstore
C. Book Club

I chose this book because of:
A. Book Reviews
B. Magazine Ads
C. WM Catalog Release
D. Friends Recommendation
Other: _____

I prefer to purchase books through:
A. Direct Mail
B. Book Store
C. Book Club

97907

PLACE
STAMP
HERE

White Mane Publishing Company, Inc.
P.O. Box 152
Shippensburg, PA 17257-0152

I..lllI..I.I.I.I.I.III....II.I.I..I.III...I

Past

Perfect. The C

The magazine. *Civil War* magazine is the cornerstone of the Society. Published bimonthly, *Civil War* features original scholarly articles covering all facets of the war. Our writers are opinionated, often conflicting in their interpretations, but that is the essence of scholarship. We work to ensure that each

Virginia Memorial, Seminary Ridge, Gettysburg National Military Park

issue is balanced in its representation of the subject matter, and covers as large a geographical area as possible. *Civil War* does not shrink from controversial or unconventional subjects, and we present the traditional topics in a fresh light to broaden understanding. Recent additions to the magazine

include Gary Gallagher's **Civil War 100,** the essential list of the Civil War classics; and a special issue devoted entirely to the Peninsula Campaign and the Seven Days Battles.

Preservation. When you join the Civil War Society, you will become part of an international network of education and preservation. Each membership gives the society the power to act on current preservation and education projects. We keep our members updated regularly through the Society's quarterly newsletter. The Civil War Society is dedicated to preserving the physical legacy of the war because we believe that tangible reminders of the conflict are vitally important to understand the total picture. We must never forget what they sacrificed. Among our many diverse preservation victories are Cedar Creek and Shiloh, where funds donated by the Society were used to help purchase important tracts of land that were slated for commercial development. We have also financed monuments at Hatcher's Run and Perryville, and the Society

ivil War Society is your link

Confederate Artillery
Gettysburg National Military Park

was the first to take a national stand against the proposed shopping center in Manassas and Disney's plan to build a theme park at Haymarket.

Our seminars. We believe

in action. Our Society seminars, held year-round, are hosted by the leading academic experts and regularly attract participants from as far as the west coast, Canada and Europe. Come to one and you'll see why. Some of our recent seminars have included an intense focus on the Seven Days Battles in Richmond, and a novel perspective of Antietam by canoe. Our seminars are excellent for deepening your appreciation of the mastery of a

successful strategy, the strengths and limitations of field command, and the personalities of the commanders themselves. They are also relaxing social events that allow members to become acquainted. Anyone can visit a battlefield—we bring it alive!

The **Civil War Society** is a unique organization: personal, yet far-reaching, impartial yet provocative, informed, yet entertaining. Our publications have won awards, our seminars have drawn praise, and our funds have

The action comes alive for seminar attendees at Gaines's Mill where Hood's Texas Brigade clashed with Morell's division.

helped save battlefields. We have a vibrant, active, and growing membership—we invite you to become a part of it!

Membership includes

- *Civil War* bi-monthly magazine

- Our historical **calendar,** thoroughly researched and really stunning

- The **Society newsletter,** where members keep abreast of preservation activities and society events.

- A personalized parchment **membership certificate**

- Our **guide** to tracing your Civil War ancestors

- The opportunity to obtain a **Civil War Society MasterCard,** with a portion of every purchase going towards preservation.

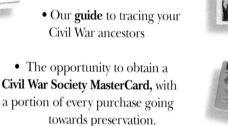

Call 1-800-247-6253
or use the order form below

- -

☐ For a Gift ☐ For Myself / ☐ 1 yr. $39.00 ☐ 2 yrs. $68.00 (save $10) ☐ 3 yrs. $89.00 (save $28)

Name _____

Address _____

City _____ State _____ Zip _____

gift card to read _____

☐ Check ☐ MasterCard ☐ VISA ☐ AMERICAN EXPRESS

Card Number _____ Exp. Date _____

Signature _____

The Civil War Society • P.O. Box 770 • Berryville, Virginia 22611
Please allow 4 to 6 weeks for delivery
For foreign shipping please add $10, $8 for Canada

Among those preparing to be baptized may be adolescents who have attended Sunday School. They were brought up in the congregation by their parents with the intention that at some point, they would decide to be baptized. They have made their way through the Sunday School curriculum, pageants and marionette plays. The youth group provided them with an opportunity to talk about ethical dilemmas. Going to the movies and discussing what they saw, provided a critical analysis of secular mores and morality. Having heard the story and the values involved, some wish to fully participate in the Christian community.

Their coming forward in Lent to prepare for baptism on Easter Eve, resembles the practice of the third-and fourth-century church. When adults in that era were baptized, they spent Lent preparing for their baptism, when they were expected to state their faith. Today young people baptized as adults are asked to make a profession of their faith. That profession will in part be an appropriation of what they have learned in their Christian education.

The pastor's task is to discover the way in which they can affirm what they have learned. To prepare for this conversation the minister looks through the old curricula books left on the shelf to find a book with that person's name written on it. Some of the stories, activities and quizzes bear not a mark. Others contain awkwardly scrawled comments, cartoon figures, and comments attributed to various individuals in the story. Sharing these with someone is a way to begin preparing for baptism. After recalling the stories that they heard, as well as the holidays they celebrated, young people may choose to articulate their faith with a particular communion's statement of faith, the congregations' covenant or a traditional creed. At that point both their parents and the minister realize that those in the congregation who said they would nurture children in the faith have kept their promise.

Some Lents adults in a congregation may decide to prepare for baptism. This may come as a bit of a surprise to their parents. Said one seventy-year-old of his adult married daughter preparing for baptism, "I don't think I can carry her to the font." When these adults present themselves for baptism, the primary pastoral task is to find the answer to the question posed in the last verse of the Good Friday hymn, "What language shall I borrow to thank thee, dearest friend?"[3] Preparing an adult for baptism involves listening to his/her pilgrimage and designing a preparatory program that will present sin and rebirth in a language each understands.

Lenten manuals make available a collection of daily prayers and meditations on a particular theme. One year it is God in the psalms and another year meals that Jesus shared with various folk. They are designed to help members of a congregation spend some part of each of the forty days meditating upon a particular passage of Scripture and commentary.

An adult, preparing to be baptized, might find that year's Lenten manual as a way into the Scriptures. Reading meditations in a Lenten booklet is the contemporary version of what Edward Taylor did in Westfield when writing preparatory meditations. The difference between the style and language of contemporary Lenten manuals and Taylor's seventeenth-century poetry reveals a marked shift in Christian language. The density of Taylor's thought turns out to be a healthy supplement to modern pieties.

Adults preparing to be baptized will also draw upon resources in the community. Said one person who presented herself for baptism at the beginning of Lent, "I'm a painter and not very articulate. I prefer to see things if I can. Would that be possible?" The answer is, "Indeed it is." Her query called for a visit to an art museum.

Museum exhibits are rarely appreciated in terms of theological tradition. When people are introduced to these works in museums, theological meanings are rarely mentioned. A guide will show a group of parochial school students a painting of "Saint Luke Drawing the Virgin and Child," unaware that very day is the feast day of Saint Luke. Church silver, including baptismal bowls, chalices and tankards, are displayed with no sense of the sacramental transactions of which they were a part. In medieval galleries, fonts and triptychs are to be seen, but little attention is paid to the particular communities of faith they enriched.

Art museum galleries exhibit art that can help adults find a language to articulate their faith. The people of God need only to go and discover meanings imbedded in paintings and objects by which earlier Christians bear witness to their understanding of the Gospel.

Someone preparing to be baptized, who visits a Cambridge museum with the minister, enters with an intention quite different from other visitors. For them a baptismal font is more than an artifact. The minister and the person to be baptized will ponder the inscriptions and figures on the font and its lid. Those signs of earlier Christians bring to mind the meaning of sin and redemption. Would Edward Taylor be more familiar with the figures on the font than the minister and parishioner examining it in a museum? Yes, undoubtedly he would be. But then those observing Lent can read both the font and Taylor's meditation.

At the Busch-Reisinger Museum, standing before the cast of a large thirteenth-century baptismal font from the Church of St. Michael in Hildesheim, Germany, they see on the middle panel a depiction of Jesus being baptized by John, complete with bold representations of the First and Third Persons of the Trinity. The scene of Jesus' baptism is familiar and straightforward. Jesus stands in the water by John the Baptist with the face and hand in heaven representing the First Person of the Trinity and the dove the Third Person. On the lid of the font just above, Jesus is shown at supper where a woman is washing his feet.

The depiction of the woman who washes Jesus' feet, while recognizable, is puzzling. From which Gospel does she come? Jesus sits between two men. The one on his left has what looks like a pretzel in front of him on the table. The man seated to the right of Jesus is depicted as asking, "Who is this who can forgive sins?" indicating that the incident is taken from Luke.

In Luke 7:49 the woman is said to be a sinner. Jesus' host thought that if he were a prophet, the Nazarene should have recognized that fact. In other words, it would have been obvious to Jesus that this woman had violated her relationship with God. For the Pharisee that was obvious in any number of proscribed actions that the woman had failed to incorporate into her life. But in what way was she a sinner?

SIN

In his 1696 triad of Easter meditations Edward Taylor presented two in-structive figures for sin. In the opening of his meditation at the beginning of Lent in the year 1696, the Westfield pastor wrote in terms of a printing press:

> Didst thou, Lord, Cast mee in a Worship-mould
> That I might Worship thee immediately?
> Hath Sin blurd all thy Print, that so I should
> Be made in vain unto this End? and Why?
> Lord print me ore again.[4]

Taylor certainly knew the opening answer of the Westminster Shorter Catechism's first question.

> What is the chief end of man?
> Man's chief end is to glorify God and
> enjoy him forever.[5]

In the figure of the press that would mean that a person's life should leave a crisp and clear impression for the glory of God. But because of sin the impression a person makes for the glory of God is blurred. Humanity does not make the im-pression God intended. The praise that is God's due is smudged.

Perhaps the woman at Jesus' feet was so smudged. Perhaps that was what Simon the Pharisee noticed, that this woman's piety was not as crisp and neat as it should have been. Who knows what manner of sin was responsible for that? At some point the woman may have taken a wrong turn. Perhaps she chose the wrong company. She may have been deceived or abused. She may have been led astray. She may have wandered away on her own devices. For whatever reason, now she was evidently a sinner—someone who did not enjoy and glorify God as her Creator had intended.

Anyone who has lived in the world and been caught up in its demands and ways knows that woman's condition. Our worship of God isn't a clear and stamped priority at the top of each week. In the rush of the week's activities and obliga-tions, the worship of God doesn't come off as sharply as it should. In other words, between the press and the page there is a blurring of the intended type.

One reason is distraction. After Christmas the "Silent Night" of Christmas and its Word may well go unheeded in the rush of other activities. There is the job to be done at work, with meetings to be attended. It is easy to wander away from the worship of God.

Taylor's Meditation 21 presents a more cosmic figure for sin. The figure is astronomical, based upon a lunar eclipse. There was a lunar eclipse in October of 1696. In his diary Samuel Sewall noted the eclipses that he could or could not see. In October of 1696 he noted that the clouds hindered him from seeing an eclipse of the moon.

> Clouds hinder our sight of the eclipsed
> Moon; though tis apparently dark by means of it.[6]

That may have been true for his friend Edward Taylor out in Westfield as well judging by these lines in Meditation 21:

> Oh! let not Earth nor its thick fogs I pray
> E're slip between me and thy lightsome
> Rayes...[7]

But in this meditation it wasn't simply the earth's clouds that obscure the moon. The earth itself can do so. In the course of a lunar eclipse the earth moves between the sun and the moon resulting in the earth's shadow blocking the sun's rays from illuminating the moon.

The rest of the stanza indicates that Taylor identifies himself with the moon.

> But let my Cloathing be thy Sunshine Ray.
> My New-Moon Trumpet then shall sound thy praise.
> I then in sweet Conjunction shall with thee
> The Sun of Righteousness abiding bee.[8]

Earlier on in the meditation he had written:

> Moon–like I have no light here of mine own.
> My shining beams are borrowd of this Sun,...[9]

Thus, Taylor in terms of the lunar eclipse imagines himself as being obscured by the earth's shadow. The earth's shadow is a figure for sin.

Anyone who has been caught up in the world's demands knows what Taylor is talking about. People encounter sickness, accidents, injustice or abusive power that overwhelms them. The clouds and shadows of earth are part of creation. To be caught up in forces that eclipse a person is to encounter the power of sin. This sin is not the result of an individual's will.

In terms of Taylor's second figure the woman anointing Jesus' feet may well have encountered the earth's shadow. She may have been overwhelmed by social systems and prejudice so that being marginalized by the powers that be she could only sit in darkness. Perhaps due to forces over which she had no control or which she could not avoid, the woman had become a sinner.

REDEMPTION

But the woman did not remain a sinner. Nor did she remain in darkness. Jesus announced that her sins were forgiven when he said, "Your faith has saved you. Go in peace." This woman had a firm and certain knowledge of God's benevolence toward her that involved the full dynamics of God. She sought Jesus out in order to express her gratitude for the sense of forgiveness he announced. Somewhere along the way, this woman had heard a parable of the lost coin, the ninety and nine sheep, or the prodigal son and grasped what was promised her. The realization of God's benevolence in the promises of those parables impressed her. The Holy Spirit having sealed those promises prompted the woman to go to Simon's house and express her gratitude.

This transaction prompted the Pharisee depicted on the lid of the font to ask, "Who is this who can forgive sins?" The panel below gives the answer.

There Jesus' baptism is depicted with the words from Matthew's Gospel inscribed above, "This is my well beloved Son." The woman anointing Jesus' feet realized that this person could forgive her sins and restore her relationship with God. The Person of Christ enabled this woman to enjoy and glorify God. The words of Taylor's lenten meditation might well have been her own.

> Thou art my Medium to God, thou art
>   My Medium of Worship done to thee,
>   And of Divine Communion, Sweet heart![10]

Or put in terms of Taylor's cosmic figure for sin this woman's eclipse was over. Whatever shadows or "Thick fogs" had cut her off from the Son, they were now gone. Her life had been redeemed. She could now go out into the world and live her life as God intended her to live rather than the way others forced her to live. Leaving the table in Taylor's words she could sing:

> ...let my Cloathing be thy Sunshine Ray.
>   My New-Moon Trumpet then
>   shall sound thy praise.
>   I then in sweet Conjunction shall with thee
>   The Sun of Righteousness abiding bee.[11]

The dynamic of the redemption as leaving one way of life behind and entering upon another is presented on both the side panels and lid of the baptismal font. The figures and their stories communicate this transition. The panel on the font to the left represents Moses' tablets under his arm, leading the people of Israel out of Egypt through the Red Sea. On the lid above, a soldier with raised sword against a child of Bethlehem represents the Massacre of the Innocents. The figures on the right side of the font depict the people of Israel crossing the Jordan by Gilgal. The figures on the lid represent the way of life that will be praised when the Son of Man comes in glory.

Both the Exodus and the Massacre of the Innocents delineate the people of God escaping from the forces of an oppressive and murderous society. Both Israel and the Holy Family escape from those evil forces in order to enjoy and glorify God. In a word, the people of God are not the victims of those who assume they rule the world.

The people of God do not simply escape. They also enter a new life. The panel on one side of the font represents the people of God entering the promised land. Joshua is leading the people of Israel across the Jordan into the land of Canaan. The ark is very much in evidence. Those carrying the ark are seen picking up the stones that will be placed in a circle at Gilgal where the people of God will meet and assemble, thus prompting the children to ask what the stones mean.

It is unclear from the biblical narrative what the Israelites did with the ark at Gilgal. In the wilderness, the ark was placed inside the tabernacle which was in part a tent-like structure. The ark inside the tabernacle constituted a holy of holies. David, shrewdly, danced the ark up to Jerusalem. Solomon placed it in the Temple.

In the New Testament the Letter to the Hebrews maintains that the tabernacle is replaced by Christ. Taking a line from the Letter to the Hebrews as the text for his 1696 Lenten Meditation, Edward Taylor links Christ and the tabernacle in an analogy of proper proportion. He elaborates the way in which the tabernacle's lavers, flames and accoutrements are types of Christ. In short, as these various liturgical elements served as a mode of worship for the people of Israel, so the person of Christ serves as the means of worship for Christians.

However, as always, worship centered in Christ involves more than Jesus. In this meditation Taylor certainly affirms the Lordship of Christ.

> Thy Son, my Lord, my Tabernacle he
> Shall be: me run in thy mould again.
> Then in this Temple I will Worship thee.

But the Temple involves the First and Third Persons of the Trinity as well. God the Father is the author not only of Christ but the tabernacle. "Thou wast their authour; Art Christs too and his." The Holy Spirit is likewise mentioned in terms of both the tabernacle and Christ:

> Thy Spirits over shaddowing form'd them, This
> Did overshadow Mary.[12]

The shadow of which Taylor here speaks is very different from that which obscures the sighting of eclipses. This one signifies the Holy Spirit. Christians worship in a congregation where they meet not only the Person of Christ alone but in the full dynamics of God. In that way the worship of faithful men and women is run again in God's intended mould.

This mould means entering a way of life characterized by the merciful actions, actions that are depicted on the lid of the Hildesheim font. Above the people of God entering the Holy Land is a figure of mercy surrounded by a person feeding the hungry, pouring a drink for the thirsty, clothing the naked, welcoming the stranger, visiting the sick and those in prison, who for all the world do appear to be in the doghouse. This is a representation of the life into which Christians are incorporated.

From the galleries of Christian art with its font, the minister and person to be baptized visit other galleries of the Busch Reisinger and their paintings. At this point the minister drops back and listens to her observations and comments. After seeing the baptismal font, certain paintings stand out in the galleries of modern art, for example, two paintings of Lyonel Feininger. Born in New York in 1871, Feininger studied in Germany and became a recognized artist. In 1919 he joined Walter Gropius at the Bauhaus as head of the graphics workshop. Feininger returned to the United States in 1937, where he died in 1956. Two of his paintings, "The Bathers" and "Bird Cloud," catch the attention of the woman to be baptized. She points them out to the minister.

"The Bathers," painted in 1912, boldly features water in its depiction of people at the beach. The waves appear to be solid blocks and the water's color is dark charcoal. The swimmers appear to be stuck in the waves. No one is moving through the water as did Israel through the Red Sea or the Jordan River. This water is more confining than that carved on the font, bringing to mind the limits of many leisure time activities. Modern folk are caught up in "the weekend" with its recreations. How many people spend time and money pursuing activities that promise regeneration but which, in the end, turn out to be quite confining? Those preparing to be baptized are leaving the recreational waters in which they are stuck for those in which they are free to live and move.

A second Feininger painting near at hand states the dynamics of baptism. "Bird Cloud" was painted in 1926. The beach, the water, the horizon and sky are dominated by the white presence of the cloud that looks like a bird. The Bird Cloud is presented with multiple planes and is descending onto the horizon and water. Although much more striking, Feininger's figure recalls the figure of the dove on the font at Jesus' baptism. Looking again, a single, thin solitary figure is spotted standing on the beach. This painting serves as a reminder of the Holy Spirit's presence at the heart of the church. Under the influence of that Holy Spirit, the solitary figure on the beach will be incorporated into a community of God's people.

The order of their itinerary through the museum's galleries is telling. The minister and woman do not begin with the figures of water and people in the modern paintings and end up at the font as though a sense of water and spirit would lead to an understanding of baptism. It went the other way round. The biblical figures on the font are primary. The paintings never become a substitute for Scripture. To the contrary, Scripture is the thread through the galleries. The figures of the water and dove are spotted in the Feininger's "Bathers" and "Bird Cloud" on this particular visit to the museum only after deciphering the font. Biblical figures in modern paintings will help those with eyes to see articulate their faith on Easter Eve. When the minister and the person to be baptized leave the museum, they take with them several strong figures to guide preparation for baptism.

The biblical figures in the museum live in a Sunday congregation. Even though people have let the thread of the Word drop from their lives and haven't sung a hymn in months, even though they have wasted their substance, coupling this experience with that experience, and their heads are filled with the images and beat of popular culture; nevertheless, when they join a congregation, the Word meets them in the worship of the congregation each Lord's Day.

Those who respond positively to the church bell, make time to sing and pray, to hear the psalms and Scriptures on the first day of the week. In the course of the service, people cordially discover meaning in different parts of a Sunday morning liturgy. For some it may be a particular prayer or kind of prayer. For others it may be a particular hymn, its words or its tune or both. For still others the readings and the anthems will strike a chord. For yet others it is the space between certain elements of the service that provide a place of meanings.

A particular line from Scripture in a lenten manual rolls back the shadows of sin.

> For with you is the fountain of life;
> In your light we see light.

[Psalm 36:9]

To know light in the world in terms of God's light is to discover an order that redeems. The people of God in the world affirm that the order of creation is neither logical, mechanical, statistical nor political. It is an aesthetic order of which music is a sign. The events of the world come together as the notes of a melody. Each event is a distinct note. Each resonates with another, sometimes in harmony, sometimes in melody, sometimes in dissonance. As the chorus in the theater of the world, the people of God recognize the consent and dissent of the various forms and realms of being in the world as notes and chords in a resounding melody building to the point of unimaginable complexity and beauty.

That sense of the world's order has direct implications for the way church members live in the world. The people of God embody the new song in the events of their community. They feed the hungry, give drink to the thirsty, clothe the naked and visit the sick as well as those in prison. Rather than being a stranger on a beach, the people of God are involved in the sufferings of the world. They become part of a community which responds to those who suffer in a vital and compassionate way. They no longer flee sickness and death as though these dark realities finally dominate all of life. Nor do they interpret accidents in terms of statistics or count on logic to establish causes. Those who spend Lent preparing for baptism move beyond superficial comments about churches being filled with hypocrites and antique ideas. Like Rahab, they are part of a congregation listening to the Word without and the Spirit within.[13]

As a result on those Sundays when the congregation sings the verse from Psalm 103:

> Praise the Lord, O my soul,...
> who forgives all thy sin,
>   and heals all thy infirmities;

these people cordially take up the melody because they know that to be true. They hear, realize and enjoy the new song in their lives inside and outside the meetinghouse.

CHAPTER 6

The Glory of Easter

On Easter morning the church is cheerfully filled. Everyone who isn't away on vacation seems to make it to church on that particular morning. Spouses who ordinarily have other things to do on Sunday are in the pew on Easter. Grandparents accompany their children and grandchildren. A bank of Easter lilies has been carefully arranged and balanced on the table at the front of the church. The minister and ushers give the arrangement a wide berth, having been warned of potential catastrophe. A trumpet can be heard as special music descends over the balcony onto the congregation. The family choir sings. A special order of service is printed for that festive morning.

Among the congregation sit people for whom this is their fourth or fifth Easter service. They were in church on Palm/Passion Sunday. They may well have attended church on Maundy Thursday and Good Friday. Most recently they will have been present at the Easter Eve Service where someone now standing in the congregation was baptized. When these members of the congregation sing "Alleluiah" in Wesley's hymn, they recognize a refrain that they will be taking up until Pentecost is celebrated with a communion service.

To spin through the local newspaper's report of Easter events for the last five or six decades on microfilm in the local library, or to thumb through a congregation's past bulletins in the parish archives, is to discover many services: the Distribution of Palms, Maundy Thursday Communion Services, Last Supper Celebrations with Services of Tenebrae; Good Friday services on the Seven Last Words of Christ from noon until three o'clock, Community Good Friday Services at noon, Vesper services in the evening, Sunrise Easter Morning Services, and Easter pageants, all with special music. When those local Holy Week services are compared with those of Salisbury Cathedral in the 1500's or Jerusalem in the late fourth century, certain liturgies in parish celebrations of Holy Week emerge as venerable and others as very recent creations.[1] The United Church of Christ's *Book of Worship* and the Presbyterians' *Book of Common Worship* draw upon this traditional material to suggest the way Holy Week is to be celebrated.[2]

However, the week before Easter has a shape of its own in the local congregation, a shape that is not always malleable. For example, so popular is Faure's anthem "The Palms," that pillars of a congregation have been known to seek out other sanctuaries on Palm Sunday where that anthem will be sung. To discover that it may be sung in their own church on a Palm Sunday is a source of great satisfaction. However, if that anthem completely dominates that Sunday's service, any sense of Christ's Passion will be difficult to hear.

Looking over the Holy Week services of past decades shows how widely the communion service has bounced throughout the week. In the course of various Holy Weeks, communion services can be found on Maundy Thursday as the Last Supper, or as part of the Good Friday liturgies. It may have been moved to Palm Sunday in order to give thanks for the life of Christ without shades of the Upper Room or Golgotha. Or it might have been celebrated on the first Sunday of March no matter when that fell in the church year because that was one of the quarterly occasions for communion.

The wandering of the communion service in the course of Holy Week celebrations is indicative of the crucial problem of so many of these celebrations— the lack of a Christological center. Holy Week services can be innovative, intriguing, poignant and dramatic. Clever ministers and their congregations can develop a variety of services at this season which they ardently appreciate and to which they certainly become attached. But in some of those services the center of Holy Week may slip into a simple identification of the sufferings of Christ with causes currently far more popular than Holy Week. Christ is enlisted to support a favorite cause rather than making his presence known. Or else these services try to repeat history by putting the readings, hymns and actions of these liturgies up for the events of Jesus' suffering under Pontius Pilate. The story is told as if for the first time, when in fact everyone knows the story. The attempt to make it more and more relevant, increases the quotient of human suffering being introduced or the dramatization of what happened. Instead the services should be directed toward realizing the significance of what happened to the person of Jesus Christ in Jerusalem.

PALM OR PASSION SUNDAY

The first question of Holy Week is whether to call the Lord's Day before Easter just plain Palm Sunday? Is it now Palm/Passion Sunday or Passion/Palm Sunday? The United Church of Christ's *Book of Worship* suggests Palm/Passion Sunday. The Presbyterians' *Book of Common Worship* designates the Sunday before Easter to be Passion/Palm Sunday.

For most congregations the designation Palm/Passion Sunday seems the better term. Even though Jesus' procession was traditionally only a part of the Sunday Gospel read in Jerusalem, the Lord's Day before Easter is a time to cordially affirm the Person of Christ. There are enough ominous signs and sayings in the gospels of Jesus' entry to preach Christ's suffering as well. The reading of the Passion, however, on the Sunday before Easter not only co-opts Good Friday, it presents the sufferings of Christ so that they dominate all other elements of his person and ministry.

However, if those who attend church on Palm Sunday do not attend a Good Friday service, they may return to church on Easter without hearing the narrative of suffering and the cross. Hence, the suggestion is made that the congregation may need to hear the story of the Passion on the Sunday before Easter. Therefore, not only is a portion of the Passion Story to be read on Palm Sunday but the choir may sing on occasion an anthem with an atoning text such as Anselm's in the anthem "Alone to Sacrifice Thou Goest, Lord."

BLESSINGS OF THE PALMS

Among the surprising suggestions in the new services for this Lord's Day is the blessing of palms. Reformed Christians have traditionally protested "the blessing of things." Their protest is against reducing the word "bless" to mean the impartation of divine favor. When the new Palm/Passion Sunday rite blesses palms, it does so with three other meanings of bless; to praise God, to authoritatively declare God's benevolence, to invoke divine favor.

In the United Church of Christ's blessing of palms and people in *The Book of Worship* before the procession, the word "bless" is an invocation that the palms might become an authoritative declaration of God's benevolence.

> We thank you for these branches
> that promise to become for us symbols
> of martyrdom and majesty. Bless them and
> us that their use this day may announce in
> our time that Christ has come and that
> Christ will come again.[3]

Nothing is imparted to the palms themselves by the blessing. God's favor being invoked upon the palms and people is based upon a promise that they would become "symbols of martyrdom and majesty." The word "promise" guards against a misunderstanding of any divine favor being automatically bestowed. The word "bless" is linked to the palms being used to announce in "our time that Christ has come and will come again." In other words, this blessing involves an authoritative statement about the Person of Christ, namely that he has come and that he will come again.

The same accent is heard in the Presbyterian service. The palms are blessed in the sense of becoming authoritative signs. That blessing declares:

> Let these branches be signs of his victory,
> and grant that we who carry them
> may follow him in the way of the cross,
> that, dying and rising with him,
> we may enter into your kingdom;...[4]

Designating the palms to be signs means that, as such, they bring to mind something else, namely, Christ's victory. In the Presbyterian prayer, instead of being symbols of final events, martyrdom and Christ's coming as in the United Church of Christ prayer, the palms signify the transition from Good Friday to Easter "in the way of the cross." Nevertheless, the blessing is in terms of an authoritative declaration of God's benevolence rather than the impartation of divine favor on things.

MAUNDY THURSDAY

The Three Great Days of Easter begin to take shape with the celebrations of Maundy Thursday. The name Maundy Thursday comes from the word *mandatum*, translated Jesus' new commandment, namely that the disciples love one another.

> I give you a new commandment, that you love one
> another. Just as I have loved you, you also
> should love one another.
>
> [John 13:34]

That new commandment is given in the fourth Gospel's account of Jesus' last days on the occasion when Jesus washed his disciples' feet. Following the footwashing, Jesus commands his disciples:

> So if I, your Lord and Teacher, have
> washed your feet, you also ought to wash
> one another's feet. For I have set you an
> example, that you also should do as I have
> done to you.
>
> [John 13:14–15]

However, when it comes to Maundy Thursday many congregations ignore the Fourth Gospel's new commandment and take up the other three Gospels' narrative of Jesus' Last Supper. Nevertheless, the recent liturgical resources do suggest a service of footwashing. Ritual footwashing is a powerful gesture that does not come easily to modern people.

A service of footwashing requires far more sensitivity and preparation than stressing the importance of tactile worship and acknowledging our cerebral forms of worship. Footwashing can easily slip into a dramatic affirmation of any loving human service. Therefore, paying close attention to the analogies involved is crucially important. A footwashing service is not based upon an analogy of proper proportion. In other words, the people washing one another's feet are not doing the same thing that Jesus did. Nor is there some intrinsic quality in the act itself which means that the actions are similar. Instead, the members of a congregation who participate in that service are doing so quite explicitly at the command of Christ. This is not a generic act. It is the act of Christians on Maundy Thursday. That service has to keep before the people the fact that the primary servant figure is Christ. Those who wash feet in a service are carrying out Christ's command of service. To keep Christology before the congregation, in the United Church of Christ's service there is a dramatic reading of the dialogue between Peter and Christ stating the meaning of the biblical gesture. But it is the communion service that accompanies the ritual of foot washing and most especially the communion prayer that accentuates the Person of Christ and places footwashing in a proper context.

The invocation of the Holy Spirit in the Presbyterian's "Great Prayer of Thanksgiving" for Maundy Thursday articulates the link between what Christ did and what Christians do.

> By your Spirit unite us with the living Christ,
> and with all who are baptized in his name,
> that we may be one in ministry in every place.[5]

The Holy Spirit is invoked in this prayer to establish a union between Christ and those united with Christ throughout the world. There is nothing intrinsic to the footwashing itself that establishes that link. It is the Holy Spirit that links the ritual action to the Person of Christ. Thus, the gesture turns on an analogy of extrinsic attribution. In other words, the similarities result from the presence of the Holy Spirit upon those following Christ's command.

However, a far more customary service on Maundy Thursday than footwashing has been a communion service commemorating Jesus' Last Supper. For those who cherish the memory of the historical Jesus, Maundy Thursday services commemorating the Last Supper are a significant event. In liberal Protestant congregations the Maundy Thursday Service may be one of the last occasions in which the communion service is celebrated. The accent falls on the Upper Room and the pathos of Jesus' last meal. Whereas the institution of the eucharist is recited as part of traditional communion prayer, in many traditional Maundy Thursday services an entire service is given over to dramatizing the Last Supper.

To capture the sense of the Last Supper, the Maundy Thursday service is sometimes connected with a church supper. The reports of Matthew, Mark and Luke that the Lord's Last Supper was a passover meal has prompted some congregations to do a *seder* of one kind or another. To present the Last Supper as a *seder* is a very dubious move. First of all, it is not by any means obvious that the Last Supper was a Passover meal when all the Gospel stories are taken into account. The synoptic Gospels Matthew, Mark, and Luke present Jesus' last meal as a Passover. But the Gospel of John does not. These biblical writers report two decidedly different chronologies of the event. There is no way to accept one as certainly superior to the other. Therefore, to embrace the synoptic account while doing a *seder* and dismiss the Johannine is to misrepresent the story. Second, since there is no Passover liturgy from Jesus' time extant, it is not possible to say what that service would have involved even if it were known to be a *seder.* Third, it is highly questionable whether or not Christians should take up and adapt a central rite of Judaism as though it were their own. While it is certainly true that Jesus was a Jew, it is not obvious that he was practitioner of Rabbinic Judaism as it was developed following the destruction of the Jerusalem Temple in the year 72 of the Common Era. At most, the historic Jesus can be presented as being in some ways close to the Pharisaic party. Even though that party became a major building block in Rabbinic Judaism, that is not all there is to that tradition. It is more accurate to say that by the time the *seder* in currently recognizable form emerged in liturgical history, the Christian Eucharist had developed in a form that was decidedly dissimilar from the *seder.* Fourth, these services are of necessity an attempt to recreate the way we think it might have been. That being the case, then the resulting service is more a reflection of the creative congregation's imaginings than a celebration of Christ's presence in their midst. Consequently, in order to restore a traditional balance to Maundy Thursday, the Presbyterian Resources suggest a service consisting of a Liturgy of the Word that includes footwashing and the Eucharist with a full communion prayer. The Maundy Thursday Service concludes with the stripping of the church in preparation for the Good Friday service.[6] This action is in anticipation of Good Friday's darkness and solemnity.

GOOD FRIDAY

The name "Good Friday" is said to be derived from "God's Friday," much the same way the word "Good bye" is derived from "God be with ye." The Good of God's Friday has to do with the event of Christ's crucifixion. But the day's services can easily move away, not only from the cross of Christ, but also from the context of Easter in which Good Friday is situated.

In Jerusalem, pilgrims had worshipped from noon to three, thus acknowledging the hours in which Christ was crucified. Recalling that precedent, three-hour midday services were held in Episcopal churches in the nineteen-thirties. By the late nineteen-fifties three hour community services had developed with ministers from the community preaching on one or two of "The Seven Last Words of Christ." Sometimes a visiting preacher would be invited to prepare homilies on all Seven Words. In some communities, by the late sixties, these services had evolved into a noon day community service. A Community Good Friday service was held so that during their noon hour people could attend the service, spending as much of that hour as possible. The liturgy itself was composed of twenty-minute units of a hymn, a prayer, silence, Scripture and sermon.

By the seventies Good Friday was an acknowledged day of low school attendance. In a community like Brookline it is not unusual for those going to the Good Friday Noon Day Service to see Jewish families coming and going from Passover services at their synagogues. Even though Good Friday with its charges and curses, has been at the root of horrible Christian anti-semitism, Christians who attend Good Friday Service and those families attending Passover services have more in common with one another than with the majority of those for whom this is just another business day. The people of God remember a history that the world chooses to respect only in its broadest outlines. Both communities of God's people are open to the presence of God acting in their history and in their lives. Living amidst the world's brutalities, these communities of God's people not only recall those brutalities, they ponder them in the context of divinity which the world cannot fathom.

Congregations on Good Friday Eve are never as large as Christmas Eve or Easter Morning. But those people who do come to hear the Passion read are, more often than not, people who have suffered: the childless couple, the abused woman, the unmarried man, the grieving parents, and the widow, people who know that there is more to life than surface amenities and obvious accomplishments.

On Good Friday the accent is to be kept on Christ's Passion. People who do not attend any service on that day miss an essential element of the Christian story. This is an event to which Christians turn in their thinking when asked why bad things happen. The understanding of God that emerges from God's Friday is very different from one that begins with God as good and all powerful. On the one hand, efforts are made to attend either a noonday or a Good Friday Vesper Service in order to hear the passion of Easter. On the other hand, the day is sufficiently solemn that such services should not become dramatic productions in which the focus slips from the sufferings of Christ to an inclusive celebration of human suffering. This can be very misleading since there is nothing analogous to the sufferings of Christ, given his Person. While it is correct to say that he truly suffered as human beings suffer, there was also more involved than human nature. All analogies between Christ and other human beings are ruled out. For example, Christ's suffering was not the same as that of the witnesses to social justice. There was more involved in his suffering than the power structures of a particular society. Nor does Good Friday hold up all that is intrinsic to human suffering. In other words, Good Friday is not a projection of human experience. The suffering of that day is set in the context of the play of Divine Being.

Therefore, an appropriate liturgy for the day involves reading of the Word with plain commentary. For the last two decades a variety of readings has been heard on Good Friday at the community service. Daniel Stevick concluded his introduction to the first *Proclamation commentary for Holy Week in Year C*:

Unfortunately for an ecumenical series,

the readings in the various churches' lectionaries

diverge more during Holy Week than during the other

parts of the church year.[7]

Some of that diversity has been eliminated. *The New Common Lectionary* now presents the same series of Good Friday Readings for each year. They are: Isaiah 52:13–53:12; Hebrews 10:16–25, or 4:14–16, 5:7–9; and John 18:1–19:42. These readings have the virtue of keeping the accent upon the person of Christ and his particular power. The reading from Isaiah is the Fourth Suffering Servant Song. Christians have traditionally read this song of Isaiah as a description of the way Christ gave himself over to death. The passages from the Letter to the Hebrews interpret the suffering of Christ in terms of the priesthood at the Temple. There is an exhortation in 10:19–25 that addresses the response of the faithful to Christ's suffering. The Gospel of John not only presents the Passion of Christ with all the drama and well wrought figures of the Fourth Gospel, this account leaves no question of who is really in charge of events as they unfold.

John's account has a noteworthy chronology. According to the Fourth Gospel, Jesus' crucifixion took place on the Day of Preparation, that is the day on which the lambs that would be used in Passover *seders* were being slaughtered in the Temple. At the time when the paschal lambs were being slaughtered, Christ was dying on the cross. Thus, the appropriateness of Paul's figure in a Letter to Christians at Corinth, "For our paschal lamb, Christ, has been sacrificed." [I Corinthians 5:7]

The metaphor of Christ as the lamb is basic to Good Friday. In Isaiah 53, it is a metaphor for the way Jesus met his death:

like a lamb that is led to the slaughter

and like a sheep that before its shearers is silent,

so he did not open his mouth.

[Isaiah 53:7]

The person of Christ is compared to a sacrificial beast. Since a human being is not a sheep, this is a metaphor resting on an analogy of improper proportion.

Apparently, sometime in 1697, Edward Taylor wrote an undated meditation on the Corinthian text, "Christ our Passover is sacrificed for us." Was this

his Easter meditation? It would have been a fitting text for an Easter meditation. Beginning with the second stanza of Meditation 22, Taylor worked out a series of analogies between the redemption of his soul and the paschal rite of Israelites in Egypt. These are analogies of improper proportion because he is juxtaposing the events in Egypt with his soul. Since the nature of the two elements of the analogy are dissimilar, they constitute an analogy of improper proportion, or in other words, a metaphor.

The reading of Christ's Passion is certainly the heart of the Good Friday service. Nevertheless, the accompanying Scriptures are telling in the way they articulate the meaning of the Passion. For example, in Lectionary Year C 1977 and 1983 the readings from the Presbyterian and the United Church of Christ lectionaries were decidedly different from those of the other communions. These Reformed churches read Hosea 6:1–6 and Revelation 5:6–14 with Matthew 27:31–50.

The six verses from Hosea speak of transition and transformation, declaring that after two days the Lord

..will revive us;
On the third day he will raise us up,
that we may live before him.
[Hosea 6:1–2]

The mention of being revived in two days and raised in three is not to be understood as a chronological calculation of the Easter event. Instead, the mention of these three days introduces the element of time into the Easter event. The words need to be taken in their straightforward sense that the people of God are not revived immediately in their sufferings. Rather the promise is that it is in the course of a short time that they expect to be revived. The phrase "three days" is taken to mean a short time.

Hosea's text is noteworthy in that it sets before a congregation God's promise of renewed life after a time of sin and suffering. It is to be noted that Hosea speaks of being revived and living before God. In the words of the psalm, God is the source or fountain of life. Thus, in the midst of the dying of Good Friday, this reading from Hosea puts forth the promise of life.

The prophet communicates God's promise to be trustworthy with a metaphor, God's "going forth is as sure as the dawn." Since God is not of the same nature as the creation, this is an analogy of improper proportion and Hosea's figure, therefore, a metaphor. In this way, Hosea affirms that God as light and life will surely overcome the darkness of death.

In a subsequent verse Hosea describes the people of God in terms of another metaphor from the land. It is likewise based on an analogy of improper proportion, comparing human beings with inanimate phenomena. When Hosea compares the love of the people of God to the morning dew which fades away, the meaning is not favorable.

...Your love is like a morning cloud,
like the dew that goes early away.
[Hosea 6:4]

This metaphor for human perseverance strikes a chord when the story of Christ's Passion is being read. The lack of human staying power, the superficial commit-

ment of people, is highlighted. Carl Wennerstrom cast Hosea's metaphor in contemporary terms by maintaining that many religious liberals would be somewhere else than at the foot of the cross on Good Friday. They would go away
early to work for an appeal of Jesus' conviction, or to investigate future supports
for the family or to petition Rome about Pilate.[8] This well intentioned activity
provides a contrast with the steadfast love God desires in the midst of suffering.
By witnessing the suffering of Christ that personifies God's steadfast love, men
would realize their own failure in contradistinction to God's triumph.

The suggested passage from the Book of Revelation describes a setting of
corporate worship. Those who meet and assemble together sing a new song around
the throne. Their praise centers on "the lamb worthy to be slain." A Good Friday
congregation would hopefully recognize an analogy of proper proportion between what John is describing and what they themselves are doing in their sanctuary. Namely, both are a congregation of praise, lauding the Person of Christ as
the Lamb of God.

But the Book of Revelation takes the metaphor of the lamb and places it in
the context of congregational praise. The accent has shifted from the lamb being
a slaughtered victim to being a lauded victor. With that note being sounded with
the Passion story, a congregation catches a sense of God's Easter victory, thereby
providing an answer to the question of why this is called Good Friday. It is God's
Friday in the sense that Christ the Lamb is victorious over death and the powers
of evil in a way that is truly praiseworthy. To hear that note on Good Friday is to
touch upon the glory of God that is all too often lost in the sweat, blood and tears
of crucifixion. While Christ's suffering and agony is not to be gilded over or
sanitized, still, the question should be raised whether those who attend Good
Friday services in this day and age need to hear more of suffering or the cordial
praise of God's victory.

As the Passion is read, the narrative grips people. It is appropriate and
informative to invite one or two members of the congregation to comment on a
portion of the Passion. A two- or three-minute commentary on a particular
episode from a member of the congregation underlines the drama. They may
speak about Jesus' concern for his mother, the compassion of a rich Pharisee or
the pain of broken promises, the failure of responsible people or the brutality
of crucifixion.

Here analogies of proper proportion and intrinsic attribution abound between figures in the Passion and their counterparts in the modern world. People
act in remarkably similar ways and manifest some of the very same attributes:
Pilate and those in authority who prefer to side-step the difficult decisions; the
High Priest and those who use a utilitarian calculus to decide what is best for the
people; Peter and those unduly confident before the pressures of a crisis; the
soldiers who brutally mock and beat the accused.

Every time the Passion is read, the darkness that the Gospel of Matthew
introduces into the story is felt.

> From noon on, darkness came over the whole land
> until three in the afternoon.

[Mt. 27:45]

That darkness is not an astronomical event but brings to mind the deep power of sin in the world of humanity. It is a power that Edward Taylor understood and presented in the abrupt and difficult first stanza of his undated paschal meditation.

> ... when the Sun's all black to see Sins pull
> The Sun of righteousness from Heaven down
> Into the Grave and weare a Pascall Crown.[9]

His basic figure is an eclipse that John Tulley had announced in his 1697 Boston almanac. Tulley reported that the only eclipse the people of Massachusetts would be able to see that year would be a lunar eclipse on April 25. A lunar eclipse meant that the earth's shadow would cut off the light from the sun reaching the moon. For purposes of the meditation Taylor imagines himself on the moon.

> I from the New Moon of the first month high
> Unto its fourteenth day When she is Full
> Of Light the Which the Shining Sun let fly...[10]

From that vantage point he imagines how the eclipse would appear. From the eclipsed moon the earth would cut off the light of the sun, thus blackening it and dragging down the sun of righteousness. Thus, Taylor described the Passion of Christ.

In terms of another metaphor, the sun is Christ. Throughout his preparatory meditations Taylor played on the words Sun and Son.[11] The Sun of righteousness, a figure from the book of the prophet Malachi is traditionally applied to Jesus Christ the Son of God. In Malachi, the sun rises with healing in its wings. This reading is sometimes heard on the Second Sunday of Advent in Year C. But in Eastertide Taylor reverses the figure.

> And when the Sun's all black to see Sins pull
> The Sun of Righteousness from Heaven down
> Into the Grave and weare a Pascall Crown.

In this situation the Son is pulled into the grave by the Sins of the earth. The "Pascall Crown" is the ring of light that surrounded the sun, eclipsed by the earth as seen from the moon. The darkness is understood as the power of sin.

Taylor's seventeenth-century poetic conceit became a commonplace of popular culture in the twentieth century. With the Apollo space flights around the moon, NASA photographs reported back what the earth looks like from the vantage point Taylor had imagined. What had been his imaginary point of view in the spring of 1697 became a postage stamp issued in May of 1969. In the posters and cards that followed, the earth was repeatedly seen floating in the deep darkness of space. That led credence to the sense of darkness on Good Friday.

The First Gospel's sense of darkness informs "A Tenebrae Service or The Service of Shadows" in the United Church of Christ's *Book of Worship*. The service is rooted in the reading of Scripture at early morning services during Holy Week in medieval cathedrals like Salisbury. A number of candles were extinguished in order to dramatize the events of Jesus' suffering.[12] This practice has carried over so that at either Good Friday or Maundy Thursday services, during the reading of the Passion, a candle is put out when incidents involving Jesus' betrayal and suffering are read.

The darkness of a Tenebrae service on Good Friday signifies the darkness of which Matthew speaks. On this holiday the people of God recognize the sin of deep darkness. The darkness of hatred and death in the world of humanity pulled Christ into the grave on Good Friday. The final darkness of the sanctuary reflects more than human decisions that were or were not made. The darkness of Good Friday touches the darkness Taylor imagined and NASA photographed. It is an overwhelming shadow.

When a Good Friday congregation sings "Were You There When They Crucified my Lord?" there are those who answer, "Yes." Their affirmation comes not from the depth of their sufferings, nor the dramatic power of the Good Friday Service itself. Their "Yes" comes from the presence of the Holy Spirit. Those who can say "Yes" to the spiritual's question, have received "the spirit of adoption," whereby they have been comforted by the Holy Spirit and conformed to the image of Christ.

Tucked in between the chapter "Of Justification" and "Of Sanctification" there is a short chapter entitled "Of Adoption" in the Westminster Confession and Savoy Declaration. The chapter mentions the "spirit of adoption" as a dynamic of the Holy Spirit. The phrase is taken from the Letter to the Romans:

> For you did not receive a spirit of
> slavery to fall back into fear, but you
> have received a spirit of adoption.
>   [Romans 8:15]

In the dark times of their life the faithful know and trust the promises of God's benevolence. That knowledge and trust is informed by the Person of Christ and sealed by the Holy Spirit in their hearts and minds. The "spirit of adoption" is one way of describing that sealing.

That Spirit is intimately bound up with Christ. When describing the "saving action of Christ" as prophet, Calvin maintains he received the Holy Spirit:

> ...not only for himself that he might carry out
> his office of teaching, but for his whole body
> that the power of the Spirit might be present in
> the continuing preaching of the gospel.[13]

Those who leave a Good Friday service saying somewhat in disbelief, "It gets me every time!" have encountered the Spirit that accompanies the Word. This is the spirit of adoption which enables them not only to empathize with the sufferings of Christ but to rely upon the promise of God's victory as well.

Those who rely upon God's promises praise the God of Comfort who strengthens them by the Comforter Jesus promised. [John 14:16] Revised translations of the English Bible do not speak of being comforted nor a Comforter. Instead they translate 2 Corinthians 1:4 and John 14:16 in terms of the people of God being "consoled" and an "Advocate." The King James' translation "Comforter" is preferable because "Comforter" basically means to strengthen. Those who say "Yes" to "Were You There When They Crucified my Lord?" have a strength that is manifest on the world. The Holy Spirit that accompanies the Passion Narrative inoculates these people with what Calvin called "the root and seed of heavenly life in us."[14] Heavenly, not in the sense of being celestial, but in terms of being in tune with the Holy Spirit in the world. These are the people of

God who live in terms of God's goodness and power. They do not cooperate with the rationalists who humiliate others by clever arguments, or make pragmatic decisions on the basis of cost benefit. Those at Good Friday services are not callous. They are the companions of doctors and nurses who remind their busy colleagues that they do not visit the sick simply to treat them. They are being present to the pain of the least of God's people.

In other words, those in the congregation who say "Yes" to "Were you there?" are conformed to the image of Christ. In a too little known interpretation of Romans 8:29, Athanasius of Alexandria maintained that the Holy Spirit was the image of the Son. Quoting Paul's line

> For those whom he foreknew he
> also predestined to be conformed
> to the image of his Son,...

toward the end of his first Letter to Serapion, Athanasius wrote, "The Spirit is said to be, and is, the image of the Son."[15] The Alexandrian Bishop interpreted the Third Person of the Trinity to be the image of the Second Person. Western Christians are quite accustomed to understanding the Second Person of the Trinity being the image of the First Person but not the Third Person being the image of the Second Person. This is an Eastern tradition developed by Gregory the Theologian.[16]

Athanasius' interpretation of the Holy Spirit being the image of Christ means that the Holy Spirit is not rooted in the movements of the world's ideologies. The Holy Spirit, as the image of Christ, defines humanity as God intends it to be. God does not intend humanity to remain in the shadow of death. Therefore, whenever the people of God encounter the "valley of the shadow," they take up Christ's promise and hope that the thread of the Word will lead to the light that dispels the darkness.

Easter Eve

A handful of the faithful, fifteen or twenty, gather at ten o'clock in the parish hall for the Easter Eve Service. They come for a variety of reasons. There are those for whom weekly and holiday worship is a part of their life. These folk are prompted to leave dinner parties or return from vacations and head for church on Easter Eve. There are those who wish to see what this service is all about. After coming once or twice, some decide that the Sunday morning service is sufficient.

The people essential to an Easter Eve congregation are the people who come to be baptized or to renew their baptism. Given the hour of the service, more often than not the persons being baptized on Easter Eve are adults who for a variety of reasons were not baptized as children and now wish to be initiated into the church. Preparing for their wedding leads some couples to think about their relationship to the people of God past and future. Intending to begin a home, the shape and dynamics of the couple's faith becomes important. They are led to reflect not only upon their own religious situation but more often than not the person with whom they have fallen in love introduces them to a communion of the church of which they have only the vaguest of understandings. That which they took for granted, i.e., where they do or do not go to church, is now cast in a whole new light.

If they are from different communions and intend to celebrate a Christian marriage, then the issue of baptism comes to the fore. When churches extend a welcome to members of other communions in Christian marriage, they do so on the basis of a shared baptism. This means finding the baptismal certificate that was put away somewhere for safe keeping. But it may also turn out that one of the engaged persons wasn't baptized as a child. After making that discovery and learning the reason why, the young adult may decide to be baptized. As one woman said, "My parents didn't have me baptized because Mom was a Methodist and Dad an Episcopalian and they could never decide where to go to church. But in a way I'm glad because now it really means something to me and my fiance." Part of that meaning is a decision in terms of understanding the theological tradition in which they were nurtured as well as one within which to celebrate their marriage. Both can be discerned during the preparations for baptism during Lent. This provides the foundation for not only the baptism and marriage, but the subsequent baptism of children as well.

The Service of Light

On Easter Eve following a word of welcome and overview of the liturgy, tapers are distributed and everyone makes their way outside to the back of the church where the service begins. At the Service of Light that begins the Easter Eve service, the congregation hears the prologue from the Fourth Gospel, and the darkness of Good Friday is rolled back. The lighting of a new fire and the tapers, with a blessing, signifies the light and life that the prologue of John's Gospel proclaims in the verses:

> In the beginning was the Word,
> and the Word was with God,
> and the Word was God.
> In him was life,
> and the life was the light of all people.
> The light shines in the darkness and the darkness
> has not overcome it.[17]

That Word leads the congregation back to the ultimate reality before all human experience—the source of light and life that defeats darkness and death. The Word that was with God and became God incarnate is both vital and dynamic. It is the source of life that bears the agony and termination of the crucifixion. Light, the quickest dynamic in the universe, signifies the vitality of the Word. The life of the Word overcomes death. The light of the Word illumines the darkness. This is the life and light that neither the darkness of death can overcome nor the deep comprehend. The verses from John are read before any of the congregation's tapers are lit because it is only in the light of the Word that those gathered on Easter Eve ignite their Easter candles.

The blessing that follows in the liturgy of the United Church of Christ describes God as the giver of light and life.

> Eternal God, giver of light and life,
> bless this new flame,
> that by its radiance and warmth
> we may respond to your love and grace,
> and be set free from all that separates us
> from you and each other;
> Through Jesus Christ,
> the Sun of Righteousness.[18]

The word "bless" in this context invokes the hope that the Easter Eve services of light may be an authoritative declaration of God's benevolence and not simply a dramatic liturgical gesture. When Reformed congregations light a Paschal candle and their tapers, then process to the sanctuary and light the darkened church, it is necessary that they keep those activities subordinate to the Scripture. These ritual actions signify the light and life of the Word.

The United Church of Christ's prayer begins by identifying God as the source of light and life and addresses the need for the people of God to walk together in that light and life free from "all that separates them from God and one another." The prayer concludes with the traditional verbal play on Christ the Sun which Taylor had turned upside down in his meditation. Thus, this blessing directs the congregation's attention toward God.

On Easter Eve, the whole sanctuary is illumined by worshippers carrying tapers. The congregation is drawn to the front of the church where the lectern, the baptismal font and the communion table are set to provide the center for the service. Whereas on a Sunday morning the Word and Sacrament may be taken for granted, emerging from the darkness of Friday into the light of Easter Eve, their significance and mission are accentuated.

THE SERVICE OF THE WORD

The transition from the darkness of Good Friday to the light of Easter is the heart of the holiday. Therefore, the primary reading in the liturgy of the Word is the Exodus of Israel from Egypt. This is the one reading that is read every year. Out of the several Old Testament lessons suggested for the Easter Eve service, the Exodus is the one narrative that must be read.

The Exodus from Egypt was the primary event that the Jewish people remembered from generation to generation after they crossed the Jordan. They remembered what happened with the signs and memorials at Gilgal. The festival of Passover kept that blessing of God before them down through the days of judges, kings and prophets, through and beyond the destruction of Jerusalem and the Babylonian captivity. It was the event of the remembered Exodus that provided the language of hope for those who returned from Babylon. That same language of sign and ritual was appropriated by Christians to describe the dynamics of Easter.

Exodus 14

The United Church of Christ's lections locate the heart of the event in Exodus 14:21–29. The initiative of God is attested in the strong east wind that held back the sea, allowing Israel to escape. This was understood as a sign of God's benevolence toward the people of Israel. The Presbyterians, by following the Common Lectionary, take up the narrative at Exodus 14:10 with the Israelites' alarm when they realize that they are being pursued by Pharaoh's army. In this reading the Easter congregation hears the bitter denunciation of Moses attesting that the people of God were not of one mind.

Christ's glorious transition from death on Good Friday to life on Easter is analogous to Israel's escape from a life of bondage in Egypt to a covenanted life in the promised land. Specifically, it is an analogy of extrinsic attribution, since, whatever quality of life these two events share, that vitality is given to the people of God by the Divine initiative. Hence the Early Church referred to Easter as the *Pascha,* that being a transliteration of the Hebrew word for Passover. The etymology was lost among those who knew no Hebrew and the word was said to have stemmed from the Greek word for suffering. This translation indicates more than a lost understanding of Hebrew. It reflects a focus upon Christ's Passion and cross that became a dominant accent in Latin Christianity. Easter is the season that articulates the dynamics of Christ's resurrection. That is why the event is depicted in terms of appearances to the disciples, sermons by the apostles, as well as analogies with events in the life of Israel. The transition of the people of Israel leaving Egypt, inscribed on the left hand side of the old baptismal font in the museum, and crossing the Jordan on the right hand side, provide the critical figure for Easter in the dynamic of deliverance and liberation.

Edward Taylor in Westfield certainly caught the initial enthusiasm of the Passover transition and imparted it to his Easter Meditation on the text "Christ our Passover is sacrificed for us" by writing:

With Staff in hand, Loins Girt, and Feet well shod
With Gospel ware as walking to my God.
I'le Goshen's Ramesis now leave apace.
Thy Flag I'le follow to thy Succoth tent.[19]

There are multiple readings at the Easter Eve service stemming from the time when catechumens were being baptized in another part of the church or down by the river and the main body of the congregation waited their arrival to join them. In that interlude, the congregation heard readings appropriate to baptism and resurrection. The presence of a person being baptized or renewing her baptismal vows is vital to the Easter Eve Service. If a baptismal rite is absent too many times, then the service on Easter Eve will either fall by the wayside or take a markedly different direction. The other Scripture readings suggested for the Easter Eve service inform the baptismal liturgies. The readings from Ezekiel chapter 36 and 37, Romans 6, and John 20, accompanying Exodus 14, speak to various individuals as well as bring out the multiple dynamics of baptism. While these themes can be presented to a congregation, it is the presence of someone actually being baptized that embodies the meaning of the texts.

Ezekiel 36

On Easter Eve, verse 25 in the reading from Ezekiel 36 brings baptism to mind.
> I will sprinkle clean water upon you
> and you shall be clean from your uncleannesses
> and from your idols I will cleanse you.

This passage presents two basic figures of baptism, the figure of cleansing and with that the Holy Spirit.

According to Calvin, the first dynamic that baptism signifies is "our cleansing."[20] Therefore, it is not surprising that question sixty-nine of the Heidelberg Catechism describes baptism's transaction:
> Christ instituted this outward washing
> and with it gave the promise that,
> as surely as water washes away the dirt from the
> body, so certainly his blood and his Spirit wash away
> my soul's impurity, in other words, all my sins.[21]

This would appear to be an analogy of proportion, an analogy of proper proportion in that the action of washing is common to both bathing and the baptismal rite. It is an analogy of improper proportion as well, in that water is not of the same substance as blood and spirit. Therefore, the element of water serves as a metaphor for the cleansing of baptism.

But then question seventy-two declares that it is not the water that does the cleansing in baptism. In the words of question seventy-two:
> Does this outward washing with water itself wash
> away sins?
> No, only Jesus Christ's blood and the Holy Spirit
> cleanse us from our sins.[22]

Baptism involves the water in conjunction with what the water signifies, the blood of Christ and the Holy Spirit. The mention of Christ's blood and the Holy Spirit being the source of cleansing in baptism makes it an analogy of extrinsic attribution. In other words, it is Christ's blood and the Spirit that are effective, not any attribute that the water of baptism may intrinsically share with those two elements. Calvin accentuated the extrinsic power of the Holy Spirit in the sacraments when he wrote:
> The sacraments properly fulfill their
> office only when the Spirit, that inward
> teacher, comes to them, by whose power
> alone hearts are penetrated and affections
> moved and our souls opened for the
> sacraments to enter in.[23]

Thus, the analogy of baptismal cleansing is not one of proportion but extrinsic attribution.

Question seventy of the Catechism indicates what is meant by being washed in the blood of Christ.
> To be washed with Christ's blood means
> that God by grace, has forgiven my sins

because of Christ's blood
poured out for me in his sacrifice on
the cross.[24]

Forgiveness of sins means that the promise of God's benevolence in Christ penetrates people's hearts so that they experience God's grace. The personal mission
of the Holy Spirit is responsible for the meaning of Christ's sacrifice reaching
them. That presence of the Holy Spirit is extrinsic to the elements of the rite.

The Heidelberg Catechism's interpretation of Christ's death on behalf of
others can be heard in Mark's report of the Last Supper where Jesus said over the
cup, "This is my blood of the covenant which is poured out for many." This is an
interpretation of Christ's death that Anselm, Archbishop of Canterbury, in the
eleventh century, developed into the satisfactory doctrine of atonement so dominant among Western Christians.

In his meditation on Paul's word, "Christ our passover is sacrificed for us,"
Edward Taylor articulates a sense of Christ's blood reaching him. He does so by
placing the figure of the blood of Christ in the context of the biblical Passover.

My Bunch of Hyssop, Faith, dipt in thy blood
My Paschall Lamb, held in thy Bason bright
Baptize my Door Posts shall...[25]

This is a reference to the Israelite practice of putting blood of the paschal lamb
over the lintels of their houses in Egypt. Taylor identifies a person's faith with the
hyssop which dabbed the blood over the lintel. In his meditation, the door posts
are not those of a person's dwelling but of their soul.

The promise of God's benevolence that Christians know and trust is understood in terms of the death of Christ. In short, Christians do not know God outside of the Good Friday portion of Easter. Any motivating sense of hope they
enjoy in the world is informed by Christ on the cross. There is no understanding
of divinity in terms of what God can or cannot do in the abstract. The common
cultural move to God as the Creator, as well as questions of why bad things
happen, is checked by a move to the cross and all three Persons of the Trinity.

Still, the Heidelberg Catechism's answer notes that it isn't the blood of
Christ alone that cleanses in baptism. The Holy Spirit is involved as well. But in
describing the dynamics of the Holy Spirit, there is a subtle difference between
questions sixty-nine and seventy. In question sixty-nine, the washing is done in
Christ's "blood and his spirit." In question seventy, washed with Christ's Spirit
"means that the Holy Spirit has renewed me and set me apart to be a member of
Christ." In question sixty-nine, the Holy Spirit is the Spirit of Christ. In the second part of the answer to question seventy it is the "Holy Spirit." At issue here is
the relation between the Second and Third Persons of the Trinity. If references to
Christ's Spirit are taken too casually, that may give the impression of subordinat-
ing the Third Person of the Trinity to the Second Person. Given the emphasis
upon the Person of Christ and his sacrificial death in Western piety, the mission
of the Holy Spirit is easily overlooked. Calvin insisted upon recognizing the
power of the Holy Spirit in terms of sacraments.

...what sight does in our eyes for seeing light,
and what hearing does in our ears for perceiving

a voice, are analogous to the work of the Holy
Spirit in our hearts, which is to conceive, sustain,
nourish and establish faith.[26]

Thus, any cleansing action of the waters of baptism is infused by the presence of
the Holy Spirit. This serves as a reminder, that in order to be effective, baptismal
rites and renewals are dependent upon the work of the Holy Spirit and checks any
enthusiasms for the rituals of the Easter Eve service. The powerful combinations
of the relighting the church after Good Friday, the multiple readings, the rites of
baptism and Holy Communion can be very dramatic. However, in the end of the
day it is the presence of the Holy Spirit that brings the congregation to life.

The mention of idolatry in the same verse Ezekiel resonates with the renunciations of the baptismal service. This is a part of the baptismal rite that
speaks to adults. Before those presenting themselves to be baptized profess what
they believe, they renounce certain aspects of life in the world. The Presbyterian
Church in Canada spells out the renunciations of candidates for baptism in the
following terms:

Trusting in the gracious mercy of God
who has been faithful to us in all generations,
do you turn away from sin,
renounce evil and all powers in the world
that rebel against God
or oppose God's rule of justice and love?[27]

The sin that the person turns away from may be their own choice. This may
be a point in their life when they publicly say "No" to a way of life that they had
tried on or explored. The renunciation of evil and all powers in the world that
rebel against and oppose God, refers to a person being caught up in situations
and circumstances whereby social structures and political forces push toward
callous rejections of God and neighbor.

Such forces can become a form of idolatry. Idolatry is much more than the
adoration of strange carvings. It is more than nationalistic and atheistic political
movements. There are also idolatries of "the weekend," when people find it all
but impossible to get to church. The secular culture has lost a sense of Saturday
being the seventh day of the week and Sunday being the first. Each year more
and more desk calendars feature Monday as the beginning of each week. Osten-
sibly the weekend is the time when people are to enjoy themselves. Recreational
industries flourish for the weekend. Feininger's depiction of bathers stuck in the
waves revealed how confining recreational activity can end up being. Since his
time, not only have bathing suits changed but motor crafts have replaced the
schooners on the horizon. But have people discovered a more perfect freedom in
their recreation?

Those adults who come to be baptized renounce the idolatries of their own
pleasure. Not that they never go to the beach on a weekend. But they realize that
in the end such activities are not true recreation. True recreation is being given
what Ezekiel called a new heart and spirit and what *Baptism, Eucharist, and
Ministry* termed "Conversion, Pardoning and Cleansing."[28]

Ezekiel describes that transaction in terms of the contrast between a heart of stone and a heart of flesh.

A new heart I will give you,
and a new spirit I will put within you;
and I will take out of your flesh the heart of
    stone and
give you a heart of flesh.

[Ezekiel 36:26]

A heart of stone is the heart of someone refusing the prompting of God's spirit. People who do not take up the melody of the church as chorus seem to have better things to do at other places. They may be busy with political or ecological affairs, not to mention sporting events. They may be too involved with the works of their own hands and their own family to take time for church. When they decide to be married, the question of church presents itself. At that point, couples who have been away from church may draw near a worshipping congregation with hearts of flesh.

Ezekiel 37

This chapter in the Book of Ezekiel begins with a valley of dry bones. The promise is that the dry bones shall come together and live. Meeting with the minister, a couple considers where they have been in terms of church. Often this conversation begins with a walk through a valley of dry bones. The conversation moves beyond casually accepted assumptions to particular recollections. Certain biblical figures and specific theological traditions are recognized as a part of the person's heritage. They recall earlier years of religious education and participation in church life. This involves an often amusing and candid evaluation of who taught what to whom. One person's narrative is punctuated by exclamations of the other such as, "You went to a Lutheran Youth Group?" or "You never told me you were confirmed!" Some of these memories hold significant meanings. Others are very dry bones indeed. Sooner or later a person puts flesh on the dry bones of their religious life and the bones come together.

In verse nine the prophet is commanded to prophecy:

Prophesy to the breath,
prophesy, son of man, and say to the breath,
Thus says the Lord God:
Come from the four winds, O breath,
    and breathe upon these slain,
    that they may live.

[Ezekiel 37:9]

There is a footnote to the Revised translations that the word "breath" could also be translated "wind" or "spirit," since the Hebrew word is the same. In the Authorized Version, verse nine in chapter thirty-seven speaks of prophesying to the wind. Either wind or breath signify the unseen power of God. However, wind is the preferable translation in that it connotes the breath of life and is most definitely outside the person.

Preparing for their wedding, couples become aware of what they learned and where they reacted to the Christian faith. They recognize that their favorite parts of Scripture have been shaped by past communities of faith they have known. Those communities are simply so many dry bones of the past, until they are touched by the Holy Spirit. The moving of the Holy Spirit through former church connections and among the memories of other congregations, invigorates the faith of a couple to be married.

Romans 6

The Easter Eve reading from Romans speaks of baptism in terms of the good news of Easter. The Christian is buried with Christ to be raised with him.

> Therefore we have been buried with
> him by baptism into death, so that,
> just as Christ was raised from the dead
> by the glory of the Father
> so we too might walk in newness of life.
>
> [Romans 6:4]

The being buried with Christ goes back to the spiritual of the Good Friday service, "Were You There When They Crucified My Lord?" The good news of Easter is Christ being raised from the dead by the glory of God the Father. Thus, the opening hymn of the Easter Eve service could well be, "Alleluia! The Strife is O'er."

Both of Paul's words, "newness" and "life," need to be heard. The resurrection has to do with new life springing out of the old. The initiating power and energy informing Christ's resurrection is the glory of God. Commenting on this verse, Karl Barth noted, "The Resurrection is the emergence of the necessity of giving glory to God."[29] The necessity springs from the fact that, in the Resurrection the power of divinity impinges upon humanity overtaking their expectations. That is why Easter cannot be equated with the predictability of spring flowers. While the Pharisees and Sadducees argued whether resurrection was possible, the Christians declared that in Christ the resurrection had happened.

The glory of God they met in Eastertide turned out to be glory shared by all Three Persons of the Trinity. It is the powerful play by and between the Persons of the Trinity that constitutes the resurrection: the Son who is raised from the bonds of death, the Spirit of holiness prompting the declaration of Christ's power, and the *arche,* the beginning, the source and principle order of divinity running counter to what moderns assume to be natural. These three strike the major chord of divinity. Christians do know a measure of the Resurrection here and now.

The result of this divine action in the Person of Christ is not restricted to him alone. Just as he was not anointed in the Spirit for his own sake so he was not raised from the dead alone. The resurrection was played out that those baptized in Christ "might walk in newness of life." A couple preparing for Christian marriage enjoy a particularly acute sense of newness. But that newness comes from that which has gone before. Thus, they have a sense of what has been left behind and what energizes them. They may be surprised to discover the power and glory that arises out of their church connections.

JOHN 20

Despite lively apposition of resurrection "with newness of life" in Paul's Letter to the Romans, all too often Christ's resurrection is enshrined in prosaic paraphrases. For a congregation to understand the presence of the risen Christ, they are to hear: the escape of Israel from the Egyptians, the gathering of the people of God out of their exiles, the purification of people from their idolatries, their renewal with hearts of holy affections, and the vital breath that enables people to walk in newness of life when before all seemed dead and dry. Whatever happened on Easter, whatever the Easter event, it is never read in a isolated way. On Easter Eve the Gospel is placed in the context of the narrative in which these texts participate.

Nevertheless, Easter is often presented as though a resuscitated body appeared to the disciples in their grief. Such misrepresentations of the event can be heard as early as the first century. Josephus wrote in *Antiquities 20:64*, "Jesus appeared to them again alive on the third day."[30] In point of fact, there is no direct Gospel chronicle of Easter that spells out what happened. The language used to describe the resurrection is not the language of an on-the-spot reporter. We do not find in the Gospels or New Testament words which describe what happened. There are no passages that declare, "After he was left in the tomb he did this... and then this... so that on the First Day of the week, when the Marys arrived, this... is what they found." Nor is there any agreed upon statement signed by all the witnesses saying, "We are convinced this is what happened." Nothing of that sort exists in the canonical Scriptures.

The earliest account of the resurrection in the canonical Scriptures speaks of Christ appearing to the disciples. The word indicates that the initiative lies with Christ. It is the surprising power of God that constitutes the Easter Event. In other words, the first move toward the disciples is decidedly from the side of Christ.[31] This dynamic informs Barth's comment regarding the emerging necessity of giving God the glory in the resurrection.[32] Hippolytus' communion prayer picks up this thrust when it declares that Christ manifested the resurrection.[33] In his farewell discourse in the Fourth Gospel, Jesus told his disciples that he would manifest himself to those who loved him and obeyed his commandments. [John 14:21] Mary Magdalene understood what that meant. The Gospel narrative from John 20, that is read on Easter Eve, describes just such a manifestation to this woman. Mary's personal grief and ardent love are overwhelmed by the appearance of the Risen Christ.

With his command that she not touch him, there comes a warning against confining the resurrection to the Second Person. The resurrection involves divine distinctions. The Father and the Holy Spirit are involved in this event as well as the Son. On the one hand, Christ is to ascend to the Father [John 20:17], and on the other hand, the disciples are to receive the gift of the Holy Spirit. [John 20:22] The glory of Easter is known in the action of both Christ manifesting himself or appearing to the disciples and the Holy Spirit reaching the grieving disciples from the realm of being that is the source of all. Or in other words, Easter involves the play between all Three Persons of the Trinity.

As a result, the language that describes Easter cannot be limited to a narrative reading of what happened to Jesus. The language that Christians borrow on Easter Eve is the language of baptismal and communion prayers as well as the Word of the Scriptures. Only the interplay of figures from the Hebrew Scriptures and the Gospels with the liturgical prayers can attest to the full dynamics of Easter. That is why the Easter Eve service moves from the homily on the Scriptures chosen for that night to the baptismal service. When the candidates present themselves for baptism, the prayer that is said at the font before the act of baptism resonates with the Scripture.

THE SERVICE OF BAPTISM

In the Prayer of Baptism one line in the invocation of the Holy Spirit is particularly significant for adults being baptized.

By your Holy Spirit
save those who confess the name of Jesus Christ
that sin may have no power over them.
Create new life in the one/all baptized this day
that she/he/they may rise in Christ.[34]

The confession of these individuals is often quite nuanced. They have had a chance to sort out their previous church encounters as well as to learn from their partner's experience of church. This will have led to an increased awareness of different pieties and traditions among the people of God. As a result they confess the name of Jesus in more inclusive terms than if they had not met the person they intend to marry.

On the other hand, adults preparing to be baptized may prepare by sorting out misunderstandings. They may have been misled somewhere along the way by their own misunderstanding or by teachings that turned out to lack authority. An adult with that preparation comes to be baptized on Easter Eve with a fuller understanding of specific elements of the faith.

Reflecting upon their pilgrimage and that of their spouse, individuals realize that they have never been utterly cut off from divinity or from the people of God in the world. They have become aware of the presence of God in the myriad communions. To have an appreciation of the way in which the Persons of the Trinity are known and enjoyed by different churches can be a saving experience. At the very least it results in an awareness of the way different traditions reflect the faith. This can prompt one to decide in what communion they will enter the church and where they will become involved.

Being incorporated into the church, they have taken the first steps toward the new life and the rising with Christ of which the baptismal prayer speaks. For couples preparing to be married, the creation of a new life is especially dramatic. One of the gifts of marriage that will be announced at the beginning of their wedding is "a new way of life, created, ordered and blessed by God."[35] Baptism is an initiation into the order of that new life.

The doxology which concludes the Prayer of Baptism affirms the glory of God in terms of time.

Glory to you, eternal God,
the one who was, and is,
and shall always be.

The sense of time is also striking for engaged couples. Reflecting upon the homes from which they came, as well as the congregations that they have known, the church in which they are being baptized, as well as the home that they intend to build, they are gratefully mindful of God's presence. Their gratitude is taken up in the communion service as they respond to the word of welcome that follows the act of baptism. In the words of Consultation on Common Texts' "Ecumenical Liturgy of Baptism":

With joy and thanksgiving we welcome you into the
Lord's family, Christ's holy church.
We are the People of God,
members of the household of faith,
a royal priesthood.
Proclaim with us the good news of Christ for all the
world.
We are one in Christ Jesus:
Share with us at the table of God's kingdom.[36]

THE SERVICE OF HOLY COMMUNION

The last half of the communion prayer from Hippolytus, as it is translated in the Presbyterian *Book of Common Worship,* expresses the "newness of life" that the Scriptures and rite of baptism proclaim. When describing Jesus' Passion, Hippolytus' prayer narrates:

In fulfillment of your will
he stretched out his hands in suffering
to release from suffering those who place their
   trust in you,
and so won for you a holy people.[37]

Those who gather around the table on Easter Eve remember what Jesus taught —that the Son of Man must suffer many things. They also recall the way in which Jesus freely accepted death on the cross. That constitutes a paradigm whereby those who trust in God endure suffering and death before they know liberation and victory. For the Christian community, the question of suffering is not posed in the abstract. It is always considered in terms of Good Friday and Easter. This congregation participates in the dynamic order of God made known in the full Easter Event from Good Friday to Pentecost. They are neither fixated upon the suffering of Good Friday nor are they vague about something called "the resurrection." Instead they participate in the transition that begins in Good Friday and ends in the various attestations of newness of life in the Easter Scriptures.

Jesus "freely accepted the death to which he was handed over." Jesus had repeatedly taught his followers that he must suffer many things and be given over to the hands of men. He lived out that fact when he did not resist those who picked him up in the garden of Gethsemane. There are several explanations of why this took place. One explanation is found in the Greek word translated "must."

It was simply necessary that the Son of Man suffer many things. That is part of his vocation.[38]

Christ realized that suffering and death would be the consequence of his life and teaching. He freely accepted that death and left his followers to interpret the significance of that death.[39] Any and all of these interpretations begin with the fact that he did not run back to Galilee. Nor did he incite a riot of protest. He trusted in God.

Those who trust in God enjoy a release from confinement. Just as the people of Israel were pressed by the armies of Pharaoh, so the followers of Jesus felt hemmed in by the events of Good Friday. The people of God know and enjoy a realm of being that transcends the confines of the world as it is administered by Pontius Pilate. Israel made it through the waters to a broader realm of being. On Easter Day, the disciples of Jesus encountered a wider realm of being beyond the confines of the tomb and the world's dominant culture.

The Atoning Acts of Christ

The next six phrases in the prayer describe Christ's move in very dramatic terms. They underline that this was not a victim. Jesus endured his suffering in order to:

> ...destroy death
>   and to shatter the chains of the evil one;
> to trample underfoot the powers of hell
>   and to lead the righteous into light;
> to fix the boundaries of death
>   and to make manifest the resurrection.[40]

This is the other side of Good Friday, a voice the culture does not amplify.

These are bold and dramatic verbs: destroy, shatter and trample, fix, make manifest. They accentuate the power of Christ as well as the victory that Easter celebrates. The holy victory was over: death, the chains of the evil one, the powers of hell, the boundaries of death. This prayer is describing a cosmic action that overwhelms basic limits and threats to humanity. The language of this prayer states the woes of humanity in as strong terms as possible.

While such language may have seemed overblown to Christians in the eighteenth or nineteenth century, it does not seem so to those of the twentieth. After the carnage of the first half of the twentieth century this generation is able to better appreciate the extraordinary forces that threaten humanity. To hear in a communion prayer that Christ has overcome those forces on Easter is indeed good news. The accent in the prayer is on the action of God. This is a real cause for thanksgiving.

The first phrase, "to destroy death," means to overcome the alienation from God. According to Calvin, Christ prayed that he might not be swallowed up by death.[41] To be swallowed up by death is to be utterly forsaken and estranged from God. Such estrangement is the Hebrew definition of Hell. In the pit of Sheol, a person is cut off and lost to God. Hence, Isaiah declared, "For Sheol cannot thank thee, death cannot praise thee." [Isaiah 38:18]

The people gathered at the table on Easter Eve have been led out of the culture's estrangement from God. They have a language with which to think and speak about the mystery of their life and its sufferings. These people are not indifferent to ultimate questions. They do not offer mild opinions as though that is the only option when it comes to God. These are a people engaged in understanding and trusting God. They aren't facile. They take religious and theological questions seriously. They do not assume that there can be no answers. Nor do they begin by inventing a new language or carving a fitting niche in the universal structure of myth. What answers these people have, begin with the language and event that they share with Christians from the first Easter morning. At church on Easter Eve, they give thanks that this is so.

The communion prayer speaks of Christ shattering the "chains of the evil one" and "trampling under foot the powers of hell." The evil one personifies all that is false. To be chained by "Old Scratch" is to be deceived into taking the false for the true. There are any number of fake substitutes for newness of life: the consumer society with its parade of new experiences that you have to try; the unrelenting exhortation to work harder against evil; a bland relativity that recognizes all religions by politely acknowledging them and leaving them alone. For those around the communion table, such chains of relativity have been indeed shattered. These are folk prepared to think with the people of God about what God intends for humanity.

The "powers of hell" are the warped affections of individuals and the unjust social structures of the world, for example, the pride of those who choose to follow the idols of this world. These are people who work very hard at projects that the world declares to be good. They are convinced that they can create a just and glorious community with the tools of their hands. They take pride in what they have accomplished as well as what they have done for others. The words of the white spiritual, "When I survey the wondrous cross," articulate liberation from such misplaced energies:

When I survey the wondrous cross
On which the Prince of Glory died,
My richest I count gain but loss,
And pour contempt on all my pride.[42]

The glory of God that triumphs on the cross consists in a consent to the world that is so extensive that it stretches human language to its limit. Christ reached out on the cross to embrace all the people of the world: those responsible for his death and execution, along with the repentant thief. That consent judges human spheres of influence to be quite limited. This includes social systems that give the appearance of doing good, but in fact are protecting, not only class interests, but a measure of earnest works–righteousness. Those who hear the communion prayer are less likely to hold up certain human efforts as the alpha and omega of compassion.

Christ at Easter "leads the righteous into light." Reformed people prefer to use the word "righteousness" despite its archaic sound. With this biblical term, the accent falls on the divine action in the biblical story. Christ leads the Reformed people of God into light just as Joshua led the people of Israel across the Jordan into Canaan. Those so led follow the action of Christ.

In the 1981 Reformed-Catholic Statement on Human Rights, this word "righteousness" appears four times. The Roman Catholic commentary notes this is a "preferred Protestant term" because it is biblically based and because it roots the discussion of human rights in God.[43] The righteous are people whose understanding of the world is informed by the glorious word and action of God. The people of God have an alternative ethic, informed by understanding and trust in God that the world dismisses as idealistic or naive.

The question of suffering is often posed in terms of God's power and goodness. That can make for a very abstract discussion. Theories are freely offered regarding suffering in terms of various attributes and purposes of God, as though such attributes and purposes were common knowledge. Those who take up their cross and follow Christ are led out of the darkness, into the light of God's countenance. Thus, the dying person who remembers hymn verses about Christ on the cross is in a very different place than someone who stoically endures the inevitable in silence.

Christ fixes the boundaries of death. The people of God recognize that there are boundaries of the realm of darkness. Having been led to the light, the people of God realize that there is a limit or boundary to darkness and its power. That is a very comforting Word in the modern world, where the powers of violence and destruction appear to be dominant. Once the Israelites passed through the Red Sea, there was no going back to Egypt. Likewise, once Easter occurred, the boundaries of Good Friday were fixed. There was no going back to the cross.

The Easter Eve service poses the question of whether a modern congregation can accept the possibility that, in the Person of Christ, a power beyond human expectation made itself known in a way that liberates men and women from fearful confines of suffering and death by leading them into a wider realm of being where righteousness is enjoyed, and all sorts of people are cordially embraced on earth in the name of God? Is it possible that there is a realm of being beyond that fenced in by political expediency, rhetoric and power, a realm of being from which Christ encourages and leads humanity to a fuller sense of life than the world assumes to exist? Sometime in the course of the Easter Eve service those gathered together answer, "Yes." They realize that the liturgy of this night of nights signifies that such a holy power and presence is not only possible but is actually present. Thus the resurrection is made manifest.

THE WORDS OF INSTITUTION

Only after having described Christ's fulfilling God's will in Jerusalem, freely accepting the death to which he was handed over and victoriously triumphing over that death, only then, does Hippolytus' communion prayer state that:

> And so he took bread, gave thanks to you, and
> said: "Take, and eat;
> This is my body, broken for you."

In the same way he took the cup, saying:
    "This is my blood, shed for you.
    When you do this, do it for the remembrance of me."[44]
Even before these words are spoken, the communion prayer has declared what
happened after the night in which Jesus was betrayed and to what purpose. At
this point the very powerful Words of Institution are said.

There are at least three reasons why these words are so powerful: they are
reported to be Jesus' own, they make a bold declaration, and the figures of body
and blood are very powerful. First, the words are said to be Jesus' own. This
gives them a definite ring of dominical authority. Moreover they make a very
specific request, namely, that the disciples do something to remember him when
they share bread and wine. The urgency of that request was accentuated by their
being spoken "on the night in which he was betrayed." To understand communion
as the carrying out of Christ's last request leads one to approach the table solemnly.

Second, the words themselves make a straightforward declaration. In the
context of the communion prayer's narration of the creation, the history of Israel,
and the life of Jesus, the words "This is...This is..." are very demonstrative. The
punch of the phrase turns as much on the demonstrative pronoun "This" as on the
verb and its object. These words point to some thing, the bread and the wine, in
a verbal context where nothing else is pointed out with such specificity.

Add to this that body and blood are signified, and the Words of Institution
become even stronger. The figures of body and blood are extremely vivid. Bishops, pastors, theologians, as well as literary critics, have recognized the tremen-
dous force of the figures. Body and blood are personal in the extreme. The body
is the most basic way a person presents himself or herself to others. Blood is a
precious bodily fluid even in modern times. Thus, to speak of a person's body
and blood is to speak in very strong terms. Moreover, "body and blood" resonate
with all kinds of archetypes. It does not take very long to trace the connotations
of those two words before primordial meanings of ritual begin to be felt.

The very mention of the Words of Institution brings to mind what is commonly called "The Real Presence." Christians have offered many explanations
and commentaries upon these words and what they really mean. In 1846, John
Williamson Nevin of Mercersburg wrote *The Mystical Presence* to remind Reformed congregations that the "real" presence of Christ in the Holy Communion
is not an alien concept but rather an overlooked part of their heritage in Calvin.
He would have said "Amen" to the statement that the World Alliance of Reformed Churches and Roman Catholic Secretariat for Promoting Christian Unity
issued in 1977 on "The Presence of Christ in Church and World." That bilateral
statement declared:
    We gratefully acknowledge that both traditions
    Reformed and Roman Catholic, hold to the belief in
    the real presence of Christ in the Eucharist.[45]
The real presence of Christ is not simply an idea in faithful people's head.
However, realizing that there are markedly different ways to acknowledge Christ's
presence in the midst of any congregation, one paragraph in *Baptism, Eucharist*

and Ministry offered a measure of consensus by describing Christ's eucharistic presence in the following words:

> It is in virtue of the living word
> of Christ and the power of the Holy Spirit that the
> bread and wine become the sacramental signs of
> Christ's body and blood.[46]

Max Thurian edited the responses to *Baptism, Eucharist and Ministry* for the Faith and Order Commission of the World Council of Churches in Geneva. In 1983, a small book that he had written was translated into English with the title, *The Mystery of the Eucharist*. In it, Thurian delineated six ways Christians have articulated the presence of Christ in the communion service. They were in effect six different conceptions of "The Real Presence": the literalist, the metabolist, the sacramental, the realistic, the substantialist and the mystery of concomitance.[47]

Of these six, the "sacramental" conception can be distinctly heard in Reformed tradition. This is a way of thinking about communion that goes back to the Early Church and speaks of the bread and wine being "sacramental signs." Calvin stated those signs are based upon some "sort of analogy."

> And so as we previously stated,
> from the physical things set forth
> in the Sacrament we are led by a
> sort of analogy to spiritual things.[48]

The bread and wine are analogous to the body and blood of Christ on the basis of an analogy of extrinsic attribution. There is no intrinsic attribute in sacramental bread and wine that links them to the body and blood of Christ. In his *Treatise on the Lord's Supper* Calvin noted:

> Therefore, when we see the visible sign
> we ought to regard what representation
> it causes and by whom it is given us...
> We must then really receive in the Supper
> the body and blood of Jesus Christ since
> the Lord there represents to us the
> communion of both.[49]

The only link between the elements of communion and the body and blood of Christ are the words Christ spoke over the bread and cup. His words are the basis of the analogy. Thus, the signs of communion signify the body and blood of Christ by virtue of an analogy of extrinsic attribution. This does not, in Thurian's words, "lessen conviction of the real and living presence of Christ."[50]

The early Reformed confessions emphasized that the bread and wine were not "empty" signs. The Scots Confession of 1560 announced, "We utterly condemn the vanity of those who affirm the sacraments to be nothing else than naked signs."[51] The Belgic Confession of Faith declared in modern translation: "Therefore the signs are not empty or meaningless, so as to deceive us."[52] Or, in other words, "Those signs then, are by no means vain or void, nor are they instituted to deceive or disappoint us."[53]

The bread and wine function as *figura*.[54] Those *figura* can be understood in terms of types and antitypes. The bread and the wine are the types. Christ's body

and blood are the antitypes. In other words, either in the context of telling the
story of Passover or along with the traditional grace, thanking God for the gift of
bread and wine, Jesus declared the bread and wine to be *figura* of his body and
blood. As a result Christians recognize the bread and the wine, body and the
blood, as type and antitype. Together these *figura*, type and antitype, create a
very powerful meaning, signifying Christ's presence.

That powerful meaning encounters people. On a Sunday morning when the
chairwoman of the flower committee strides into the sanctuary to inspect the
floral arrangements and sees the bread and wine on the communion table, she
can be heard to exclaim, "Oh, we're doing that this morning!" The woman could
not ignore the typology of the bread and wine. Nor did she have to have it pointed
out to her. In that setting she knew whom the bread and wine signified. The floral
arrangement that she had come to inspect no longer dominated the church.

It is by hearing the "living word of Christ"and the presence of the Holy
Spirit that those who gather know the bread and wine to be the types of Christ's
body and blood and thereby realize his presence in the breaking of the bread.
That "living word of Christ" embraces the entire communion prayer. It springs
from the Scriptures read in the Liturgy of the Word as well. The living word
includes the types of resurrection and the Easter stories. These Scriptures keep
the unity of Good Friday and Easter before people as well as hand on the figures
and stories which communicate the way in which Christ's presence can be enjoyed. Jesus' repeated phrase "for you" communicates that his life is not irrel-
evant to those who know the story. Paul's phrase "newness of life" names the
sustaining gift that is offered with the types of the body and blood of Christ. It is
in part due to these living words that the people of God know the promise of
God's benevolence as being really present to them.

THE INVOCATION OF THE SPIRIT

In addition to "the living words of Christ" the Reformed tradition accentuates "the power of the Holy Spirit" to realize Christ's presence in the communion
service. The Scots Confession made the point with a measure of pastoral concern:

> Further we affirm that although the faithful,
> hindered by negligence and human weakness, do
> not profit as much as they ought in the actual
> moment of the Supper, yet afterwards it shall
> bring forth fruit, being living seed sown in good
> ground; for the Holy Spirit, who can never be
> separated from the right institution of the Lord
> Jesus, will not deprive the faithful of the fruit of
> that mystical action.[55]

The Belgic Confession declared the sacraments to be:

> ...visible signs and seals of an inward
> and invisible thing, by means whereof God works
> in us by the power of the Holy Spirit.[56]

With this understanding of the communion, the invocation of the Holy Spirit in the communion prayer is crucial. That portion of the communion prayer in Presbyterian's "Great Thanksgiving G" does so in these words:

> We ask you to send your Holy Spirit
> upon the offering of the holy church,
> Gather into one all who share these holy mysteries,
> filling them with the Holy Spirit
> and confirming their faith in the truth,
> that together we may praise you and give you glory,
> through your Servant, Jesus Christ.[57]

When the prayer speaks of the "offering of the holy church," it is important that the word "offering" not be restricted to the bread and the cup but include the people present. Too often the communion prayer is understood only in terms of the bread and the wine set apart from those who gather about the table. The "offering of the holy church" is not just those things that are on the table. The congregation itself is to present themselves as a "living sacrifice, holy and acceptable to God" which is their "spiritual worship." [Romans 12:1] In other words, the congregation does not put the bread and cup on the table and then step back to watch what happens. The Holy Spirit is invoked upon them as well.

The prayer asks that those present might be gathered into one with all who share these "holy mysteries." The presence of Christ in Word and Sacrament not only brings people to the font and table from year to year, that presence also unites those who attend in extraordinary ways. To witness adults being baptized and to share the signs of communion with them, in the remnant that is an Easter Eve congregation in a candle-lit church, produces a profound fellowship. That shared communion is initiated by the promptings of the Holy Spirit and sustained by the presence of Christ in the intimate and grateful worship of God. To have come to church on that night, to witness a baptism and take communion with those gathered, is to know a sense of unity that is different from that of a church service without these sacraments.

The sentence, "All who share these holy mysteries," includes other congregations as well. When his daughter's friend gets up from the table on Easter Eve and says she has to go to church, the Methodist father may very well file that comment away. The next time they see the Congregational minister at a meeting, they might ask, "Do you have an Easter Vigil at your church?" When the minister responds, "Yes," the father replies, "I thought so," and recalls his daughter's friend leaving his house on Easter Eve. Just beneath the surface of those apparent pleasantries is the recognition that the people in these two congregations share a measure of the unity for which Christ prayed.

The portion of the communion prayer that invokes the Holy Spirit is decisive for Reformed congregations. The German Reformed Church wrote an original epiclesis for the 1857 Mercersburg Liturgy. For them, the Holy Spirit being present means that the congregation really and truly partakes in the "blessed life" of Christ "through the power of the Holy Ghost."[58] The life of Christ is blessed in the sense that it is not only praiseworthy, but it is an authoritative statement of Emmanuel, God's being with us. This statement imparts the vitality of Christ to the congregation.[59] That results in their steadfast patience to trust in the benevolence of God in daily life rather than to cower before the destructive powers of the world's darkness.

The Holy Spirit makes a vital impression upon those who are regenerated and renewed. It is the Holy Spirit that teaches the people of God to be still and know that God is the alpha and the omega, the beginning and the end. While the Holy Spirit moves in the liturgy, it is ultimately the Holy Spirit's work that speaks, not that of the liturgy. No liturgy can automatically dispense the life of Christ. That is why the communion prayer requests the Holy Spirit.

The Holy Spirit is invoked upon the congregation in order to confirm its knowledge and trust of God's benevolence to humanity. This promise is known in the death and resurrection of Christ. With all of the stories and their types that surround and interpret that event, there is a strengthening in Word and Sacrament that comes from concentration of the biblical figures. Still, the truth that Easter presents and manifests is not so obvious that those who gather about the table fail to have doubts. In the course of their lives from year to year, new experiences, new situations, new crises, new relationships test the truth of God's promised benevolence in Christ.

Each Easter Eve, the central truth is confirmed in the Word and Sacrament. A different mix of the Old Testament stories as well as the people who come to be baptized and the different parts of the communion prayer, all communicate the promise of God's benevolence. In the course of the weeks it is easy to forget the sense of God's being with us that is at the heart of Easter. Hence, the prayer is that the congregation will be filled with the Holy Spirit and thus strengthened in their knowledge and trust of God's benevolence toward them and the world.

This portion of the prayer blesses God by giving praise and glory. Giving God the glory in this setting means affirming that it is by the virtue of the Word and the Holy Spirit that those gathered about the table have encountered the dynamics of divinity in sufficient measure, so that they can not only be grateful, but can now bless God. They are not alone in an indifferent world but together have been drawn to the truth of Christ's promises of God's benevolence. On the one hand, the Easter Eve congregation blesses God by gratefully acknowledging all that has been done in the Person of Christ who trampled the powers of hell underfoot. On the other hand, they pray that they might be anointed to walk in the newness of life, "fill us with thy Holy Spirit confirming our faith in the truth." All of which praises the God whom they know to be the source, medium and presence of those victories.

Hippolytus' prayer declares that these people are standing in God's presence and serving as the Lord's "priestly people" on Easter Eve. Those who consider what they do in church, primarily in terms of hearing and studying the prophetic Word, are unaccustomed to being addressed as a "priestly people."

Remembering therefore his death and
resurrection,

we set before you this bread and cup,
thankful that you have counted us worthy
to stand in your presence
and serve you as your priestly people.[60]

Those around the table stand because that is a bold and enthusiastic posture of prayer. The congregation has in fact been standing since singing "Father we thank thee who has planted," to the Genevan tune "Rendez a Dieu," just before the communion prayer. Standing is a venerable Christian posture of praise in which the congregation expresses its gratitude that God has counted them worthy to serve as a priestly people.

This phrase in the prayer, describing the congregation's action toward God, is translated differently by different communions. The Presbyterian text addresses God as a congregation being worthy to "serve you as your priestly people." But the Roman Catholic International Committee on English in the Liturgy translated the phrase to mean the congregation will show God "priestly service."[61] Geoffrey Cuming, the Anglican scholar who prepared a study guide to Hippolytus, translated this line:

...giving you thanks because you have held us
worthy to stand before you and minister to you.[62]

These differences in translation depend not only upon the different received texts but theological traditions as well. There is no text recording the Greek word Hippolytus used. The Latin and Ethiopic texts each offer different words at this point. There is no question in any of the translations but that God is the one who has counted the people of God worthy to celebrate the communion. In other words, it is God who initiates and sustains liturgical action. A congregation is "priestly," not by virtue of what they do, but by virtue of their participation in the life of Christ. The Heidelberg Catechism would say by sharing in his anointing[63] as their only priest.

However, the Presbyterian's translation "priestly people," rather than "priestly service," does place the accent on the people, the congregation, rather than the bread and cup. That accent will follow through the remainder of the prayer. In fact, when the Holy Spirit is invoked in this communion prayer, there is no mention of that Holy Spirit affecting the bread and the wine. Instead, the prayer speaks only of the Holy Spirit's impression upon the priestly people gathered as one congregation about the bread and cup.

The prayer speaks of the bread and cup being set before God. That means they are simply on the communion table. In Reformed congregations there is no procession of the bread and wine nor are either elevated in the course of the prayer. They are holy in the sense of being set apart in the worship of God. There is no particular attempt to draw attention to them as though they were the essence of the service.

This is not to ignore or slight the bread and the cup. As types of Christ's body and blood, they are the sacramental signs without which holy communion would not be. Very soon in the church, the types of bread and wine took on meaning in terms of the congregation's relation to Christ. Therefore, before the signs of communion are distributed, the words of Paul to the church in Corinth are said:

Because there is one loaf,
we who are many are one body,
for we all partake of the one bread.

[I Corinthians 10:17]

Those who are gathered together, partaking of the one bread of communion, are one body, not in their hopes, not in their hurts, not even in their friendships, but in Christ. In Holy Communion the members of a congregation share the bread on the table. Being united in the sharing of the bread is a type of the body of Christ. That is to say, those who share in the bread also share in the life of Christ. The bread not only bears meaning as a type of the person of Christ, it bears the meaning of the communion which the congregation enjoys in Christ's presence.

So, likewise, Paul comments in the same letter on the cup.

The cup of blessing that we bless
is it not a sharing in the blood of Christ?

[I Corinthians 10:16]

A "cup of blessing" is a cup of wine that has been part of a religious table rite. Note that Paul speaks of the cup being blessed, not by an individual, but by the congregation: "the cup of blessing that *we* bless." This blessing is the act of together giving God praise and glory. In other words, an authoritative statement of divine favor has been pronounced over the cup, namely that Christ is God with us and has communicated newness of life for which the congregation is heartily grateful. That newness of life comes from the person of Christ who in the words of the Genevan Catechism was:

filled with the Holy Spirit and
loaded with a perfect abundance
of gifts that he might impart
them to us, according to measure
of course which the Father knows
to be appropriate.[64]

The Holy Spirit links those in whose name the blessing is pronounced and the cup is being blessed. This bond of the Holy Spirit is signified when the cup is passed among the members of the congregation. In other words, the cup is not a separate offering that the congregation adores. The cup signifies Christ's life, a life which those at the table are given at communion and which they share.

The final sentence of the communion prayer begins "through your Servant, Jesus Christ." The designation "Servant" fits the sense of Christ's mission as it is narrated in this prayer which speaks of Jesus stretching out his hands in suffering and freely accepting the death to which he was handed over. But the prayer goes on to affirm that Jesus Christ was much more than a victim:

Through him all glory and honor are
yours, almighty Father, with the Holy Spirit
in the holy church now and forever.

The Easter Eve congregation is a cordial gathering where the Holy Spirit dwells and in which God is given the glory through Christ. This is the place where the essential activities of God on behalf of human beings are communicated and praised. It is where the Scriptures, bread and wine prompt insights that secular people dismiss as impossible and incredible. To indicate that this is the meal of God's Kingdom, the congregation goes directly from the communion prayer to the Lord's Prayer.

Having given thanks to almighty God for the deeds of liberation, having recalled the victory of Jesus Christ over death, having prayed for the Holy Spirit to be present, those who have gathered on Easter Eve, the old-timers and the newcomers, the familiar faithful as well as the stranger, share the signs of communion and participate "in God's mission to the world."[65] This city upon the hill is visible. The candle is on the candlestick and the darkness is pushed back. After singing "Joy Dawned Again on Easter Day," the congregation goes out into the world.

Easter Morning

Easter Morning comes early, with the youth group preparing the Easter Morning Breakfast and the organist-choir director rushing about, striving to get all the rehearsals in on time. First the trumpet soloist and then the choirs rehearse. In the meantime, families begin to arrive at the parish hall and the breakfast is served. Hopefully there are enough tables set so that adolescents, and not the grandparents, will sit in the very low chairs.

At the conclusion of breakfast, the fifth graders present their Easter marionette play. Behind the curtains of the stage there is much whispering, checking of script and props, all hopefully with a minimum of tangled strings. The youngest children sit up front. Then come the parents. In the back row are one or two college students who took the story with them when they left home for school. Writing an art history paper on a sculpture of Mary at the tomb, they remember the marionette play the year they did it. Now they watch to see if the marionette they made seven years back has been given a role in this year's play.

The narrator stands in front of the stage where he can easily spot any delays backstage; this year's Gospel account is on the lectern. Each Gospel has its special characters and moves, the angel or the two men in "dazzling apparel," or Mary Magdalene and "the other Mary" or Mary Magdalene, Mary the mother of James and Salome.

Each play has its special effects. "And he went to a garden called Gethsemane": enter Jesus, then, ZIP thud, ZIP thud, ZIP thud. The garden is dramatically produced by flowers taped to darts flying down into the styrofoam which surrounds the figure of Jesus. Several scenes later the Marys make their way to the black box of a tomb to be surprised. In some plays they are too afraid to say anything. Other years they go back and tell the disciples. Sometimes two of the disciples set out on the road to Emmaus.

The Easter Breakfast concludes with a hymn sing. This is the time to heartily sing the favorite hymns, accompanied by piano and banjos. It's a time to sing the praises of God with all kinds of folk hymns and spirituals: "Rocka my Soul in the Bosom of Abraham" along with "He's Got the Whole World in his Hands,"

"Swing Low Sweet Chariot," "Lord of the Dance," "When the Saints Go Marching In," concluding with a perfect Easter hymn that combines the Exodus with Easter:

O Mary, Don't You Weep.
O Mary, don't you weep, don't you mourn,
O Mary, don't you weep, don't you mourn,
Pharaoh's army got drowned
O Mary, Don't you weep.

The hymns are a cordial way to give God the glory and enjoy the spirit of Easter.

The Sunday morning service is festive and stirring, beginning with a prelude with brass, the greeting "Christ is risen" and the congregational response "He is risen indeed," followed by Wesley's "Christ the Lord is Risen Today." The larger than usual congregation is taken seriously. Where have the members of this congregation been since last Easter? Have they found a measure of forgiveness in the world? Are the rulers of this world more just than Pontius Pilate? Have they found light in the darkness?

Easter Sunday is an opportunity to preach a sermon that presents part of the Easter story in a way that will either catch the attention of those who rarely attend or remind them that the resurrection is not what they assume it to be. The sermon may point out that the earliest canonical statement about the resurrection in the New Testament is not the Gospel but the epistle for Easter, I Corinthians 15:1-11. Paul's letter tells just what he received and what the apostle passed on to the Corinthian congregation about "Easter." Was this the tradition of the Jerusalem Church or Antioch? It may not have occurred to the people in the pews to think of Easter in terms of specific geography of the Roman Empire. Nor may it have occurred to them that Easter is not a universal myth but an event that particular congregations in particular cultures described in very particular ways. In other words, Easter is not one more way of recognizing that spring is here. The New Testament doesn't present Easter in strokes of watercolor but in hard bits of mosaic. Becoming acquainted with that mosaic has the advantage of bringing the resurrection down to earth. Instead of experiencing the glow of a spiritual theme, Easter congregations encounter the edge of a historical event. Instead of a message of cosmic optimism, they hear Matthew's impression of what happened after Good Friday.

The choice of the Gospel reading for the day will depend on the year of the Lectionary. The Easter congregations will hear the story as it is told by Matthew, Mark and Luke, and perhaps John somewhere in between. However, it is important to note that for the most part, these Easter narratives turn on the empty tomb and the initial appearances of Christ. This is one way of expressing the Easter story. Those who only hear those stories without the complement of Good Friday, have a very truncated understanding of the crucial Christian holiday.

In order to preach any of the Easter traditions, it is necessary to think critically in terms of the Scriptures. That means pointing out the difference between a letter of Paul and one of the gospels. It means rooting the particular Scripture in the history of the people of God. All of this is done in the hope that some insight will accompany the hearing of the Word. This is very different from trying to explain the resurrection by analogies to flowers, butterflies or grief therapies.

Easter is not an event to be measured either by common sense or human experiences, however profound. Rather Easter is an event in which the power of God breaks in upon humanity in glory. Nothing is gained in smoothing up the story by eliminating one or the other parts of the narrative. The tension in the tradition that Paul received and passed along, contrasts Jesus' dying and being buried with Jesus' being raised up and appearing to the disciples.[66] The tension of those two elements has to be maintained.

Since this is the day when all but the smallest children sit with their parents through the sermon, parents are glad when the older children can follow it as well. In other words, when the Easter sermon is graphic and not too long, it is appreciated. After the benediction, when the lilies are distributed and the parish hall picked up and the last load of dishes put in the dishwasher, the church empties out. To those sitting on the front porch across from the church, that would seem to be the end of Easter. Therefore, it comes as a surprise to many when the tape on the church telephone says that there are fifty days to Easter.

The Great Fifty Days

The resurrection is not a simple event. Therefore, for the next seven Sundays, stories are told about the way Easter was experienced and known to the disciples, beginning with Doubting Thomas, a fitting Gospel for that Sunday since those who return, come back with questions. Easter is not a *fait accomplis* for the people of God. The singing of the hymns, prayers, hearing the Word, celebrating communion and witnessing baptism do not immediately or automatically bear fruit. In the course of the seven weeks, the Narrative of Easter continues. Again, it is not a simple event given to prosaic descriptions. Rather, there are decidedly different ways to interpret and present "The Resurrection."

The First Readings on the Lord's Days of Easter in the Revised Common Lectionary do not come from the Old Testament but from the Acts of the Apostles. Resurrection is one of the critical issues that marked the parting of the ways for Christians and Jews. The Pharisees and the Sadducees were divided on that issue in Jesus' own time, a fact he and his disciples turned to their advantage. After Easter, Christ's own resurrection became a contested point between Christians and Jews. Today Christians realize that they cannot find proof texts for the resurrection in the Hebrew Scriptures. In recognition of that exegetical fact, the first readings for the Sundays in Easter are taken from the Book of the Acts of the Apostles.

The significance of that move is twofold. First, contemporary congregations encounter the structure and witness of the early church and hear fragments of the sermons they preached in and around Jerusalem. On Easter morning Peter is heard preaching to a centurion of the Italian Cohort in Caesarea that:

...God anointed Jesus of Nazareth with
the Holy Spirit and with power; how
he went about doing good and healing

all those who were oppressed by the
devil, for God was with him.
[Acts 10:38]
The descriptions of the first church:
Now the whole group of those who believed
were of one heart and soul, and no one
claimed private ownership of any possessions,
but everything they owned was held in common.
[Acts 4:32]
create a stir of discomfort in the pew and a temptation to preach economics in the
pulpit. When what happened to Judas after Good Friday is taken up, the congregation becomes aware there were disciples other than the twelve.

The stories of the apostle's preaching to those in and about Jerusalem, such
as the Ethiopian official and the centurion posted at Caesarea, portray the church
in the world. That is the second significant point of readings from the Book of
Acts: to tell the story of the church in the world.

It was not at the Lord's Supper, but only in the days following Easter, that
the disciples became effective witnesses in the world. In the words of the Scots
Confession, they brought forth fruit being living seed sown in good ground. The
point of the parable of the Sower is not the seed that fell by the wayside, or had
no roots, or was choked by thorns, but the seed that fell on good soil and brought
forth a hundred, sixty and thirty fold. The disciples, as well as those who followed them, are the parable's "good ground." However, they do not bring forth
fruit immediately. The yield has to do with the:
Holy Spirit who can never be separated
from the right institution of the Lord
Jesus, will not deprive the faithful of
the fruit of that mystical action.[67]
It is the illumination and prompting of the Holy Spirit in the days following
Easter that bears fruit in the world in deeds of compassion and acts of righteousness. When the Word is being preached, no one can tell when and where it
will bear fruit. But the promise and presence of the Holy Spirit insures that it will
bear fruit in peoples' lives. They make that fact known by the way they take up
the melody of divinity in the world.

Easter concludes with the festival of Pentecost. Edward Taylor indicated
that he was well aware of this sequence, when halfway through his Easter medi-
tation, he wrote:
But now I from Passover do pass.
Easter farewell, rich jewells
thou did shew,...[68]
As a poet, Taylor has a delightful homely figure to mark the passing of the season.
And come to Whitsuntide; and turn the Glass
To search her Sands for pearles therein anew.[69]
The hour glass of which he speaks was a fixture in early New England
pulpits and turned in the course of the sermon. In May of 1697 the Westfield
minister had arrived at a new season. Having written a meditation at the begin-

ning of Lent and one on Easter, it was time to do so for Pentecost. Whitsunday is the Anglo-Saxon word for Pentecost.

The latter part of the Pentecost meditation incorporates the transition passage in the Easter meditation with a few telling changes. Taylor changed the word "Passover" to "the New Moon Feast."

　　　But now I from the New Moon Feast do pass

Taylor's text for this meditation was taken from the Letter to the Colossians 2:16, 17 and spoke of holidays and new moons. The sermon Taylor preached dealt with the typology of Jewish festivals. In point of fact, Meditation 21 turns out to have been written on Pentecost or Whitsunday of 1697, May 16. At the same time, Sam Sewall was busy with the printing of his first book. At the beginning of May the initial sheets of *Phoenomena Apocalyptica* were being "wrought off."[70]

Pentecost was one of the Jewish pilgrimage festivals. The Israeli editors of the *MacMillan Bible Atlas* are interested in the story of Pentecost in the Book of Acts because the apostles' listeners came from Jewish communities scattered around the empire. Later when Christians in their ministries admitted "all nations to the entrance of life,"[71] that marked a new beginning in the history of the people of God. The apostles in Jerusalem realized that going to the Gentiles with the Word was a radical departure. Encountering the apostles preaching in Jerusalem, Rabbi Gamaliel allowed that what the Christians were about might very well be of God. Therefore, he advised the Jewish Council:

　　　...in the present case, I tell you keep
　　　away from these men and let them alone;
　　　because if this plan or this undertaking
　　　is of human origin, it will fail; but if it is of
　　　God, you will not be able to overthrow them—
　　　in that case you may even be found fighting against
　　　God.
　　　　　　　　　　　　　　　　[Acts 5:38–39]

Thus, a chord is struck with Rahab.

The Jewish festival is associated with the Giving of the Torah at Mount Sinai and the harvest of winter wheat. Taylor was aware of all these traditions and played with them in his meditation. He compares the giving of the Torah at Sinai with what he calls "the Law of Spirit and of Life"[72] that was given on Pentecost. In the meditation he asks to be a guest at this feast.

　　　Then make me to this Penticost repare.
　　　Make me thy Guest, Lord, at this feast and live
　　　Up to thy Gospell Law.[73]

This Lord is not Christ alone but the three Persons of the Trinity. This accent can be heard in Communion Prayer A of the United Church of Christ's "Word and Sacraments Service II." Thanksgiving is given for God as creator who gives breath to all of life, the Son who is begotten by God and born of Mary, and the Holy Spirit that is active in the witness of the people of God to the world. In each of these activities the Holy Spirit is acknowledged as a personal presence for life.

Pentecost is a communion Sunday. This is a time to celebrate communion, rejoicing in the Holy Spirit that touched the followers of Jesus after the first Easter at the festival of *Shavuot*. Pentecost is the Greek name for the Jewish festival of Shavuot. In this holiday, after Passover and Easter, the people of Israel and the Christian church continue to share a calendar. The fifth graders who help distribute the bread and wine are alerted to listen for the prayer for the Holy Spirit in the prayer of thanksgiving. This is the prayer that articulates the meaning of what Taylor called the Gospel Law.

> Gracious God, we ask you to bless
> this bread and cup and all of us
> with the outpouring of your Holy Spirit.
> Through this meal,
> make us the body of Christ, the church,
> your servant people, that we may be
> salt and light, and leaven
> for the furtherance of your will in the
> world.[74]

The word "bless" here is an invocation to God that the Holy Spirit will touch the congregation, sending them back into the world where they will function as salt, light and leaven: "salt" in that they will witness to a flavor of mystery in the world that users and consumers do not taste; "light" in the sense that they know the limits of darkness and have a lamp at their feet with which to make their way; "leaven" in that they will work in and through the structures of the world, providing alternatives and doing in compassion what the world assumes can never be done. The words of the prayer indicate that, even when touched by the Holy Spirit, Christians define themselves in the world in terms of Christ who has made them "household disciples of God."[75]

As was his custom, Taylor concluded this meditation on a musical note.

> If th'Prophets Seedtime spring my harvest I
> Will, as I reape't, sing thee my harvest joy.[76]

The Word that the sower went forth to sow did fall on good ground in Edward Taylor. The poet pastor did share in the anointing of Christ. On Pentecost he sang songs of harvest joy to his Lord. Those in church on Pentecost take up the melody and join the chorus. Having heard the Word and been impressed by the Holy Spirit, at the end of Easter season they stand and sing:

> Frail children of dust and feeble as frail
> in thee do we trust nor find thee to fail.
> Thy Mercies how tender, how firm to the end!
> Our Maker, Defender, Redeemer and Friend.

Chapter 7

The Test of the Hospital

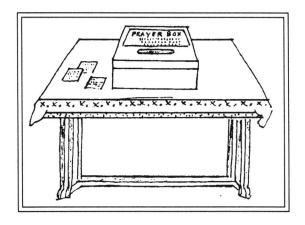

hen a member of the family has to go to the hospital "for some tests," a feeling of uneasiness ensues. We hope they don't find anything serious but if they should, media reports of modern medical advances come vaguely to mind. If the tests call for a procedure that can be done right then and there, the neighbors help out with food and child care. Family, friends and the minister drop by to visit. In this way the hospitalized persons maintain contact with their local congregation. Before long they are back at their daily routine and are seen in church. Before very long the neighbors stop asking about the operation.

However, this is not always the case. Some illnesses demand more extensive diagnosis and treatment. That may require the person to be transferred to a larger hospital, in all probability a medical center with advanced and specialized facilities. People are sent to these centers from all over the world. The languages spoken, as well as the pieties represented, are many. One's neighbor down the hall or the nurse on the floor are often as strange and good as Samaritans. Contact with home and church is much less immediate. The tests are more prolonged and elaborate. Uncertainties and tensions increase. At that point the observation of the retired pastor comes into play, "It takes three years of going to church to survive one major hospitalization."

If someone is in a hospital for long, away from home, they will benefit from a book of familiar prayers. Therefore, when going into the hospital, it is well to pack a prayer book and a Bible. It may be that they will find various prayers and pamphlets in the hospital chapel. But given the diverse populations of hospitals, one cannot assume that these prayers will be familiar and therefore comforting. Having a book of prayers from their home congregation on hand will provide a variety of prayers. The shape of those prayers will place the person's situation in the context of their community's prayers.

The United Church of Christ's *Book of Worship* contains a section at the back of the book, entitled "General Resources." These are a selection of prayers and Scripture placed in the order of a worship service. Among the prayers of confession and assurance, of thanksgiving, intercession and general prayers, there are prayers that would be helpful to someone in the hospital. The arrangement of these prayers in terms of a worship service as well as the resonances with Scripture in the prayers themselves communicate a sense of the worshipping congregation to the person in the hospital. These prayers place the patient's immediate aches and pains in a context beyond the medical center.

The Presbyterians' *Book of Common Worship* provides prayers to accompany psalms as well as prayers of thanksgiving and intercession. This book also provides a shortened order of daily prayer, consisting of reading a psalm, a portion of Scripture, followed by prayers of thanksgiving and intercession. This can be very helpful. In a hospital setting, with a member of the family or friend, this shortened form of daily prayer may gratefully acknowledge the passing of time. Or alone amid the comings and goings of staff and visitors, someone in a hospital can say their prayers with one of these books as the opportunity presents itself.

141

In the course of any hospitalization the people of God are sustained by many prayers. There are morning and evening prayers, as well as the prayers that accompany psalms. There are pastoral prayers and personal prayers. An abbreviated morning or evening service, said by the hospitalized person and their family, can complement the pastoral prayers of a visiting minister or chaplain. Outside the patient's hospital room, members of the family may seek out the hospital chapel. In that sanctuary they will ponder the crisis and offer prayers for those they love. At the heart of every Christian's prayer is the Lord's Prayer. If death does come, then the seven fold gift of the Holy Spirit makes its presence felt. When the family returns home, it is amidst the worshipping congregation that their grief is eventually healed.

PRAYERS TO MARK THE DAYS

In a hospital time takes on a new measure. It can be time before and after a particular procedure. Or time can mean long periods of waiting. A difficult medical situation may call for an arduous vigil that seems interminable. One of the purposes of daily prayer at such times is to shape the passing days with strength, hope and thanksgiving.

Daily prayers are said primarily in the morning and evening. They can be quite simple, straightforward, and free. A morning prayer can be as simple as "It is morning and I'm still here." It may be more introspectively elaborate and unhaltingly ardent. Someone might look up a general prayer of intercession in the United Church of Christ's *Book of Worship* and find one that touches their circumstances. For example,

> O God, the refuge of the poor,
> and the hope of the humble,
> the salvation of the needy;
> hear us as we pray for those who
>   are worn by illness,
> for all who are wronged and oppressed,
> and for the weary and heavy-laden,
> that they may be strengthened by your grace
> and healed by your consolations.
> Let the dayspring from on high
> visit those who sit in darkness
> and in the shadow of death,
> to guide their feet into the way of peace;
> through Jesus Christ. Amen.[1]

Sometimes the reading of a single prayer at some point in the day is quite sufficient to sustain a hospitalized person.

On the other hand, if the hospital stay is prolonged it may be that the Presbyterians' abbreviated order of morning prayer in their *Book of Common Worship* is not only possible but helpful. This order consists of a Psalm, Scripture reading with silent reflection, followed by prayers of thanksgiving and intercession, all of which are in the book.[2]

In periods of hospitalization the people of God have time to be attentive to the Scriptures. While this is not the occasion for extended Bible study, it is a time when the words of the psalms may speak with authority. The United Church of Christ's *Book of Worship* suggests a number of psalms under the heading, "Words of Comfort from Scripture." Among those suggested are Psalms 121 and 130.

Filled with the affections of the people of God, the psalms are especially appropriate for those in the hospital. A person can read a suggested psalm morning or evening and ponder that particular text. After so reflecting, they can make a prayer in their own words with the images or refrains of the psalm which struck them. Or they can read the psalm prayer at the conclusion of the psalm.

From Psalm 121:

> I lift up mine eyes to the hills,
> From whence does my help come?...

The psalm prayer in the *Book of Common Worship* accentuates God's presence to those feeling vulnerable and thus prays:

> God, our helper,
> you are strength greater than the mountains;
> you look to our needs and watch over us
>   day and night.
> Teach us to hold confidently to your grace,
> that in times of fear and danger
> we may know you are near and depend on you,
> our sure deliverer.[3]

The psalm prayer for Psalm 130 casts the figure of the psalm's opening line, "Out of the depths I cry to thee, O Lord!" in terms of Christ's passion and resurrection, so that the dynamic of Easter is felt.

> O God,
> you have come to us in the depths of our darkest despair,
> in the sufferings of Jesus Christ.
> By the rising of your Son,
> give us new light to guide us,
> that we may always praise your holy name;
> through Jesus Christ our Lord.[4]

On the other hand, someone in the hospital may be sick and tired of thinking about their condition. These folk will look forward to a refreshing Word in the course of the day that does not necessarily dredge up their situation. For example, they might enjoy a psalm of praise such as Psalm 97 with the following concluding prayer.

> O God,
> you clothe the sky with light,
> and ocean depths with darkness.
> You work your mighty wonders among us.

Claim us for your purposes, that we may be among those
who see your glory and give you praise,
for you live and reign,
now and forever. Amen.[5]

The author of this psalm and its prayer, like the person in the hospital bed, are to be numbered among those who give God the glory, realizing that their being is not the beginning and end of creation.

There are seasons of rejoicing in a hospital when patients enjoy a new lease on life. They may go home with psalms and prayers of thanksgiving ringing in their hearts. For example, Psalm 116 is the traditional psalm read, giving thanks for the birth of a child. The prayer for that psalm in the *Book of Common Worship* serves as a reminder of fervent intentions:

God our Redeemer,
you have delivered us from death in the resurrection
  of Jesus Christ
and brought us to new life by the power of your
  Spirit.
Give us grace to keep our promises
to praise and serve you all our days;
through Jesus Christ our Lord.[6]

Following the psalms there are a number of Scriptures that might be read. For the days of the week there is a daily lectionary at the back of the *Book of Common Worship*. This will provide three biblical readings for each day. People can read one or all three pericopes. If they do read all three, they are divided between morning and evening prayer. This can be an opportunity for someone to make their way through an epistle, a book in the Old Testament or a Gospel. It is beneficial to have a text of Scripture to ruminate upon in the course of a hospital day. While waiting for X-ray, one might ponder the makeup of the Corinthian congregation.

The third portion of morning and evening prayers includes the prayers of thanksgiving and intercession. These prayers for each morning and evening of the week are noteworthy in that they begin with thanksgiving. The note of thanksgiving is a mark of Reformed piety. When the Book of Common Prayer was being revised in 1662, it was a bishop "with Puritan sympathies" who wrote a prayer of thanksgiving. When in 1789 the American Episcopal Church revised the prayer book, they moved the prayer of General Thanksgiving from the occasional prayers to the conclusion of morning prayer.[7] Whereas Morning Prayer in the Anglican rite concludes with the Prayer of General Thanksgiving, Morning Prayer in the Presbyterians' *Book of Common Worship* begins with thanksgiving.

The note of thanksgiving is followed by intercessions. The intercessions conclude with a prayer for the church in a particular part of the world. Thus, the person who prays these prayers of thanksgiving and intercession articulates their own situation in the communion of those who have known God's benevolence in Christ and who pray for a fresh measure of the Holy Spirit.

Said in the course of the week, the prayer for Monday morning is:
We praise you, God our creator, for your handiwork

in shaping and sustaining your wondrous creation.
Especially we thank you for
the miracle of life and the wonder of living...
particular blessings coming to us in this
        day...
    the resources of the earth...
    gifts of creative vision and skillful craft...
    the treasure stored in every human life....
We dare to pray for others, God our Savior, claiming
your love in Jesus Christ for the whole
world, committing ourselves to care for those around
us in his name. Especially we pray for
    those who work for the benefit of others...
    those who cannot work today...
    those who teach and those who learn...
    people who are poor...
    the church in Europe....[8]

These prayers are designed so that a person can add personal phrases and thoughts that will fill out various thanksgivings and intercessions.

The language of prayers presents a renewed sense of a person's situation. For example, it is one thing to be generally thankful for nurses and doctors. But a prayer that mentions the "creative vision and skillful craft" gives a more vivid sense of those who minister in a hospital. The phrase recalls the unseen technicians upon whom doctors and nurses depend. A poetic phrase like "the treasure stored in every human life" can give a new sense of gratitude that can be lost in the daily medical statistics. Likewise, the intercessions are particularly instructive with their references to those who work for the benefit of others and those unable to work. Those prayers not only recognize the needs of those who labor in less than exalted positions, they also acknowledge the limitations of the patient.

A prayer on a morning following tests earlier in the week, might on the one hand give particular meaning to the thanksgiving for "the gifts of creative vision and skillful craft." On the other hand, the results of that morning might call for the opening and concluding paragraphs of a prayer in the United Church of Christ's *Book of Worship*:

Almighty and most gracious God,
whose very nature is to be present in good times
    and in bad;
in warm days and cold;
in wind, rain, and sunny life;
in laughter and in pain;
in joy and in despair;
in work and in play;
and in all those things that
    are a joy of life,

open our hearts and our minds to the realities
of the present here and now...
We ask not that you make the hard moments of life
easier,
except that our burdens are eased by the assurance
of your companionship,
heightened by the knowledge of your loving care,
strengthened by hope,
and shaped by love,
even as was the one in whose name we pray,
Jesus Christ,
our Lord and Savior.[9]

Daily prayers tied to the day of the week help maintain a sense of time independent of the hospital routine. When the activity level slows down over the weekend, the prayers for Friday and Sunday mornings mark the transition that is the heart of Easter.

Eternal God,
we praise you for your mighty love given in
Christ's sacrifice on the cross,
and the new life we have received by his
resurrection.
Especially we thank you for the presence of Christ
in our weakness and suffering...
the ministry of Word and Sacrament...
all who work to help and heal...
sacrifices made for our benefit...
opportunities for our generous giving...
God of grace, let our concern for others reflect
Christ's self-giving love,
not only in our prayers but in our practice.
Especially we pray for
those subjected to tyranny and oppression...
wounded and injured people...
those who face death...
those who may be our enemies...
the church in Latin America....[10]

Then the prayer for Sunday morning:

Mighty God of mercy,
we thank you for the resurrection dawn bringing
glory of our risen Lord who makes every day new.
Especially we thank you for
the beauty of creation...
the new creation in Christ and
all gifts of healing and forgiveness...
the sustaining love of family and friends...
the fellowship of faith in your church...

Merciful God of might, renew this weary world, heal
the hurts of all your children, and bring about your
peace for all in Christ Jesus, the living Lord.
Especially we pray for
those who govern the nations of the world...
the people in countries ravaged by strife or
warfare...
all who work for peace and
international harmony...
all who strive to save the earth
from destruction...
the church of Jesus Christ in every land.[11]

For the Christian the healing that occurs is not so much a question of repair as it is of being recreated in the image of Christ. The image of Christ involves taking up one's cross as well as enjoying the new creation after the hospital. In the darkness of illness these prayers orient the person toward the light of God's New Song. They do so in terms of the passover from Good Friday to Easter Sunday.

Prayers for the evening can be as straightforward as those of the morning. "It is evening and here we still are." But evenings are often a very lonely time in a hospital. The day's major medical activities have ceased. Hospitalized people are away from their families, when at home they sit down for supper. The Taize Community's prayer book, *Praise God*, addresses that evening loneliness in terms of Jesus and Emmaus.

Remain with us, O Lord,
since the day is far spent and
the evening is coming;
kindle our hearts on our way,
that we may recognize you in the Scriptures and
in the breaking of bread,
for you live and reign forever.[12]

A prayer from the synagogue liturgy in the Presbyterians' *Book of Common Worship* touches upon the transition from day to night.

You are the Creator of both night
and day, making light recede
before darkness, and darkness before light.[13]

The word "recede" might be better translated "roll away light from darkness and darkness from light." The Hebrew verb translated "recede" shares the same root as the name Gilgal and Golgotha, meaning "circle" or "round like a skull." The word communicates the promise of being able to give thanks after suffering.

The Presbyterians' Thursday evening prayer touches the faith of those anxious from probes or just plain waiting.

To you, O God
we give up the burdens of this day,
trusting your love and mercy.
To you, O God,

we surrender ourselves,
    trusting our risen Lord to lead us always
    in the way of peace,
  today, tomorrow, and forever. Amen.[14]

That trust does not materialize out of thin air. It is informed by the promises of the risen Christ. A meditation of Thomas Merton casts Christ in the same figure.

    ...you will lead me by the right road, though
    I may know nothing about it. Therefore, I will
    trust you always though I may seem to be lost
    and in the shadow of death. I will not fear, for
    you are with me, and you will never leave me to
    face my perils alone.[15]

A Friday prayer articulates the reign of God over the darkness of any day.

    As you have made this day, O God,
    you also make the night.
    Give light for our comfort.
    Come upon us with quietness and still our souls,
    that we may listen for the whisper of your Spirit
    and be attentive to your nearness in our dreams.
    Empower us to rise again in new life
    to proclaim your praise,
    and show Christ to the world,
    for he reigns forever and ever. Amen.[16]

The juxtaposition of "listening to the whisper of the Spirit" and "being attentive to dreams" reminds Christians that some insights are communicated in ways other than a lab report.

    The prayer for Sunday evening expresses the hope of many in a hospital in terms of returning from exile and being brought to their families and friends.

    Great God, you are one God,
    and you bring together what is scattered
    and mend what is broken.
    Unite us with the scattered peoples of the earth
    that we may be one family of your children.
    Bind up all our wounds,
    and heal us in spirit,
    that we may be renewed as disciples
    of Jesus Christ, our Master and Savior. Amen.[17]

Daily prayers in a hospital help Christians to mark the passing of time in times of darkness and to keep a grip on the thread of God's promises in the light of Christ.

    The minister from home may make a call at the medical center in the course of the week if the stay is long and the distance reasonable. He or she will keep in touch with the family and friends by phone and mutual grapevines. In those circumstances a good pastoral prayer counts.

PASTORAL PRAYERS

A pastoral prayer communicates the sense of being understood and accompanied in the presence of God. These prayers may be the result of a long association with the person as a member of the church community. One mother, a long way from home, with a sick child, reported, "Our minister called and she said a prayer with us over the phone." The tone and animation of her voice attested to the power of that pastoral prayer. Not because of what it did or did not do in the hospital. Rather because the words of that prayer communicated the embrace of the people of God outside the medical center.

On Sunday pastoral prayers are spoken in church on behalf of those hospitalized. There is an order of prayer that informs congregational pastoral prayers. It is an order that the Rabbis passed on to Christians. These pastoral prayers begin with praise, move to petition, and conclude with thanksgiving. For example,

> We praise thee for the gift of life and space;
> -for the Word that calls us to look again;
> -for the Spirit that prompts the truth.

The petitions follow:

> We pray this day for:
> -those who are making adjustments to new
>   surroundings,
>   that they may find their bearings,
> -those caught up in a web of circumstance
>   unable to move as they would like,
>   that they may learn and be encouraged.
> -those recuperating,
>   that they may not rush into their old ways
>   without learning from their sickness;

The pastoral prayer concludes with thanksgiving:

> We give Thee thanks for:
> - those who move to act decisively
>   with compassion,
> - for kindnesses shown in little ways,
> - for the peace of reconciliation
>   within Thy Kingdom.
> - and above all for the call to love Thee
>   and our neighbor as ourselves.

When the people of God are in a major medical center, in addition to their own minister, they may be visited by a hospital chaplain. By visiting patients and their families and hearing as much as these folk wish to share, a chaplain may receive the elements of a prayer.

On the one hand, he or she may not be welcome. In a large hospital with all kinds of people coming at them, patients may wish to keep their distance from some of those who enter their room. The chaplain is easier to keep at arm's length than a nurse or doctor. The person may communicate that fact openly or talk of nothing more than the weather or the news. Chaplains and ministers are trained to be sensitive to those signals and to carry on the conversation, as it is directed by the patient. They may leave after a short visit.

On the other hand, the chaplain may be welcome as a relative stranger or as someone to whom the person or their family may speak more freely than others. Others in the hospital may be just as sensitive as the chaplain to the needs and crisis of a patient and family. But the chaplain places those needs and concerns within the context of the Kingdom of God. One way they do that is to offer pastoral prayers. A pastoral prayer does more than articulate the person's feelings. It places the affections of that person in the realm of the Holy as that person understands and trusts the Holy One. In addition to the feelings and concerns being expressed, the chaplain in a conversation will also come to understand the piety of the person with whom he or she is speaking and praying. When the person speaks of "having prayer" or requests a collect, he or she is asking for a particular kind of prayer language. A true pastoral prayer places the patient's needs away from home and family in the context of God's promises in the key of their faith. The chaplain needs to be able to recognize the person's piety and to incorporate that tone into the pastoral prayer.

CHAPEL PRAYERS

At some point in a long hospital stay, the members of a family will find the chapel. It can usually be found in a corner somewhere on the first floor, noticeably quiet, apparently empty, removed from the main medical workings of the hospital. Unlike most areas of the hospital, this room is not large, bright, busy or technically wired. Quite to the contrary, chapels are small, still and furnished with basic tones. The walls have warm textiles and colored glass. The furniture is dominated by a lectern, or an altar. For the wide variety of people who come to the chapel, there will be a shelf of books and texts. Out of this literature, someone lost in their particular labyrinth may pick up the thread of the Word. For some it will be a Bible, for others a hymnal, for others a prayer book of one sort or another, for still others one of the pamphlets.

People slip into the chapel at different times of the night or day. Often they come simply to get away from the sick room and the caring people that are working on that floor. In the quiet of the chapel a person finds solitude to evaluate, to weep and to pray, to think and to plan. Leafing through a prayer book, searching for words to express what is happening to them, they might find a short prayer that "collects" up their thoughts and affections. These prayers enjoy a definite literary form.[18] God is first invoked and then described in terms of an action or attribute. This opening of praise is followed by a petition and concludes with the name of the One in whom we pray.

Among the collects that are prayed in the *Book of Common Prayer*, there is one for the Monday of Holy Week written by William Reed Huntington, a nineteenth-century Episcopal bishop, that speaks in a hospital with authority.

> Almighty God, whose most dear Son went not
> up to joy but first he suffered pain, and entered
> not into glory before he was crucified; mercifully
> grant that we walking in the way of the cross,
> may find it none other than the way of life and
> peace;...

Huntington drew the line "went not up to joy but first he suffered pain and entered not into glory before he was crucified" from the 1549 Anglican Order for Visitation of the Sick.[19] In the prayer he balanced Christ's joy and glory with the life and peace of the one praying. This collect goes right to the heart of the paradigm of Good Friday and Easter, no crown without the cross. It places the issue of suffering in the appropriate context; the life of Christ. Beginning with Jesus' saying, "Take up your cross and follow me," Christians have been learning the harder lessons of suffering and pain that the cross signifies. The hope is that they do so with faith and fortitude.

In a hospital chapel there is often an open notebook or a pad of paper next to a box. There people are invited to leave their own prayers. Many do so. The prayers themselves vary widely. They can be very cryptic or quite explicit. Sometimes words of frustration close to blasphemy cry out with the vehemence of Job. Not all are petitions. There are prayers of thanksgiving and praise as well. Sometimes only a name will be written and placed in the box. Other slips contain a description of the person or of a very specific procedure. Some prayers chronicle a person's stay in the hospital, beginning with their arrival and diagnosis, ending with prayers of thanksgiving a week or so later. Other prayers are pensive reflections of a parent in crisis. Requesting prayers for the person in the next room whose name is not known, reveals a love of neighbor. Others simply ask for prayers of the community, seeming to assume that those who gather will know what to say. Among the prayers there are several voices of profound gratitude.

These prayer notations are left to be shared with a liturgical community. People leave their prayers behind, expecting them to be incorporated into a weekday service. In the context of either a gathered weekly prayer service or a eucharistic liturgy the prayers will be spoken. Even though they may not be in the pews at that time, the prayers people request make them integral members of that particular gathering of God's people in the hospital.

The Lord's Prayer

Whenever Christians come to pray, it is the Lord's Prayer with which they begin and end. The prayer has always come in different translations and versions, beginning with Luke and Matthew. Some say debts; some say trespasses. Some end with "For thine is the kingdom and the power and the glory forever and ever." Others do not. In 1970, the International Consultation on English Texts brought out another translation which was introduced to people in the more recent liturgies and prayer books. This translation asked that "our" sins be forgiven as well as being saved "from the time of trial." In whatever translation, the Lord's Prayer speaks with both comfort and authority.

This prayer, along with the Ten Commandments and the Apostles' Creed, was considered by the Reformed Churches to be the heart of what a baptized Christian should know. Therefore, in the first edition of the *Institutes,* published in 1536, Calvin commented upon the Ten Commandments in the first chapter, the Apostles' Creed in the second and the Lord's Prayer in the third chapter. Subsequent commentaries on the Lord's Prayer were written. However, in a hospital the accent of Calvin's early commentary can still be appreciated.

"Our Father who art in heaven," or in other words,

"Our Father in heaven."

The opening words of the Lord's Prayer involve neither an analogy of proportion nor attribution. This "Father" is not one metaphor among many for God. Nor is there any hidden quality of human paternity that human fathers share with God. Rather it is to address God as did Jesus of Nazareth and thus to acknowledge a relationship to Christ. To address God as Father is, in Paul's words, to cry "Abba." Calvin said, "...in calling God 'Father' we assuredly put forth Christ's name."[20] Specifically, it is to presuppose that the person praying has been adopted by God in "the Spirit of Adoption." Those who pray this prayer have been adopted as the children of God in Christ. Thus, "Father" in the Lord's Prayer is an analogy of extrinsic attribution. It is invoked as the way Christ taught his disciples to pray.

The word "Our" acknowledges that those who pray the Lord's Prayer do not do so as individuals but as members of the whole church. Christians do not turn aside from their community in prayer but bear it in mind with the very first word of the Lord's Prayer. This is especially important in a hospital because the use of "Our" brings to mind one's congregation outside the hospital.

Matthew added the phrase "who art in heaven," which is a way of affirming the glory of God. But, Calvin notes, that does not mean that God is somehow shut up in heaven or confined to some lofty realm.[21] Calvin noted that, at the dedication of the Temple [I Kings 8:27], Solomon praised God as the One whom the heaven of heavens could not contain, maintaining that God "is not confined to any particular region."[22] In other words, however exalted and praiseworthy the God of Israel might be, the Holy One is not removed from dwellers upon the earth. Those who pray in Jesus' name do so because God is with them in the world.

God is the One in whom the people of the earth live, move and have their being. [Acts 17:28] Living and operating as he did in a very cosmopolitan city, Solomon also prayed that, in the Temple he built, God would hear the prayers of the "foreigner," that is someone not of thy covenanted people, someone "who comes from a far country." [I Kings 8:41] Certainly the same can be said of a hospital chapel. There are people who find themselves in that sanctuary who are a very long way from home.

"Hallowed be thy name," or in other words

"Hallowed be your name,"

The first line of the prayer, "Hallowed be thy name," indicates that, whatever their circumstances may be, the people of God honor God's name in that they realize and praise the power of God. God's power is not mechanical. The hospital has no need of the *deus ex machina*, a deity that reaches down to fix things with the sudden flip of a switch or the deft stroke of a blade. With serious illness, quite another paradigm comes to mind. God's power is signified by the cross where there is no manipulating the transition from Good Friday to Easter. That power is like the measured, sustaining and solemn phrases of Gregorian chant. It is comforting and substantial, neither difficult to follow nor quickly over. God's power isn't heard as a thrilling solo performance but as a sustaining common melody. Calvin said, those who hallow God's name want God's power to "be truly recognized and magnified."[23] To do so, these folk have found their way to the chapel.

One of the first manifestations of God's power is the realization that human life is a gift. After the initial efforts and excitement are over, in the quiet of a chapel, the people of God somehow manage to blurt out their gratitude for the gift which they are in danger of losing. The beauty of God is that, even in the midst of a medical crisis, the faithful are able to acknowledge the glory of God's power.

"Thy Kingdom Come," or

"your kingdom come."

Calvin defines the Kingdom of God as the Holy One acting and ruling over the people of God by the Holy Spirit in order to make God's goodness and mercy conspicuous.[24] That is indeed the prayer of someone in a medical center, that the goodness of life and the mercy of healing might be bestowed upon those confined by sickness. A measure of the kingdom coming would be the light of the Holy Spirit penetrating the darkness of sickness and bringing those in the shadow of death back to a playful and joyful life.

There is a distinct note in this part of the prayer that the Kingdom of God is in the world but not of it. That is to say, because of the shadows of sin, the order of the world is not the order that God intends. Nevertheless, there are sufficient indications of God's holy order in the world to enable the saints to hear the promise of God's benevolence within the hospital and those who staff it. Those who pray "Thy Kingdom come" cordially acknowledge those notes of hope.

"Thy will be done, on earth as it is in heaven," or

"your will be done, on earth as in heaven."

Much of the time in a hospital is spent waiting and watching for the will of God to be discerned, here and now, on this floor, in this bed with this person. When the people of God are engaged in that vigil, they realize that they may not make their way in the world as they would like. Like Peter, they may not be able even to gird themselves. Moreover, they may be carried where they "do not wish to go." [John 21:18] Calvin described this verse of the prayer in terms of the new heart of flesh of which Ezekiel spoke. At this point, the people of God listen for the Holy Spirit teaching them to graciously consent to realms of illness from which they had previously fled in fear.

Thus, the first three petitions of the Lord's Prayer are directed toward God. Reformed Christians direct their prayers toward God out there and even over and against them in power and glory. Prayer is not only the voicing of an individual's religious affections, it is the praise of God's beauty in the theater of the world. When Christians pray in Jesus' name, God is first of all praised:

> Our father, who art in heaven,
> Hallowed be thy name.
> Thy kingdom come.
> Thy will be done on earth as it is in heaven.

"GivE us This dAy ouR dAily bREAd," oR iN oThER woRds,

"GivE us TodAy ouR dAily bREAd."

This petition can be very misleading. Commentators following Calvin have concluded that this bread represents the necessities of life. This has led to warnings about not stuffing oneself or one's barn. In Calvin's words:

> ...we are taught not to long with immoderate
> desire for those fleeting things, which we
> afterward flamboyantly squander in sensual
> pleasure, show, or other appearance of luxury.[25]

In this line there is a whole tradition of thinking of bread in terms of daily necessities.

In a hospital chapel, people are acutely aware of necessities both large and small. The gift of life from today to tomorrow, as well as a normal temperature and an appetite, become an object of sincere prayer. But for those praying the Lord's Prayer, the request for daily necessities is made in the context of not of just this week, or month, but the Kingdom. Our daily bread is the bread of tomorrow, in that it is given and received in the ultimate shape of our life with God and with others.

Thus, for some Christians, the phrase "our daily bread" held a much more dramatic meaning than daily needs. Translating from the *Gospel to the Hebrews,* Jerome noted the word we translate as "daily" in Hebrew was *machar,* meaning tomorrow. Thus, the daily bread may be the bread of tomorrow, the day of God's coming Kingdom.

Luke relates that one of the guests remarked, "Blessed is anyone who will eat bread in the Kingdom of God." By this the person meant that anyone who could share in the banquet that was part of the Kingdom of God would be profoundly happy. Jesus responded by telling the parable of the great banquet, the point of which was, maybe not. For when a certain man invited guests to a banquet they sent back the message that they had other fish to fry.

> The first said to him, "I have bought a
> piece of land, and I must go out and see
> it; please accept my regrets." Another said,
> "I have bought five yoke of oxen, and I am
> going to try them out; please, accept my
> regrets." Another said, "I have just been
> married and therefore I cannot come."
>   [Luke 14:18–20]

All of these are certainly worthy activities in and of themselves. However, Jesus' point was that these activities kept those invited from coming to the banquet of the Kingdom.

In a hospital chapel such refused invitations may be recalled. People may very well turn a deaf ear to invitations regarding the Kingdom of God, on the assumption that, of course, the gift of life would always be there, and surely there would always be time for God at the end of it all. But now in a medical crisis, "daily bread" signifies not only life's necessities but an invitation to live life as God, the Creator, intended life to be lived. Calvin maintained that the Kingdom of God involved the Holy Spirit acting in the people of God so that the riches of God's goodness and mercy become conspicuous in the work of their hands.[26] One of the most common understandings of healing is that inexplicable healing is somehow more praiseworthy in the church than the healing done in the course of regular treatment.[27] That attitude denigrates the glory of God that is shown forth in the theater of the world. Since God is not circumscribed in heaven, the glory of God can be known in an Operating Room. Those in the medical center administering healing and hope, are signs of the Kingdom. They are distributing in their care the bread for tomorrow.

"Forgive us our trespasses

as we forgive those who trespass against us," or

"Forgive us our debts as we forgive our debtors,"

or in other words,

"Forgive us our sins as we forgive those who sin against us."

The new translations of the next two petitions are helpful in their terseness. The "sins" being spoken of here have to do with the forces of darkness as well as the turns on the road that have led people into the shadows. People in a crisis can become very self-incriminating and hostile toward others. They tend to remember those things that they ought not to have done and as well as those things that they have left undone. The petition addresses that condition by asking that we be forgiven for the sins we have knowingly and unknowingly committed. More-over, in the context of a sudden illness or accident, the relationships that were strained or broken suddenly have to be mended or at least tolerated. People who have not spoken for years, suddenly find themselves in the same intensive care unit. They would like to be delivered from a continuing alienation that isolates and hurts. There is a palpable need for forgiveness, not only of self, but of others as well.

The forgiveness of sins is a mark of the new covenant. But forgiveness is rarely completely or suddenly done. Forgiveness is more often gradual and in-complete. Forgiveness in a hospital chapel is no different from forgiveness any-where else. People may intend to change their ways. Whether they actually do so, remains to be seen. Thus, people pray for forgiveness in the chapel as they have in church, and the way they will certainly pray in the future.

Calvin thought the reciprocal phrase was added, "as we forgive those who sin against us," not as a condition of God's forgiveness of us but as a description of our response to neighbor. People can become bitter and angry in a hospital situation, especially after an extended stay and when events do not seem particu-larly promising. To pray, "forgive those who have sinned against us," means relinquishing the harsh affections of frustration and anger. The bitterness toward others is best relinquished. Saying the Lord's Prayer in the hospital chapel and pondering this phrase is one way to begin doing so.

"Lead us not into temptation but deliver us from evil,"

or in other words,

"Save us from the time of trial and deliver us from evil."

In the new translation, temptation is described as more than dabbling in the moral mud puddle. The time of trial is not a matter of subjective indiscre-tions. Rather at this point the prayer articulates Christians' fear that they may not be able to withstand their confrontation with the shadows of disease in this world, shadows that are capable of separating a person from God. "The time of trial" has to do with crises that drive people to apostasy, that is, to curse God and reject any sense of the promise of divine benevolence toward them. In very serious illness, members of a family may fear that they will not be able to be there, come what may. In that situation Calvin spoke of temptations on the left and tempta-tions on the right. Those on the right had to do with forgetting God and banking on accomplishments, achievements and honors. The temptation of the left is to be so worn down by adversity as to finally be estranged from God.[28] Hence, the new translation of this portion of the prayer is "Save us from the time of trial." That is, don't put us in such a situation that we will not be able to keep the faith and love those near and dear.

These three petitions, "Give us our daily bread," "forgive us our sins," and "bring us not to the time of trial" are public, according to Calvin, in the sense that, when Christians pray for these blessings, they pray not for themselves alone but for others as well. In the hospital, that means the staff, family members, neighbors and friends back home. All of these folk are gathered up in the Lord's Prayer said by someone in a far off place.

"For thine is the Kingdom and the power and the glory for ever and ever.

Amen." or in other words,

"For the kingdom, power and the glory are yours now and forever. Amen."

According to Matthew, the Lord's Prayer ends with this doxology. In a hospital, the words kingdom and power put the situation in context. What sustains the people of God is their sense of participating in God's realm even when they are pressed in the hospital, knowing that the power of life and death ultimately belongs to God. The people on the floor will do what they can, the best that they can. But in the end the gift of life comes from God, the source and fullness of all being.

The glory always belongs to God. This is the glory that reaches people in the medical center and makes known to them a sense of God's benevolence in terms of the promise of Easter, when the shadows of Good Friday are all too evident. It is the mission of the Holy Spirit to prompt the people of God to spend a few moments in the chapel to search out the situation in terms of one's relations to neighbors as well as God, to listen to the words of Scripture as well as of other people, to appreciate the anointing of men and women with the Spirit and to be hopeful.

One says "Amen" because, according to Calvin, that word attests the warmth of the desire to obtain what has been asked of God.[29] Many an "Amen" is breathed in a hospital chapel even by people who have not been in church for some time. In the silence of their time in that sanctuary where the Lord's Prayer is recited, they will be given a heart of flesh to enjoy a sense of the presence and intention of Almighty God in the particular room where the one they love meets the way of life and the way of death. They slip out of the chapel and they make their way back up to that room, having visited a tabernacle in which to worship God.

The majority of persons who are sent to a medical center will return home with and to their families. Before they go home, a few of these folk, like the Samaritan leper, will stop by the chapel, write a prayer of thanksgiving and put it in the box. But for others, the hope of returning home is the size of a mustard seed. The efforts of the staff hopefully will bear fruit. But there are times when tares begin to show up in the charts and the valley of the shadow looms ahead. That is a frightening prospect, to every generation of God's people.

Death and Restoration

When the condition of a patient takes a turn for the worse, the sixfold Spirit that Isaiah mentions is recognized. The Spirit of Wisdom informs the skill and knowledge at the heart of a medical center. Solomon's wisdom was prover-bial. People came from miles around to draw upon it. The modern medical center accumulates incredible medical wisdom in the delivery of care. The cases that they see and from which they learn are far more extensive than those in local health facilities. When they are uncertain, people come from considerable dis-tances to benefit from that wisdom.

As a medical situation becomes increasingly specialized, the Spirit of In-sight is also evident. Insight is the ability to penetrate a particular problem and solve the riddle. The Spirit of Insight was attributed to Solomon in abundance. It is said that he could solve the most difficult of riddles. The Spirit of Insight is celebrated within modern biological science. This Spirit is what drives people in the center's laboratories to ponder and discover what had baffled the doctors back home.

Likewise the Spirit of Counsel is recognized in a medical center. This is the ability to consult and to receive advice. Unlike his son Rehoboam, Solomon from the first proved to be quite capable of taking advice from all sorts of people. Not only that, Solomon developed and directed a very elaborate administrative structure in Jerusalem. The staffs of medical centers make deliberate attempts to seek the advice of others. The involvement of nurses, social workers, child life specialists, dieticians and chaplains is an indication of the breadth of counsel that is brought to bear on a situation. Should the issues become even more com-plex, ethical counsel will be sought as well.

The Spirit of Might is recognized in the courage and tenacity that is pa-tience. There is a tradition that says, when Solomon was a young man, he wrote the Song of Solomon, when he was middle aged, he wrote Proverbs, and when he was an old man, he wrote Ecclesiastes. In the book of Ecclesiastes 7:8, it is written, "the patient in spirit is better than the proud in spirit." The word trans-lated "patient" is "long." A stay in a hospital can be very trying simply in terms of the time and pace. A long Spirit is required on all sides. The idea that someone can check into a medical center and get a quick answer to what ails them is soon dispelled. The routine tests and the more subtle tests take time. Stays stretch over weekends when the lobby and floors are noticeably empty. The time required to interpret the tests and do what needs to be done puts a strain on the patients and their families. It is at that point that the Spirit of Might manifests itself, in the strength of waiting.

The Spirit of Knowledge is present, knowledge in the sense of experience. That Spirit of Knowledge is evident in what the Hebrew Scripture calls an under-standing heart. When he dedicated the Temple, Solomon prayed that he might be given just that—an understanding heart. This is the ability to appreciate those elements of a person's life that are beyond the hospital. Those with the Spirit of Knowledge do not treat patients as "the left breast" to be radiated, but recognize them as persons with a life to lead and a schedule to keep. When those who are sick turn to nurses, ministers and chaplains, part of what they hope to find is the Spirit of Knowledge in them.

As a situation becomes more grave, the sixth sense of the Spirit is felt—that which is traditionally called "the fear of the Lord." When people begin to realize that they are on the borders of life and death, they acknowledge a sense of being in the presence of truly ultimate realms of being.

At the point when those involved begin to ponder what needs to be done, some professions will speak in terms of calculus. For example, Justice Liakos of the Massachusetts Supreme Judicial Court wrote, in an important case deciding life support in a hospital, regarding the preservation of life:

The calculus shifts when the issue is
not "whether, but when, for how long, and
at what cost to the individual that life
may be briefly extended."[30]

The word "calculus" is employed in order to take into account a mode of reasoning in which multiple factors can be coordinated. But for the people of God, more than a formula with many variables is invoked.

At this crucial juncture Christians pray for the Holy Spirit that searches "everything, even the depths of God." [I Corinthians 2:10] That means it is time to grasp the realms of being that surround this crisis beyond the wisdom, insights, counsel and knowledge of those who care for the person. Christians begin such thinking with the understanding that life is a gift, not a given. Their sense of God as the Lord who gives and who takes away not only humbles people, it gives them what one minister called "the ontological shakes."

As the time to die draws near, the Holy Spirit prompts the faithful to meditate upon the transition to the ultimate realms of God's Being. The family has already moved from home to the hospital, and from hospital to medical center. Within that realm of being, they have gone from their room to the intensive care unit. There is a passover of death.

Many figures have articulated that transition, the Johanine passage of the house of many mansions being one of the best known. The Revised Standard Version translates that favorite phrase, "In my Father's house are many rooms," because after the seventeenth century the word "mansion" carried too grand an architectural meaning. For Jesus to say, "In my Father's house are many rooms," is to say that Christians are not confined to those realms of being delineated between birth and death. At the threshold that is death, they move to another room, another realm of being which Christ entered before them. This is a realm of being the proportions, boundaries and limits of which are within the depths of God.

As death draws near, the family and hospital staff approach the door of the wider and unfamiliar realm that borders human existence. Those who die go through that door, leaving others on the threshold. In the course of their vigil, the faithful must recognize when it is time to let go. The question is really not when to stop doing all that can be done. The question of those who wait upon the Holy Spirit is: when has the person reached the threshold where they move from the realm of suffering and death to fullness of being that is a measure of God's Kingdom? To discern that moment, the people of God rely upon the insight of the Holy Spirit. It is most definitely not an autonomous decision. Nor is it the result of some technical formula. Rather it emerges in a communion of knowledge, wisdom and insight as well as silence and prayer.

The Holy Spirit communicates a sense of timing when the person dying is finally being drawn into the life of God. It is not simply a question of feeling that those dying are leaving. There is the sense that they are entering the life of God, that a new life is being created for them in the play between the source of all life, the promise of Christ and the Holy Spirit that is upon and within them. Rather than being the end, death is a crossing over to realms of being, deeper and wider than those over which the Holy Spirit moved in the beginning. These are the realms of being that Christ's death and resurrection pioneered.

The United Church of Christ's *Book of Worship* has an "Order for the Time of Dying." The opening prayer speaks of the light filling the eyes of the dying so that they may see beyond human sight. In other words, at the moment of death, it is in God's light, the source of light, that human beings see light. A psalm is read and the Lord's Prayer is said. These Words are sources of comfort for all who gather in the room. But the Order then specifically offers a prayer of thanksgiving for those who have cared for the sick person. That prayer concludes:

> As death draws near
> and there is no more they can do,
> let them hear again the words of Jesus Christ:
> As often as you did it to one of the least of
>   these, you did it to me;
> and fill them with the joy of your Holy
>   Spirit.[31]

In the midst of the valley of the shadow of death, this prayer thankfully remembers and acknowledges those who have manifest the restored image of God and personified the new life of Christ.

Truth to tell, were it not stated in the *Book of Worship*, the sense of thankfulness could very well be lost. The shock and the trauma of death numbs people and overwhelms them. Given all of the burdens of that experience, it is very difficult to immediately think in terms of gratitude and thanksgiving. The insights and teachings of psychology have led people to expect and accept harsh displays of grief as not only understandable, but even necessary. The times around death are no time for empty phrases or proscribed reactions. Samuel Miller's prayer for the grieving, resonating with the twenty-third psalm, sets forth the promise of faith while still recognizing the pain. Addressing the Lord, it concludes:

> As you walk in the valley of every shadow,
> be our good shepherd
> and sustain us while we walk with you,
> lest in weakness we falter.
> Though the pain deepens,
> keep us in your way
> and guide us past every danger;
> through Jesus Christ our Savior.[32]

The Order concludes by commending the person who has died into the care of the Lord, with a benediction upon those who have gathered in that place.

To lose the gift of life in a medical center is a blow for everyone left behind. Those gathered about the bed are the people who will have to try to resume their lives, coping with a sense of loss of a life that was given and taken. It is not only the family and friends who grieve. Those who cared for the person and struggled against the disease, doing the best that they could, are left with a sense of loss.

The family leaves to make arrangements for the funeral back home. These arrangements keep a family very busy. They may be involved in three kinds of services. There is a Christian service for the burial of the dead with the body or the ashes being present. There is the committal service, when the body or ashes are placed in the ground, or the ashes in a memorial garden. There may be a memorial service which does not involve the ashes or body being present and may be held sometime after the committal service.

At any of these services in a church, three notes are struck. The first is the acknowledgment that death comes to all men and women. Psalms 90, whether read or sung in the hymn "O God Our Help in Ages Past," makes that point as does the passage from Ecclesiastes:

> For everything there is a season
> and a time for every matter under heaven.

These passages are followed by the affirmations of the church. Here the Gospel is proclaimed and hopefully preached. This will include parts of Jesus' farewell discourses to his disciples as well as Paul's declaration of our life in the Spirit, and Christians being immersed in the Love of God in Christ. The third note of the service is thanksgiving, thanksgiving for the person who has lived. Thanksgiving can be expressed in poems, recollections and favorite passages of Scripture which the family wishes to share with the congregation.

At the grave site, the ashes or the body is placed in the ground. The family and friends gather around and a few short verses of Scripture are read with the words of committal and one or two prayers and a benediction. As the family members move away from the grave, sometimes having placed a flower upon it, they recognize and remember certain names on the stones and point them out to the younger members of the family. Memories are renewed and connections made, before everyone takes their leave and returns to the house where neighbors have brought over food. In the weeks that follow, the death is slowly forgotten by many, but not by others.

After answering notes and letters, meeting with various people having to do with the estate, those who have lost a loved one continue to grieve. It is very hard work whether they realize it or not. At any point, in a supermarket or in the house, overwhelming memories may be triggered. It is impossible to tell what will set them off. The grieving person stops whatever they happen to be doing and responds to the memory, concluding with the realization "But they are dead," and then continues to grieve. While working through their grief, the people of God attend church and hear the hymns, prayers and Scriptures in their need. But it is not always easy to join in wholeheartedly. Those in the congregation understand.

In 1690 Edward Taylor had been a widower for six months. Samuel Sewall was thirty-seven. The smallpox in Boston had taken a nine-year-old boy, Richard Dummer, whom Sewall called a "flourishing youth." Telling his own son, Samuel, age eleven or twelve, about the boy's death, Sewall spoke of "what need he had to prepare for Death." Part of that preparation meant "to really pray when he said over the Lord's Prayer." The young man listened to his father's admonitions while eating an apple. But when they started to pray, the boy burst into tears at the words "Our Father." Old Sam asked Young Sam what was the matter. When he could speak, the boy said, "he was afraid he should die." The moment of truth and mortality had struck. Any parent knows the truth of that incident. The senior Sewall prayed with his son and read those portions of the Scripture that were comforting against death. He notes in his diary one of the passages being, "All things yours."[33] This text was from I Corinthians 3:21–23:

> For all things are yours, whether Paul or
> Apollos or Cephas or the world or life or
> death or the present or the future, all are
> yours; and you are Christ's and Christ is God's.

Out in Westfield at this time, Edward Taylor was composing meditations on that same passage of Scripture. The minister began the series in February of 1688 and ended in May 1690. His eighth child, Hezekiah, died on March 3, 1689, having been born on February 18. Then on July 7, 1689, his first wife, Elizabeth Fitch died, they having been married almost fifteen years. Five of her eight children had died.[34] The poet pastor of Westfield meditated on the words of Paul in preparation for serving Holy Communion.

Four months after his wife died, Taylor wrote his fourth meditation on I Corinthians 3:22. It was on the phrase "Death is yours." He began by acknowledging that he really couldn't praise God at all well.

> ...Impossibilities blocke up my pass.
> My tongue Wants Words to tell my thoughts,...
> ...Hence little Praise is brought.[35]

The issue was not simply Taylor's Calvinist sense of God's glory being beyond all human measure and capability. There was the unmistakable note of personal grief in the November meditation's opening lines.

In the body of the meditation he criticized the depictions of death done by a "Painter." He may have been describing the carvings of the gravestones at the burial ground that he visited. Their depictions of death struck Taylor as too harsh. The minister noted that:

> The Painter lies who pensills death's Face grim
>   With White bare butter Teeth, bare staring
>   bones,
> With Empty Eyeholes, Ghostly Lookes which fling
> Such Dread to see as raiseth Deadly groans,...[36]

By November, Taylor was beginning to recognize in his visits to God's Acre that the grimness of death was not the complete story. As a poet he began to metaphorically describe the grave as a "Down bed" or a "Golden Door."

Heavens brightsom Light shines out
in Death's Dark Cave.
The Golden Dore of Glory is the Grave.
Later in the poem Taylor compares the grave to a bed.
The Grave's a Down bed now made for your clay.[37]
This suggests that Taylor may have been reading George Herbert's poem, "Death,"
for comfort. At the end of his poem, Herbert takes up the same conceit, referring
to a pillow of "either down or dust." In other words, five months after his wife's
death, Westfield's first minister could write that the grave is not the end but may
be a transition. Even so, Taylor doesn't elaborate upon the glory toward which
the grave leads.

Taylor had both his feet planted firmly in the Connecticut Valley. While he
certainly believed that death has been "Tamde, Subdude, and Washt fair by his
Lord," still Taylor did not go soaring off into speculative raptures. Instead Taylor
prayed for a change from the tolling of the bell at a funeral to a ringing of praise
and trust. Taylor ended this meditation:
...How should our Bells hereby
Ring Changes, Lord, and praises trust with joy.
Say I am thine, My Lord: Make me thy bell
To ring thy Praise.[38]
Three months later his next meditation began:
Oh! that I ever felt what I profess.
'Twould make me the happi'st man alive.[39]
This was a meditation upon the phrase "Things Present" from the same epistle,
I Corinthians 3:22. He wanted to be able to see the Glory of God, but there was a
film over his eyes. Thus, he could not reflect God's praise in his soul even though
he could say the words as the minister.

In the spring matters were little better. In the opening stanza, this time on
the phrase, "Things to come yours," Taylor noted:
I am many months do drown in Sorrows Spring
But hardly raise a Sigh to blow down Sin.[40]
The references to sin suggest the terms in which Taylor was thinking of his wife's
death. He found himself caught up in sin in the sense that he could not cordially
and wholeheartedly worship God.
For now I wonder t'feele how I thus feele....
Cold Sorrows fall into my Soule as Steel,...
I scarce know what t'make of myselfe....[41]
Coming up on a year of his wife's death, he noted in his May meditation,
that his "Wedden Ring" was slack.[42] This was the final meditation in the series on
I Corinthians 3:23. The next two meditations were based on the line from John's
First Letter, "If anyone sin we have an advocate with the Father." He elaborated
upon a forensic sense of sin in which Christ is the sinner's advocate. In the Feb-
ruary 1690 meditation, he took up the second verse of I John's second chapter.
That meditation began:
Still I complain; I am complaining still.
Oh! woe is me! Was ever Heart like mine?[43]

After approximately a year and a half, Edward Taylor was still grieving, wondering this time if there was something wrong with him. Why couldn't he snap out of it? Was he losing his mind?

It is not until May of 1691, his wife died in July of 1689, that a strong note of joy returns to Taylor's meditation in preparation for the Lord's Supper. The text is from John 14:2, "I go to prepare a place for you." Taylor speaks in this meditation of glory—the glory that reaches him despite his out-gushing grief. There is a place of divine beauty beyond his suffering and pain. That glory is based upon God's good will. The Westfield minister was back to his usual ways, seeking words in which to sing of God's "glory out." The glory that he wished to set forth and praise was based upon God's goodwill, an element that he had not been able to grasp in his grief.

> Lord screw my faculties up to the Skill
> And height of praise as answers thy good will.[44]

The good will of God, i.e., God's benevolence, is set forth in the promises of Christ articulated in Word and Sacrament. After meditating upon texts from I Corinthians and I John, a line from the Gospel of John resonated with the Westfield minister and poet. In this text Christ set forth the promise of God's benevolence in phrases that Edward Taylor heard in terms of Christ preparing a place where the people of God can hopefully resign those who have died. This is where "glorie glowes." That is to say, it is a realm of being wherein the delightful order of God welcomes and embraces those who die in the Lord. Having discovered that lovely dwelling place which encompasses those who have died, those left behind on earth are set free to move on gratefully with their lives. In May of 1691, almost two years after Elizabeth's death, Edward Taylor's heart and mind were sufficiently impressed with Christ's promise of God's benevolence that he could write a meditation in preparation for his approach to the Lord's Supper that sang of God's multiple glories.

Just when and where those who mourn in a congregation will hear God's comforting Word cannot be predicted. Not only is grief one of the most complicated of all human dynamics, the Spirit blows like the wind in that the people of God do not know whence it comes or whither it goes. The process takes at least one year, with all of its anniversaries and holidays. For those who come to church through Advent, Christmas, Lent and Easter, there will come a Sunday, when, with Samuel Miller, they discern a glory, "... not gross or flamboyant, but quite sufficient to sustain our courage and enable us to sing despite our tears."[45] At that point they will rejoin the chorus in the orchestra of the world and sing the everlasting song. The song they sing is everlasting because God's glory calls the tune, that divine glory in which members of a congregation find healing, courage and joy.

When the communion service is celebrated on Sunday of All Souls and All Saints at the end of October or the beginning of November, those in the congregation who have died are remembered. The communion prayer praises God as the source of all creation, gives thanks for the person of Christ, his ministry, death, and resurrection, and invokes the Holy Spirit upon the congregation, as well as the bread and wine. In this prayer, the names of those who have most recently died are spoken along with those who died decades earlier. At that point the congregation take up the notes of memory and gratitude, notes that underly and sustain every local church in holy communion.

ENdNOTES

PREFACE

1. Thomas Frank, Book Reviews in *Eden Events*, vol. VI, No.2 (1987), p. 7.
2. John Williamson Nevin, "The Liturgical Movement," *The Mercersburg Review*, I (November 1849), pp. 611–612.

CHAPTER 1

1. John Calvin, *The Institutes of the Christian Religion*, ed. John T. McNeill and trans. Ford L. Battles, The Library of Christian Classics XX (Philadelphia: Westminster, 1960), p. 714.
2. Augustine, *On Christian Doctrine*, trans. J. F. Shaw, Nicene and Post-Nicene Fathers II (Buffalo: Christian Literature, 1887), p. 536.
3. Brevard S. Childs, *Memory and Tradition in Israel* (Naperville, Illinois: Alec R. Allens Inc., 1962), p. 54.
4. Williston Walker, *The Creeds and Platforms of Congregationalism* (Pilgrim: Philadelphia, 1969), p. 213.
5. Edward Taylor, *The Diary of Edward Taylor*, ed. Francis Murphy (Springfield: Connecticut Valley Historical Museum, 1964), p. 25.
6. Ibid., p. 28.
7. Ibid., p. 35.
8. William Bradford, *Of Plymouth Plantation*, ed. Samuel Eliot Morison (New York: The Modern Library, 1967), p. 63.
9. Taylor, *Diary*, p. 35.
10. Samuel Sewall, *The Diary of Samuel Sewall*, ed. M. Halsey Thomas (2 vols. New York: Farrar, Straus and Giroux, 1973), II, p. 1090.
11. Taylor, *Diary*, pp. 35–36.
12. John H. Lockwood, *Westfield and Its Historic Influences 1669–1919* (2 vols. Springfield: By the Author, 1922), pp. 1, 134.
13. Taylor, *Diary*, p. 39.
14. Ibid., p. 39.
15. Ibid., p. 39.
16. Edward Taylor, *The Poems of Edward Taylor*, ed. Donald E. Stanford (New Haven: Yale University Press, 1968), p. xlii.

17. Ibid., p. xliii.
18. Lockwood, *Westfield*, I, p. 148.
19. Ibid., p. 149.
20. *Edward Taylor's "Church Records" and Related Sermons*, eds. Thomas M. and Virginia L. Davis, vol. 1 of the Unpublished Writings of Edward Taylor (Boston: Twayne, 1981), p. 179.
21. Ibid., p. 188.
22. Ibid., p. 470.
23. Ibid., p. 205.
24. Ibid., p. 212.
25. Ibid., p. 474.
26. Ibid., p. 227.
27. Lockwood, *Westfield*, I, p. 312.
28. Taylor, *Poems*, p. xlviii.
29. Lockwood,*Westfield*, I, p. 148.
30. Ibid., p. 147.
31. Thomas and Virginia Davis, "Edward Taylor's Library: Another Note" *Early American Literature*, vol. 6 (1971–72), p. 272.
32. Taylor, *Poems*, pp. 508–509.
33. Davis, *Church Records*, p. 97.
34. Williston Walker, *Creeds and Platforms of Congregationalism* (Boston: Pilgrim, 1960), p. 433.
35. Edward Taylor, *Edward Taylor's Treatise Concerning the Lord's Supper*, ed. Norman Grabo (Michigan State Press, 1965), p. xxiv.
36. James A. H. Murray et al. eds., *The Oxford English Dictionary* (Oxford: Clarendon, 1933), vol. VII, p. 892.
37. Thomas M. Davis, "Edward Taylor's 'Valedictory' Poems," *Early American Literature*, VII:1 (1972), p. 40.
38. Taylor, *Poems*, p. 99.
39. Ibid., p. 11.
40. Edward J. Kilmartin, *Christian Liturgy* (Kansas City: Sheed and Ward, 1988), p. 139.
41. Anglican-Reformed International Commission 1984, Report of the Commission *God's Reign and Our Unity* (London: SPCK, 1984), p. 27.
42. Clement of Alexandria, *Exhortation to the Heathen*, eds. Alexander Roberts and James Donaldson, The Ante-Nicean Fathers II (Buffalo: Christian Literature Publishing Company, 1885), p. 172.
43. An *epiclesis* is that part of a prayer that invokes the Holy Spirit. It is a crucial element in prayers of communion and baptism.
44. *Theological Dialogue Between Orthodox and Reformed Churches*, Thomas F. Torrance, ed. (Edinburgh and London: Scottish Academic Press, 1985), p. 4.
45. Taylor, *Poems*, p. 10.
46. Ibid., p. 11.
47. John Calvin, *Calvin's Commentaries upon the Book of Psalms*, trans. Henry Beveridge (Grand Rapids: Associated Publishers and Authors Inc., n.d.), p. 1089.

CHAPTER 2

1. John Williamson Nevin, *The Liturgical Question* (Philadelphia: Lindsay & Blakiston, 1862), p. 12.
2. Eric Routley, ed., *Rejoice in the Lord, A Hymn Companion to the Scriptures* (Grand Rapids: Eerdmans, 1985), p. 7.
3. James Lenhart et al., *The Pilgrim Hymnal* (Philadelphia: Pilgrim Press, 1958), p. 491.
4. *Rejoice in the Lord*, No. 556. *The Pilgrim Hymnal*, No. 514.

5. Edward Taylor, *The Poems of Edward Taylor*, ed. Donald E. Stanford (New Haven: Yale University Press, 1968), p. 111.
6. Ibid., p. 113.
7. Ruth C. Duck, ed. *Bread For the Journey: Resources for Worship* (New York: Pilgrim, 1981), p. 69.
8. Cf. Chapter 1, p. 6.
9. Northrop Frye, *The Great Code: The Bible and Literature* (New York and London: Harcourt Brace Jovanovich, 1982), p. 15.
10. Battista Mondin S. X., *The Principle of Analogy in Protestant and Catholic Theology* (The Hague: Martinus Nijhoff, 1963), p. 52.
11. Marjorie Proctor-Smith, "Lectionaries-Principles and Problems:Alternative Perspectives," *Studia Liturgica* 22, No. 1 (1991), p. 95.
12. Karl Barth, *Church Dogmatics II/1*, eds. G. W. Bromiley and T. F. Torrance and trans. T. H. L. Parker (Edinburgh: T&T Clark, 1957), pp. 237–243.
13. Taylor, *Poems*, p. 96.
14. Ibid., p. 83.
15. John Calvin, *The Institutes of the Christian Religion*, ed. John T. McNeill and trans. Ford L. Battles, The Library of Christian Classics XX (Philadelphia: Westminster, 1960), p. 73.
16. Consultation on Common Texts, *The Revised Common Lectionary* (Nashville: Abingdon, 1992), p. 34.
17. United Church of Christ, *Book of Worship* (New York: Office for Church Life and Leadership, 1986), p. 330.
18. Taylor, *Poems*, p. 111.
19. The Theology and Worship Ministry Unit for The Presbyterian Church (U.S.A.) and the Cumberland Presbyterian Church, *Book of Common Worship* (Louisville: Westminster/John Knox, 1993), p. 89. This prayer is a variation of a prayer of confession in *The United Methodist Book of Worship* (Nashville: United Methodist Publishing House, 1992), p. 35.
20. The Joint Office of Worship for the Presbyterian Church (U.S.A.) and the Cumberland Presbyterian Church, *The Service for the Lord's Day, Supplemental Liturgical Resource 1* (Philadelphia: Westminster, 1984), p. 54.
21. The United Church of Christ, *Book of Worship*, p. 273.
22. Routley, *Rejoice in the Lord*, p. 561.
23. The United Church of Christ, *Book of Worship*, p. 82.
24. Calvin, *Institutes*, p. 551.
25. Taylor, *Poems*, p. 99.
26. Calvin, *Institutes*, p. 541.

CHAPTER 3

1. Samuell Sewall, *The Diary of Samuel Sewall*, ed. M. Hasley Thomas (2 vols. New York: Straus and Giroux, 1973), I, p. 497.
2. Ibid., I, p. 497.
3. Daniel Stevick, "Types of Baptismal Piety," *Worship*, 47 (January, 1973), pp. 11–26.
4. Faith and Order Paper No. 111, *Baptism, Eucharist and Ministry* (World Council of Churches, Geneva, 1982), p. 2.
5. John Calvin, *The Institutes of the Christian Religion*, p. 1345.
6. Arthur B. Ellis, *The History of the First Church in Boston 1630–1880* (Boston: Hall and Whiting, 1881), p. 3.
7. Ibid., p. 3.
8. Williston Walker, *The Creeds and Platforms of Congregationalism* (Boston: Pilgrim, 1969), p. 318.
9. The United Church of Christ, *Book of Worship*, p. 139.

10. *Baptism, Eucharist and Ministry*, Baptism IV B 14, p. 6.
11. United Church of Christ, *Book of Worship*, p. 134.
12. Ibid., p. 135.
13. Edward J. Kilmartin S. J., *Christian Liturgy* (Kansas City: Sheed and Ward, 1988), p. 161.
14. United Church of Christ, *Book of Worship*, p. 141.
15. Presbyterian Church, *The Book of Common Worship*, p. 411.
16. The Church Hymnal Corporation, *Proposed Book of Common Prayer* (New York: Seabury Press, 1977), p. 307.
17. United Church of Christ, *Book of Worship*, p. 142.
18. Thomas Talley, "From *Berakah* to *Eucharistia*: A Reopening Question," *Worship* 50 (March, 1976), p. 125.
19. James Lenhart et al., *Pilgrim Hymnal* (Philadelphia: Pilgrim Press, 1931), No. 230.
20. Calvin, *Institutes*, p. 551.
21. Killian McDonnell, OSB, *John Calvin, the Church and the Eucharist* (Princeton: Princeton University Press, 1967), p. 273.
22. United Church of Christ, *Book of Worship*, p. 142.
23. Geoffrey Wainwright, "The Perfection of Salvation in Wesley and Calvin", *Reformed World*, vol. 40 No. 2, (1988), p. 906.
24. Calvin, *Institutes*, p. 189.
25. Roman Catholic/Presbyterian-Reformed Consultation, *Ethics and the Search for Christian Unity* (Washington-Princeton: United States Catholic Conference, 1981), p. 26.
26. Edward Taylor, *The Poems of Edward Taylor*, ed. Donald E. Stanford (New Haven: Yale University Press, 1960), p. 186.
27. Basil, *Epistle 125:3*, trans. Blomfield Jackson, Nicene and Post-Nicene Fathers, eds. Philip Schaff and Henry Wace, vol. 8 (New York: Christian Literature Company, 1896), p. 195.
28. Tertullian, *Apology xviii*, The Ante-Nicene Fathers III, eds. Alexander Roberts and James Donaldson (Buffalo: The Christian Literature Publishing Company, 1885), p. 32.
29. Harry Murray Stokes, "Unitarian Prayers" *The Unitarian Universalist Christian* vol. 39 Nos.1–2, (1984), p. 72.
30. Inclusive Language Lectionary Committee, *An Inclusive Language Lectionary Reading for Year A* (Atlanta, New York, Philadelphia: John Knox Press, Pilgrim Press, Westminster Press, 1983) "Ascension."
31. Mondin Battista S. X., *The Principle of Analogy in Protestant and Catholic Theology* (The Hague: Martinus Nijhoff, 1963), p. 67.
32. Thomas F. Torrance, "Commentary on Agreed Statement on the Holy Trinity" in the Joint Statement of the official Dialogue between the Orthodox Church and the World Alliance of Reformed Churches, (typescript given to author; Edinburgh, March 1991), p. 1.
33. J. A. McGuckin, "Perceiving Light from Light In Light" (paper presented at a Conference on Saint Gregory the Theologian, Patriarch of Constantinople, The Hellenic College, Brookline, Massachusetts, April 21, 1991), p. 17.
34. The United Church of Christ, *Book of Worship*, p. 510.
35. Anyone interested in studying these terms may do so with the Commission on Faith and Order's "Apostolic Faith Project." This is Faith and Order's Study Document Paper No. 140, published in Geneva 1987; it presents the articles of the Nicene Creed in terms of its biblical roots and contemporary challenges and issues.
36. Taylor, *Poems*, p. 187.

CHAPTER 4

1. Northrop Frye, *The Great Code* (New York: Harcourt Brace, 1982), p. 80.

2. The 199th General Assembly of the Presbyterian Church (U.S.A), *A Theological Understanding of the Relationship Between Christians and Jews: A Paper Commended to the Church for Study and Reflection* (New York: Office of the General Assembly, 1987), p. 16.

3. Philip Birnbaum, *Daily Prayer Book* (New York: Hebrew-Publishing, 1977), p. 192.

4. The International Reformed/Methodist Consultation, "Together in God's Grace," *Reformed World*, vol. 39 No. 8 (1987), p. 825.

5. Carl Sandburg, "Silver Star" in *The Complete Poems of Carl Sandburg* (New York: Harcourt Brace Jovanovitch, 1970), p. 685.

6. Northrop Frye, *Anatomy of Criticism* (Princeton University Press, 1957), p. 365.

7. Thomas, S. Eliot, *The Complete Poems and Plays 1909–1950*, (New York: Harcourt Brace, 1956), p. 65.

8. The Office of Worship for the Presbyterian Church (U.S.A.) and the Cumberland Presbyterian Church, *Daily Prayer, the Worship of God Supplemental Liturgical Resource 5* "Music for Daily Prayer" (Philadelphia: Westminster, 1987), no. 102.

9. See page 27 for the figure of light attesting God's glory in terms of an analogy of proper proportion. See page 24 for an example illustrating the four kinds of analogy.

10. The Rev. Dr. Harry Hoehler, Pastor in The First Parish in Weston, Massachusetts, 1964–1995.

11. Faith and Order Paper No. 153, *Confessing One Faith, An Ecumenical Explication of the Apostolic Faith as it is Confessed in the Nicene-Constantinopolitan Creed (381)*, (Geneva: World Council of Churches, 1991), p. 49.

12. Clement of Alexandria, *Exhortation to the Heathen*, eds. Alexander Roberts and James Donaldson, The Ante-Nicene Fathers II (Grand Rapids: Eerdmans, 1957), p. 172.

13. Frank Moore Cross, *Canaanite Myth and Hebrew Epic* (Cambridge: Harvard University Press, 1973), p. 299. The NRSV translation "Lived with us" likewise lacks the dynamic sense of being on the road.

14. Edward Taylor, *The Poems of Edward Taylor*, ed. Donald E. Stanford (New Haven: Yale, 1960), p. 125.

15. Ibid., p. 125.

16. Ibid., p. 126.

17. James Lenhart et al., *The Pilgrim Hymnal* (Philadelphia: Pilgrim Press, 1958), p. 496.

18. Three critical editions of *The Apostolic Tradition* are available; two in English and one in French. Gregory Dix published an English version in 1937 and Geoffrey Cuming in 1976. Dom B. Botte published a critical edition in French in 1963.

19. The Office of Worship for the Presbyterian Church (U.S.A.) and the Cumberland Presbyterian Church, *The Lord's Day Service Supplemental Liturgical Resource 1* (Philadelphia: Westminster, 1984), p. 106.

20. The Theology and Worship Ministry Unit for The Presbyterian Church (U.S.A.) and the Cumberland Presbyterian Church, *Book of Common Worship* (Louisville: Westminster/John Knox, 1993), p. 150.

21. Ibid., p. 150.

22. See pages 22–26 for an illustrated listing of the four kinds of analogy.

23. Gregory of Nazianzus, *Oration on Holy Baptism*, trans. Charles Gordon Browne and James Edward Swallow, Nicene and Post-Nicene Fathers of the Christian Church VII, eds. Phillip Schaff and Henry Wace (Grand Rapids: Eerdmans, 1955), p. 375.

24. The Presbyterian Church, *The Service for the Lord's Day*, p. 106.

25. John Calvin, *Catechism of the Church of Geneva*, Calvin: Theological Treatises, trans. J. K. S. Reid, Library of Christian Classics XXII (London: SCM, 1954), p. 97.

26. Zacharius Ursinus and Caspar Olevianus, *The Heidelberg Catechism* (Grand Rapids: Board of Publications of the Christian Reformed Church, 1975), Q. 35, p. 15.

27. Presbyterian Church (U.S.A.), *The Constitution Presbyterian Church (U.S.A.) Part I The Book of Confessions*, "The Shorter Catechism" (New York: Office of The General Assembly, 1983), 7.022.

28. Taylor, *Poems*, p. 11.

29. Ibid., p. 126.
30. John Calvin, *The Institutes of the Christian Religion,* ed. John T. McNeill and trans. Ford L. Battles, The Library of Christian Classics XX (Philadelphia: Westminster, 1969), p. 537.
31. George B. Emerson letter to Francis Greenwood Peabody in *The Annals of King's Chapel,* ed. Henry Wilder Foote (Boston: Little Brown, 1896) II, p. 495.
32. James C. Humes, *My Fellow Americans* (New York: Praeger, 1992), p. 222.
33. *The Bay Psalm Book,* Wilberforce Eames, ed. (New York: Lenox Hill, 1973) Psalm 16.
34. Samuel Sewall, *The Diary of Samuel Sewall,* ed. M. Halsey Thomas (2 vols.; New York: Farrar, Straus and Giroux), I, p. 384. To "dehort" is to dissuade a person by means of exhortation.
35. The Savoy Declaration in *Creeds and Platforms of Congregationalism,* ed. Williston Walker (Boston, Philadelphia: Pilgrim, 1969), p. 379.

CHAPTER 5

1. F. L. Cross and W. E. A. Livingstone, eds., *The Oxford Dictionary of the Christian Church* (Oxford: Oxford University Press, 1983), p. 1037.
2. Puritans designated months by numbers since names of the months were derived from pagan Roman deities. Wendy Kaplan, *New England Begins: The Seventeenth Century,* vol. 2, Mentality and Environment, (3 Volumes; Boston: Museum of Fine Arts, 1982), p. 148.
3. Paul Gerhardt, "O Sacred Head, Now Wounded" in *The Pilgrim Hymnal* (Philadelphia: Pilgrim Press, 1958), No. 170.
4. Edward Taylor, *The Poems of Edward Taylor,* ed. Donald E. Stanford (New Haven: Yale University Press, 1960), p. 114.
5. Presbyterian Church (U.S.A.), *The Constitution Presbyterian Church (U.S.A.) Part I The Book of Confessions*, "The Shorter Catechism" (New York: The General Assembly of the Presbyterian Church (U.S.A.), 1983), 7.001.
6. Samuel Sewall, *The Diary of Samuel Sewall,* ed. M. Halsey Thomas (2 vols; New York: Farrar, Straus and Giroux), I, p. 358.
7. Taylor, *Poems,* p. 118.
8. Ibid., p. 118.
9. Ibid., p. 117.
10. Ibid., p. 116.
11. Ibid., p. 118.
12. Ibid., p. 115.
13. John Calvin, *The Institutes of the Christian Religion,* ed. John T. McNeill and trans. Ford L. Battles, The Library of Christian Classics XX (Philadelphia: Westminster, 1960), p. 322.

CHAPTER 6

1. The comparison can be made in J. Gordon Davies, *Holy Week: A Short History* (Richmond: John Knox, 1963) passim.
2. United Church of Christ, *Book of Worship* (New York: Office for Church Life and Leadership, 1986), pp. 185–243. The Theology and Worship Ministry Unit for the Presbyterian Church (U.S.A.) and the Cumberland Presbyterian Church, *The Book of Common Worship,* (Louisville; Westminster/John Knox, 1993), pp. 252–314.
3. United Church of Christ, *Book of Worship,* p. 189.
4. Presbyterian Church, *Book of Common Worship,* p. 253.
5. Ibid., p. 276.
6. Ibid., p. 279.

7. Daniel B. Stevick and Ben Johnson, *Proclamation Holy Week* (Philadelphia: Fortress Press, 1973), p. vi.
8. James Luther Adams and Seward Hiltner eds., *Pastoral Care in the Liberal Churches*, (Nashville: Abingdon, 1970), p. 37.
9. Edward Taylor, *The Poems of Edward Taylor*, ed. Donald E. Stanford (New Haven: Yale University Press, 1960), p. 119.
10. Ibid., p. 119.
11. Robert Reiter, "Poetry and Typology: Edward Taylor's Preparatory Meditations, Second Series Numbers 1–30," *Early American Literature*, V, No.1 (1970), pp. 111–123.
12. Davies, *Holy Week: A Short History*, p. 46.
13. John Calvin, *The Institutes of the Christian Religion*, ed. John T. McNeill and trans. Ford L. Battles, The Library of Christian Classics XX (Philadelphia: Westminster, 1960), p. 496.
14. Ibid., p. 538.
15. Athanasius, *The Letters of Saint Athanasius Concerning the Holy Spirit*, translated C. R. B. Shapland (London: The Epworth Press, 1951), p. 127.
16. J. A. McGuckin, "Perceiving Light from Light in Light: The Trinitarian Theology of St. Gregory Nazianzen," lecture given at The Hellenic College, Brookline, Massachusetts; April 21, 1991, Mss. p. 15.
17. Presbyterian Church, *The Book of Common Worship*, p. 298.
18. The United Church of Christ, *Book of Worship*, p. 229.
19. Taylor, *Poems*, p. 121.
20. Calvin, *Institutes*, p. 1304.
21. Zacharius Ursinus and Caspar Olevianus, *The Heidelberg Catechism* (Grand Rapids: Board of Publications of the Christian Reformed Church, 1975), p. 27.
22. Ibid., p. 29.
23. Calvin, *Institutes*, p. 1284.
24. Ursinus, *The Heidelberg Catechism*, p. 27.
25. Taylor, *Poems*, p. 120.
26. Calvin, *Institutes*, p. 1285.
27. E. Margaret MacNaughton, ed., *The Book Of Common Worship: The Presbyterian Church in Canada* (Toronto: The Worship Committee Board of Congregational Life, The Presbyterian Church in Canada, 1991), p. 139.
28. Faith and Order Paper No. 111, *Baptism, Eucharist, and Ministry* (Geneva: World Council of Churches, 1982), Baptism No. 5, p. 2.
29. Karl Barth, *The Epistle to the Romans*, trans. Edwyn C. Hoskyn (London: Oxford, 1953), p. 30.
30. Josephus, *Antiquities*, in C. K. Barrett, The New Testament Background: Selected Documents (New York: Harper, 1961), p. 199.
31. Edward Schillebeeckx, *Jesus: An Experiment in Christology*, trans. Hubert Hoskins (New York: Seabury, 1979), p. 347.
32. Barth, *Romans*, p. 30.
33. Presbyterian Church, *Book Of Common Worship*, p. 150.
34. United Church of Christ, *Book of Worship*, p. 142.
35. Presbyterian Church, *The Book of Common Worship*, p. 842.
36. The Consultation on Common Texts, *A Celebration of Baptism* (Nashville: Abingdon Press, 1988), p. 32.
37. Presbyterian Church, *Book of Common Worship*, p. 150.
38. Schillebeeckx, *Jesus*, p. 282.
39. Ibid., p. 318.
40. Presbyterian Church, *Book of Common Worship*, p. 150.
41. Calvin, *Institutes*, p. 516.
42. *Pilgrim Hymnal*, No. 177.
43. Roman Catholic/Presbyterian-Reformed Consultation, *Ethics and the Search for Christian Unity*, p. 35.
44. Presbyterian Church, *Book of Common Worship*, p. 151.

45. Secretariat for Promoting Christian Unity, *The Presence of Christ in Church and World Dialogue between the World Alliance of Reformed Churches and the Secretariat for Promoting Christian Unity: 1970–77,* Information Service No. 35 (1977/iii-iv), p. 30.

46. Faith and Order, *Baptism, Eucharist and Ministry,* Eucharist 15, p. 13.

47. Max Thurian, *The Mystery of the Eucharist* (Grand Rapids: Eerdmans, 1984), pp. 32–46.

48. Calvin, *Institutes,* p. 1363.

49. John Calvin, *Treatise on the Lord's Supper,* trans. J. K. S. Reid, Library of Christian Classics XXII (London: SCM Press, 1954), p. 148.

50. Thurian, *The Mystery of the Eucharist,* p. 39.

51. The Presbyterian Church (U.S.A.), *The Scots Confession,* The Constitution of the Presbyterian Church (U.S.A.) Part I Book of Confessions (New York: General Assembly, 1983) no. 3.21.

52. Belgic Confession, *Ecumenical Creed and Reformed Confessions* (Grand Rapids, Board of Publications of the Christian Reformed Church, 1979), p. 80.

53. John Williamson Nevin, *The Mystical Presence,* eds. Bard Thomspson and George Bricker (Philadelphia, Boston: United Church Press, 1966), p. 63.

54. Max Thurian, *The Mystery of the Eucharist,* p. 38.

55. Scots Confession, *Book of Confessions,* no. 3.21.

56. Belgic Confession, *Ecumenical Creeds and Reformed Confessions,* p. 80.

57. Presbyterian Church, *Book of Common Worship,* p. 151.

58. Jack Martin Maxwell, *Worship and Reformed Theology* (Pittsburgh: Pickwick Press, 1976), p. 449.

59. John Williamson Nevin, "The New Creation in Christ," *The Mercersburg Review* vol. II, No. 1 (1850), pp. 1–11.

60. Presbyterian Church, *Book of Common Worship,* p. 151.

61. International Commission on English in the Liturgy, *Eucharistic Prayer of Hippolytus, Text for Consultation* (Washington, D.C.; Catholic Bishops' Conferences, 1983), p. 9.

62. Geoffrey J. Cuming, *Hippolytus: A Text for Students* (Grove Books, Bramcote Notts., 1984), p. 11.

63. Ursinus, *Heidelberg Catechism,* Q. 32, p. 13.

64. John Calvin, *The Genevan Catechism,* The Library of Christian Classics XXII (London: SCM Press, 1954), p. 95.

65. Faith and Order, *Baptism, Eucharist and Ministry,* Eucharist 25, p. 15.

66. Schilebeeckx, *Jesus,* p. 347.

67. Presbyterian Church, *Book of Confessions,* no. 3:21.

68. Taylor, *Poems,* p. 121.

69. Ibid., p. 121.

70. Samuel Sewall, *The Diary of Samuel Sewall,* ed. M. Hasley Thomas (2 vols, New York: Straus and Giroux, 1973), I, p. 372.

71. Irenaeus, *Against Heresies,* The Ante-Nicene Fathers I, (Grand Rapids: Eerdmans, 1973) p. 444.

72. Taylor, *Poems,* p. 118.

73. Ibid., p. 119.

74. The United Church of Christ, *Book of Worship,* p. 71.

75. John Calvin, *The Genevan Catechism,* p. 96.

76. Taylor, *Poems,* p. 119.

CHAPTER 7

1. United Church of Christ, *Book of Worship* (New York: Office for Church Life and Leadership, 1986), p. 536.

2. The Theology and Worship Ministry Unit for the Presbyterian Church (U.S.A.) and the Cumberland Presbyterian Church, *Book of Common Worship* (Louisville: Westminster/John Knox, 1992), p. 496 ff.
3. Ibid., p. 756.
4. Ibid., p. 761.
5. Ibid., p. 721.
6. Ibid., p. 748.
7. Massey Hamilton Shepherd, Jr. *The Oxford American Prayer Book Commentary* (New York: Oxford University Press, 1950), p. 19.
8. Presbyterian Church, *Book of Common Worship*, p. 497.
9. United Church of Christ, *Book of Worship*, pp. 545-46.
10. Presbyterian Church, *Book of Common Worship*, p. 499.
11. Ibid., p. 496.
12. The Taize Community, *Praise God Common Prayer at Taize* (New York: Oxford University Press, 1977), p. 284.
13. *The Book of Common Worship*, p. 508.
14. Ibid., 521.
15. Thomas Merton, *Thoughts in Solitude* (New York: Farrar Straus & Cudahy, 1958), p. 83.
16. Presbyterian Church, *The Book of Common Worship*, p. 520.
17. Ibid., p. 521.
18. Shepherd, *The Oxford American Prayer Book Commentary* , p. 70.
19. Ibid., p. 138.
20. John Calvin, *Institutes of the Christian Religion 1536 Edition*, Ford Lewis Battles translator, Collins Flame Classics (Grand Rapids: Eerdmans, 1986), p. 76.
21. Ibid., p. 78.
22. Ibid., p. 78.
23. Ibid., p. 78.
24. Ibid., p. 79.
25. Ibid., p. 81.
26. Ibid., p. 79.
27. Charles W. Gusmer, *The Healing Ministry in the Church of England,* (Great Wakering: Alcuin Club No. 56, 1974), p. 57.
28. Calvin, *Institutes of the Christian Religion 1536*, p. 83.
29. Ibid., p. 84.
30. *Brophy v. New England Sinai Hospital Inc.*, 388 Mass. 417 (1986), p. 21.
31. United Church of Christ, *Book of Worship*, p. 364.
32. Ibid., p. 364.
33. Samuel Sewall, *The Diary of Samuel Sewall 1674–1729*, ed. M. Halsey Thomas (2 vols.; New York: Farrar, Straus and Giroux, 1973), I, p. 249.
34. Norman Grabo, *Edward Taylor*, Twayne's United States Authors Series (New Haven: College and University Press, 1961), p. 30.
35. Edward Taylor, *The Poems of Edward Taylor,* ed. Donald E. Stanford (New Haven: Yale University Press, 1960), p. 54.
36. Ibid., p. 55.
37. Taylor, *Poems*, p. 55.
38. Ibid., p. 55.
39. Taylor, *Poems*, p. 56.
40. Ibid., p. 57.
41. Ibid., p. 58.
42. Ibid., p. 60.
43. Taylor, *Poems*, p. 64.
44. Ibid., p. 68.
45. Samuel H. Miller, *Man the Believer* (Nashville: Abingdon, 1968), p. 140.

Acknowledgments

Scripture quotations are from the Revised Standard Version of the Bible, copyright 1946, 1952, 1971 and the New Revised Standard Version, copyright 1989, by the Division of Christian Education of the National Council of the Churches of Christ in the USA. Used by permission.

Prayers and blessings from Book of Common Worship, copyright 1993, Westminster/John Knox Press. Used by permission of Westminster/John Knox Press.

Poems of Edward Taylor from *The Poems of Edward Taylor*, copyright 1960, Yale University Press. Used by permission of Yale University Press. Lines from Edward Taylor's Meditation 40 first series is reprinted by permission of the *New England Quarterly*.

The prayers and blessings from the *Book of Worship* United Church of Christ, copyright 1986, United Church of Christ, Office for Church Life and Leadership, New York, New York. Used by permission.

The translation of Matthew 3:13–17 adapted from the *Good News Bible* is used by permission of the American Bible Society.

The prayer for Psalm 97 from the *Lutheran Book of Worship: Minister's Desk Edition*, copyright 1978, by permission of Augsburg Fortress.

The baptismal renunciations reprinted from The Book of Common Worship, copyright 1991, is used by permission of The Presbyterian Church in Canada, 50 Wynford Drive, North York, Ontario, M3C 1J7.

The greeting "Why are we here" is reprinted by permission of the publisher from *Bread For the Journey*, ed. Ruth C. Duck, copyright 1981, The Pilgrim Press.

The prayer "Remain with us" From *Praise God*, copyright 1977 is reprinted by permission of Oxford University Press.

Index